STUDIES IN THE ECONOMIC POLICY OF FREDERICK THE GREAT

T0313145

STUDIES IN THE ECONOMIC
POLICY OF FREDERICK THE GREAT

W.O. HENDERSON

Routledge
Taylor & Francis Group

LONDON AND NEW YORK

First published in 1963

Published in 2006 by
Routledge
2 Park Square, Milton Park, Abingdon, Oxfordshire OX14 4RN
711 Third Avenue, New York, NY 10017

First issued in paperback 2014

Routledge is an imprint of the Taylor and Francis Group, an informa business

British Library Cataloguing in Publication Data
A CIP catalogue record for this book
is available from the British Library

Studies in the Economic Policy of Frederick the Great
ISBN 0-415-38203-3 (volume)
ISBN 0-415-37907-5 (subset)
ISBN 0-415-28619-0 (set)

ISBN 13: 978-1-138-86520-4 (pbk)
ISBN 13: 978-0-415-38203-8 (hbk)

Routledge Library Editions: Economic History

STUDIES IN THE
ECONOMIC POLICY OF
FREDERICK THE GREAT

The Lancashire Cotton Famine (*Manchester University Press, 1934*).

The Zollverein (*Second Edition, Frank Cass, London, 1959*)

Britain and Industrial Europe, 1750-1870 (*Liverpool University Press, 1954*)

The State and the Industrial Revolution in Prussia, 1740-1870 (*Liverpool University Press, 1958*)

The Industrial Revolution on the Continent, 1800-1914 (*Frank Cass, 1961*)

Studies in German Colonial History (*Frank Cass, 1962*)

The Genesis of the Common Market (*Frank Cass, 1962*)

EDITED WITH W. H. CHALONER

Friedrich Engels, The Conditions of the Working Class in England (*Basil Blackwell, 1958*)

Engels as Military Critic (*Manchester University Press, 1959*)

STUDIES IN THE ECONOMIC POLICY OF FREDERICK THE GREAT

W. O. HENDERSON

FRANK CASS & CO. LTD.,
1963

First published in 1963 by Frank Cass & Co. Ltd.
10, Woburn Walk, London, W.C.1.

TO
FAY HENDERSON

Acknowledgements

THE AUTHOR thanks the editors of *Business History*, the *Economic History Review*, and the *Zeitschrift für die Gesamte Staatswissenschaft* for permission to reprint articles which have appeared in those journals. The maps have been drawn by Miss Lowcock of the University of Manchester and by Mr. Alan Hodgkiss of the University of Liverpool. Maps 1, 6 and 9 have been reproduced by permission of the Liverpool University Press from my book on *The State and the Industrial Revolution in Prussia, 1740-1870* (1958). Maps 13 and 14 are based on maps in R. Forberger, *Die Manufaktur in Sachsen vom Ende des 16en bis zum Anfang des 19en Jahrhunderts* (1958). The author thanks Dr Chaloner and Dr Aldcroft for reading the proofs of the book.

W.O.H.

Contents

Contents

Introduction

THE period between the death of the Emperor Charles VI and the outbreak of the French revolution was dominated by Frederick the Great. He was largely responsible for the drastic change that occurred in the balance of power in Europe after 1740. He was the greatest of the enlightened monarchs and he showed how the *ancien régime* of the eighteenth century could adapt to its own purposes some of the ideas of the French philosophers. His personality and his achievements left their mark on Prussia, on Germany, and on the Continent. He completed the work begun by the Great Elector and gained for Prussia the status of a Great Power. He defied the Habsburgs and challenged their position as head of the leading state in Germany.

Many accounts have been given of Frederick II's reign and there are numerous detailed studies of particular aspects of his career. But the king's biographers have generally concentrated their attention upon Frederick the philosopher king, Frederick the statesman, and Frederick the general. On the other hand Frederick's economic policy has, to some extent, been neglected. This may be because Frederick showed much more originality in his conception of monarchy, in his diplomacy, and in his military strategy, than in his work as an administrator or an economist. For the idea of enlightened monarchy in the eighteenth century owed much to Frederick. He showed how a king could put into practice the ideas of some of the most progressive thinkers of his day. His conception of the ruler as the first servant of the state, his rigid standards of economy at Court, his policy of religious toleration, his reorganisation of the administration and the legal system, and his efforts to prevent peasant clearances were all facets of a new idea of kingship. As a statesman Frederick wrought great changes in the map of Germany and in the European balance of power while as a soldier he earned the admiration of Napoleon.

In economic affairs, on the other hand, Frederick showed less originality and he appears to have learned little from experience. He never seems to have questioned the principles of economics which he was taught as a young man by his tutor Hille. The views of the Physiocrats and of Adam Smith did not deflect Frederick from pursuing the mercantilist policy which he had inherited from his father. When Ursinus ventured to question the king's wisdom in subsidising the Berlin silk industry, which was far from efficient, he was clapped in prison. Despite the public outcry against the extortions of the French tax collectors Frederick retained the services of the head of the *Regie* until the end of his reign. Many of Frederick's successes in stimulating the Prussian economy were achieved simply by following policies already adopted by earlier Hohenzollerms. The establishment of colonies of religious refugees, the draining of marshes, the improvement of sandy heaths, the construction of canals, the encouragement given to the woollen industry, and the promotion of overseas commerce were not new policies. On the other hand the economic exploitation of weak neighbours—Poland, Saxony and Mecklenburg—was a policy which Frederick's predecessors had not seriously attempted to follow.

The real significance of Frederick's economic policy lay in the extraordinary vigour with which it was carried out. The establishment of new villages peopled with foreign immigrants, the extension of farmland by draining fens and improving wastes, the expansion of existing industries of the introduction of new branches of manufacture, the stimulus given to the fisheries and to overseas trade—all this was done on a scale never before attempted in Prussia. The fact that so much was achieved in spite of adverse conditions made Frederick's achievements all the more remarkable. He waged two great wars and by 1763 many of his provinces were devastated and the merchants of Berlin faced a commercial crisis of unprecedented severity. Thirteen years after he ascended the throne Frederick had to start again to plan for the reconstruction and the expansion of the economy. Yet at the end of his reign Prussia had a larger population, a more efficient agriculture, numerous new branches of manufacture, a balanced budget, and a favourable balance of payments in international trade.

Frederick had to face considerable opposition to his plans. The force of tradition was strong and there was resistance to many of the changes that he wished to bring about. For one progressive landlord who was prepared to try out new farming ideas on his estate there were a dozen who preferred the ways of their forefathers. New industrial processes and new methods of business organisation and finance were held up by the inertia of manufacturers, merchants and artisans who were as hidebound in their ways as landowners and peasants. Frederick was disappointed with the merchants of his capital who failed to withstand the commercial crisis of 1763 and with manufacturers who clamoured for subsidies instead of trying to stand on their own feet.

Among those who, at one time or another, opposed some aspect of Frederick's economic policy mention may be made of the fenmen who objected to the drainage of marsh lands; the officials who complained of the arrival of foreign immigrants who were difficult to assimilate with the local population; the merchants and artisans who resented the privileges accorded to State corporations and specially favoured manufacturers; and the citizens who resisted de Launay's tax collectors. The establishment of the salt and coffee monopolies, the depreciation of the coinage during the Seven Years War, and the too rapid deflation after 1763 did not enhance Frederick's popularity with his subjects. But the king was not to be deflected from his purpose. The louder the outcry against his actions the more determined was Frederick to carry out his economic policy. Nine times out of ten he succeeded. But even Frederick was unable to overcome the opposition of the landed gentry to the abolition of serfdom and his instruction to Brenkenhof to free the peasants of Pomerania remained a dead letter.

Another factor that delayed the changes desired by the king was the problem of finding officials capable of carrying out his plans. The early difficulties of the Bank of Berlin and the Overseas Trading Corporation were due largely to the incompetence—even the dishonesty—of the men placed in charge of these institutions. Frederick sometimes had to wait for many years before he could find the right men to place in charge of government departments and State corporations.

The way in which Frederick was able to carry out so many of his plans to stimulate the Prussian economy compares very favourably with the achievements of other monarchs in the second half of the eighteenth century. At that time a number of enlightened rulers were pursuing economic policies not very different from those of Frederick. But they were generally less successful than the king of Prussia. The failure of many of their plans was due to their inability to face resolutely the kind of difficulties that Frederick so often surmounted. Failure to balance the budget, inability to find suitable officials, and irresolution in the face of the opposition of vested interests led to the downfall of many imposing schemes of economic reform. Thus one of his biographers has written of Joseph II that " seldom did reforming efforts meet with less success than did his largely-conceived and well-intentioned measures". Alone among his contemporaries Frederick left his country with a far more flourishing economy than it had been when he ascended the throne.

By the 1780's the changes that had taken place in the Prussian economy in the past forty years were being studied by contemporary observers. Hertzberg summarised the economic progress of the reign in addresses to the Royal Academy of Sciences in Berlin while Mirabeau's book on the Prussian monarchy contained a wealth of information on the recent progress of the country's agriculture and industries. Fifty years later Preuss wrote his life of Frederick to which had added five volumes of documents. The period of economic reconstruction after the Seven Years War was discussed in some detail. A careful study of the records bearing upon Frederick's economic policy was initiated by Schmoller and his pupils in the last quarter of the nineteenth century. A detailed account of the Prussian silk industry appeared in the *Acta Borussica* in 1892 and this was followed by studies of the coinage and of taxation in Frederick's reign. Numerous articles on various aspects of Frederick's economic policy appeared in such journals as *Schmoller's Jahrbuch* and the *Forschungen zur Brandenburgischen und Preussischen Geschichte*. An excellent survey of the means by which Frederick stimulated the industrial expansion of his kingdom was made by Matschoss (1912) while biographical studies of some of Frederick's officials—Heinitz and Reden —appeared in the *Beiträge zur Geschichte der Technik und Industrie* (edited by Matschoss). Koser's standard biography of Frederick, which was completed in 1925, included a full account of the king's economic policy. For English readers Carlyle's biography will always be the best introduction to a study of Frederick the Great. In matchless prose he described the struggles of the king against seemingly impossible odds and he did not neglect the economic problems that Frederick had to solve before Prussia could secure for herself the status of a Great Power.

CHAPTER I

The Rise of the Metal and Armament Industries in Berlin and Brandenburg

IN the reigns of Frederick William I and Frederick II of Prussia the house of Splitgerber and Daum rose to the position of one of the leading mercantile, financial and industrial undertakings in Berlin and the Mark Brandenburg. The firm was engaged in a variety of enterprises and it played an important part in promoting the expansion of the production of metal goods, cutlery and refined sugar in Prussia. It was, however, as armament manufacturers and army contractors that Splitgerber and Daum made their greatest contribution to the rise of Prussia in the eighteeneth century.[1]

The firm of Splitgerber and Daum was established in 1712 when David Splitberger was 29 and Gottfried Adolf Daum was 33 years of age. Splitgerber was a bookkeeper who had served his apprenticeship in Stettin before coming to Berlin, where he was employed by the firm of Gregori[2] while Daum appears to have served in the army as a non-commissioned officer. The partners started with only a little capital and conducted their business from two furnished rooms. In 1713 Daum married the daughter of a prosperous tailor and her dowry helped to finance the firm in its early days. Splitberger and Daum were not burghers of Berlin[3] and they could not open a shop or engage in

---

[1] For Splitgerber and Daum see König, *Versuch einer historischen Schilderung der Hauptänderungen der Religion, Sitten, Gewohnheiten, Künste, und Wissenschaften der Residenzstadt Berlin seit den ältesten Zeiten bis 1786* (1793-98), IV, Part 2, pp. 201-3; F. Lenz and O. Unholtz, *Die Geschichte des Bankhauses Gebrüder Schickler* (Berlin, 1921); and W. Treue, 'David Splitgerber, Ein Unternehmer im preussischen Mercantilstaat' in *Vierteljahrschrift für Sozial- und Wirtschaftsgeschichte*, XLI, iii, (1954); H. Rachel and P. Wallich, *Berliner Grosskaufleute und Kapitalisten*, II, (Berlin, 1938), Otto Wiedfeldt, *Statistiche Studien zur Entwicklungsgeschichte der Berliner Industrie von 1720 bis 1890* (1898), H. Rachel, *Das Berliner Wirtschaftsleben in Zeitalter des Frühkapitalismus* (1931), and M. Arendt, E. Faden and O. F. Gaudert, *Geschichte der Stadt Berlin* (Berlin, 1937).

[2] For Gregori see H. Rachel and P. Wallich, op. cit., pp. 20-21.

[3] Splitgerber came from Pomerania and Daum came from Saxony.

crafts over which a guild enjoyed a monopoly. So they began their business careers as commission agents, which was one of the few business activities open to them, and they eventually became wholesalers, financiers, bankers and industrialists. Neither partner had any predominance in the firm though it was David Splitgerber who handled the 'public relations' aspects of the firm's activities, presented memoranda to the King from time to time and advised the authorities on questions of currency, public finance and foreign trade.[1]

Shortly after the partnership had been formed Splitgerber and Daum secured two orders from Augustus the Strong[2] to supply the Dresden arsenal with a consignment of cannon balls and bombs, and before long the firm was also delivering military supplies to the Prussian army. Some bombs were purchased from the royal foundry at Neustadt an der Dosse[3] and from ironworks near Grabow in Mecklenburg while most of the copper came from the Rothenburg mine in the Prussian part of the County of Mansfeld.[4]

These orders from the King of Prussia and the Elector of Saxony gave the young partners a flying start. New clients soon came forward to do business with a firm that had so quickly gained the confidence of two crowned heads. In July 1713 Splitgerber and Daum began to buy wines, tapestries and 'colonial goods', such as tea and cocoa, from de Almeyda of Lisbon for sale in Germany and Poland, transactions which amounted to 26 million thalers in the five years 1713-18. A few years later they were handling the sale of various English manufactured products—such as cloth, stockings and hats—which had been imported by Johann Witte of Berlin. The partners travelled widely to secure new orders. Between 1712

---

[1] W. Treue, 'David Splitgerber . . .', *Vierteljahrschrift für Sozial- und Wirtschaftsgeschichte*, XLI, iii, (1954), p. 254.

[2] Augustus the Strong was Elector of Saxony (1694) and King of Poland (1697).

[3] The Neustadt an der Dosse foundry in the Neu Ruppin district (*Kreis*) had been founded jointly by the Great Elector and the Landgraf of Hesse-Homburg. In 1698 it became the sole property of the Elector of Brandenburg.

[4] The Rothenburg mine was operated by the *Rothenburger Erz- Schiefer- und Steinkohlenbergbau* and had at this time an annual output of between 250 and 300 tons. It was taken over by the Prussian State in 1768.

and 1715 Daum visited Dresden, Hamburg, Denmark and Lisbon while Splitgerber was in Königsberg and Dresden. The partners raised capital to expand their business by borrowing from various sources.[1] On the other hand Splitgerber and Daum were also lending money.[2] The balance sheet for the first six years of the partnership showed a profit of 10,450 thalers.

One cause of the rapid progress of the firm in the early days of Frederick William I's reign was the fact that the partners appreciated more clearly than some of their rivals the peculiar nature of the Prussian State at this time. They realised that success in business could be achieved only within the framework of a strictly organised mercantilist economy. They saw that the key to advancement lay in securing the support of a soldier-king who was engaged in building up an army more powerful than Prussia had ever seen before. Splitgerber and Daum realised that by sharing in the patriotic task of supplying the needs of the army they might hope to secure access to Court circles where valuable commissions might be picked up. The monarchy was the fountain from which new orders and valuable privileges flowed. Just as Gotzkowsky[3] secured the patronage of Frederick the Great by helping to establish the silk and porcelain industries in Berlin so Splitgerber and Daum entered the small circle of those who enjoyed royal favours by fostering the development of the metal and armaments industries of the province of Brandenburg. The modest commissions which Splitgerber and Daum carried out for the military authorities in the early period of the firm's existence were a prelude to much more ambitious undertakings in later years.

The commercial, financial and industrial activities of Splitgerber and Daum expanded in the 1720's and 1730's. The firm handled many commodities on a commission basis. They purchased 'colonial goods' in Lisbon, Amsterdam and Hamburg; copper at Rothenburg and Breslau; and silk in Leipzig. They

---

[1] For example Eugeling (Daum's father-in-law), Weyl (a Jew from Halle), Stephen Caesar and the Countess of Vitzthum made loans to Splitgerber and Daum in the early period of the firm's history.

[2] For example Anton Götsch, the agent of the estate of the late Duchess of Strelitz, deposited some of the Duchess's jewels with Splitgerber and Daum as security for a loan.

[3] For Gotzkowsky see below, ch. 2.

had correspondents all over the Continent[1] and they helped to finance trading voyages such as those of the *Potsdam* (1725) and *Kronprinz* (1732).

Although they had no previous experience of trading in cloth Splitgerber and Daum were pioneers in fostering the expansion of the export of Prussian woollens to Russia. Hitherto the Russian military authorities had generally obtained army cloth from England. In the early eighteenth century, however, the output and the quality of coarse Yorkshire woollens declined. Prussian and Silesian cloths now compared favourably with those of Yorkshire as regards price and quality. The rupture in Anglo-Russian diplomatic relations in 1720 gave Mardefeld (the Prussian ambassador in St. Petersburg) an opportunity to persuade the Russians to buy Prussian instead of English cloth. His efforts were successful. In 1722 he secured an order for 9,300 yards of Prussian cloth and in 1724 the Russian authorities decided to buy no more English cloth. In that year the Russia Commercial Company was set up by a consortium of Berlin merchants and the majority of its shares were soon held by Splitgerber and Daum. Frederick William I granted the company a twelve-year monopoly of the export of Prussian army cloth —but not of all woollen cloth—to Russia. He also gave the company permission to import Russian goods (such as leather) duty free to warehouses in Stettin and Frankfurt an der Oder. In 1725 two representatives of the company went to St. Petersburg and secured an order for 520,000 yards of army cloth.

The Berlin company had to overcome many difficulties. It had to set up its own dyeworks at Drossen and Landsberg. The transport of cloth to Russia proved to be hazardous and costly. Insurance premiums were high. The prices charged by the cloth-makers—which were regulated by the government—sometimes left only a small margin of profit when the cloth was sold to the Russians. Nevertheless the Berlin company traded successfully with the Russians between 1725 and 1727. Army cloth worth 485,000 thalers was delivered and the Russians paid a third of this sum in specie. Considerable quantities of Russian leather were sold by the company in Austrian territories—particularly

[1] For example Almeyda in Lisbon, the Krusemarck brothers in St. Petersburg, Joseph Ressany in Hamburg; and Schubarth and Dassdorf in Leipzig.

in Silesia. English intrigues in St. Petersburg led to a virtual suspension of the trade but after 1728 some new orders were received. In 1733 Britain and Russia resumed diplomatic relations and the new British envoy in St. Petersburg made every effort to recover the army cloth contract for British merchants. An Anglo-Russian agreement of 1734 reduced the Russian import duty on coarse Yorkshire woollens to 2*d.* per yard and this gave English clothiers a decisive advantage over their Prussian rivals. For a time the Berlin company continued to receive some orders for Russian army cloth but by 1738 British influence had finally triumphed in St. Petersburg and all orders for Prussian cloth were cancelled. Nevertheless Splitgerber and Daum continued to maintain an agency in St. Petersburg and some private trade with Russian merchants continued.[1]

Splitgerber and Daum were also financiers and bankers who carried out many commissions for the King such as making payments to a recruiting officer in London who enlisted tall men for the Prussian army; providing silver for the royal mint;[2] distributing money from the royal charity; and administering the finances of the Royal Salt Fund. Between 1726 and 1738 the firm's turnover rose from 189,649 thalers to 641,582 thalers while the capital account rose from 92,640 thalers to 278,461 thalers.

Splitgerber and Daum also became industrialists by taking over the management of several royal manufactures. In 1719 they took over the state copperworks at Neustadt-Eberswalde which turned out boilers, pipes, brewing-pans and engraving

---

[1] For the Russian Commercial Company of Berlin see P. B. Struve, 'The Anglo-Russian Trade Treaty of 1734', *Russian Review*, I (1912); D. K. Reading, *The Anglo-Russian Commercial Treaty of 1734* (1938), ch. 2; Gustav Schmoller, *Umrisse und Untersuchungen zur Verfassungs-Verwaltungs-und Wirtschaftsgeschichte besonders des Preussischen Staates im 17en und 18en Jahrhundert* (1898), pp. 457-529. Schmoller's essay first appeared—with an appendix of documents—in the *Zeitschrift für Preussische Geschichte und Landeskunde*, XX, (1883). In the 1730s there were quarrels among the members of the consortium of Berlin merchants and Splitgerber and Daum formed a new company which was known both as the New Russian Commercial Company and Splitgerber and Buder. In 1735 Splitgerber and Daum held shares to the value of 125,000 thalers in the company.

[2] For the contracts of 1752-3 for the supply of silver to the Prussian mint see Friedrich von Schrötter, *Das Preussische Münzwesen im 18en Jahrhundert: Münzgeschichtlicher Teil*, I (*Acta Borussica: Denkmäler der Preussischen Staatsverwaltung im 18en Jahrhundert*, 1904), pp. 229-31, 452-3 and 481.

plates. The partners enjoyed a monopoly of the sale of these products in the Mark Brandenburg. In 1726 the lease of the copperworks was renewed and the monopoly of the sale of copper products was extended to Pomerania, Magdeburg, Halberstadt and Mansfeld.

When the Crown established small arms workshops at Spandau and Potsdam their management was entrusted to Splitgerber and Daum (1722). The manufacture of gunbarrels, swords, daggers and bayonets took place at Spandau while the assembling of guns was carried out at Potsdam. Daum engaged 70 skilled artisans at Liège but in Solingen the authorities of the Duchy of Berg put difficulties in his way. The King paid the fares of the Liège workers and granted them various privileges. Some of the immigrants however failed to settle down and returned to their homes.

By March 1730 the men employed in the Spandau and Potsdam workshops included 76 masters, 135 journeymen and 41 apprentices. Some of the younger workers were boys from military orphanages. The King of Prussia prohibited the import of guns and blades (so as to give the royal workshops a monopoly of supplying the army) and allowed the export of arms to Denmark, Poland, Russia and Austria. The lease was not very profitable because although Splitgerber and Daum had to pay more for their Swedish iron the King insisted upon a reduction in the prices they charged for the guns which they sold to the Crown. Between 1724 and 1736 their profits fell from 30,000 thalers to 5,000 thalers a year despite an expansion of output. Daum stated that the capital invested in these workshops would have earned three times as much profit in some other commercial venture.

In 1725 Splitgerber and Daum took over the management of three other royal industrial establishments—an iron furnace at Zehdenick,[1] a forge at Peitz[2], and ironworks at Neustadt-

---

[1] The Zehdenick furnace lay on the River Havel in the Templin district (*Kreis*). It had been leased to a Frenchman named Jacques Julien between 1700 and 1704. The ironworks were operated by the State between 1704 and 1708 and were then leased again.

[2] According to L. Beck, *Die Geschichte des Eisens*, Vol. III (1897) the Peitz ironworks were 'of exceptional importance'. They lay in the district (*Kreis*) of Cottbus.

Eberswalde.[1] Frederick William I hoped to expand the output of these works so that Prussia would be less dependent upon Sweden for the pig-iron and other iron products required for military purposes.[2] The Zehdenick plant made cannon balls, bombs and grenades which were stored in a warehouse established by Splitgerber and Daum at Spandau. Royal brass works (1727) and ironworks (1732)[3] at Hegermühle were leased to them—the former being operated in conjunction with adjacent copper works at Neustadt-Eberswalde so that in thirteen years Splitgerber and Daum had come to operate eight nationalised undertakings.[4]

In Frederick the Great's reign the house of Splitgerber and Daum went from strength to strength. Frederick had no very high opinion of merchants and bankers, for he held that men whose actions were guided by the profit motive were inferior to soldiers and civil servants for whom financial rewards were a secondary consideration as compared with the efficient discharge of their duty. In his letters to Fredersdorf the King criticised the mercantile classes and referred to Splitgerber in derogatory terms such as 'Spitzbube' and 'Spitzbubegerber'.[5] Nevertheless, like his father, Frederick the

---

[1] In 1698 a Frenchman named Moyse Aureillon secured a concession to erect ironworks and wire-drawing shops at Neustadt-Eberswalde. The former began operations in 1700, the latter in 1702. The ironworks are described as an *Eisenspalterei*, i.e. a rolling and slitting mill. Aureillon was also responsible for setting up tin works at Hegermuhle (near Neustadt-Eberswalde). The ironworks at Neustadt-Eberswalde had been largely destroyed by fire in 1707. The state had taken over this establishment in 1719.

[2] At this time the Mark Brandenburg, the New Mark and Pomerania imported iron from Sweden while the districts of Magdeburg and Halberstadt obtained iron from the Harz. An edict of 5 July 1699 forbade the export of scrap iron and an edict of 12 May 1703 forbade the import of certain types of iron products. The prohibition of imports, however, could not be effective until the output of Prussia's own ironworks was sufficient to meet the home demand.

[3] The Hegermühle ironworks—built in 1698 and nationalised in 1719 —were rolling and slitting mills.

[4] For the metalworks of Brandenburg in the reign of Frederick William I see Hugo Rachel, *Die Handels-, Zoll- und Akzisenpolitik Preussens 1713-1740* (*Acta Borussica: Denkmäler der Preussischen Staatsverwaltung im 18en Jahrhundert*), II, Part i, (1922), pp. 429-432.

[5] J. Richter (ed.) *Die Briefe Friedrichs des Grossen an seinen vormaligen Kammerdiener Fredersdorf* (1926). 'Spitzbube' means 'rogue'.

Great frequently made use of the services of Splitgerber and Daum who now took their place among the leading bankers, merchants and entrepreneurs in Berlin. When Daum died (1743) his heirs left their capital in the business but had no influence over its management. David Splitgerber was now left in charge of the firm and he engaged Johan Jacob Schickler of Strasbourg and Friedrich Heinrich Berendes of Berlin as his assistants. In due course Schickler and Berendes married Splitgerber's daughters and became partners in the firm.

As a commercial concern Splitgerber and Daum continued to prosper in the 1750's and 1760's despite the interruptions to trade brought about by two wars. The firm dealt in tropical products purchased in Lisbon, Cadiz, Bordeaux, Amsterdam and Hamburg; grain and timber from the Baltic ports; pig-iron from Sweden; linen from Silesia and Westphalia; and copper from Rothenburg and Magdeburg. Trade with France expanded and a representative of the firm at Bordeaux purchased sugar from San Domingo as well as lead, timber and tallow. Some of this trade was carried in the firm's own ships. In the 1740's Splitgerber and Daum owned four vessels and in the 1760's they operated a fleet of five ships and also had a half share in a sixth. The financial activites of the firm included dealings in bills of exchange (particularly with Dutch and Hamburg firms), the purchase of specie and coins, and also dealings in British annuities and consols. Between 1740 and 1762 the assets of the firm amounted to two million thalers. The wide experience of the firm in matters of commerce, industry, currency and finance led Frederick the Great to consult Splitgerber on many occasions. His advice was sought on commercial negotiations with France,[1] Spain[2], and Portugal and on projects concerning the establishment of overseas trading companies.

Commissions from Frederick the Great were received as soon as he came to the throne. As Crown Prince he had dealt with

---

[1] Splitgerber pressed the King to secure for Prussian merchants the same trading rights in France as those enjoyed by the Hansa merchants. A Franco-Prussian commercial agreement was signed in February, 1753.

[2] R. Koser in his *Geschichte Friedrichs des Grossen*, II, p. 410, states that a commercial treaty between Spain and Prussia was signed in 1782. This is incorrect.

Splitgerber and Daum, having asked them to purchase books and other articles, and at the age of 15 he already owed them 7,000 thalers. When he ascended the throne he lifted the ban imposed by his father on the import of cereals—for supplies were low and prices were high—and instructed Splitgerber and Daum to spend up to 150,000 thalers on grain in Amsterdam or elsewhere. On the day after he heard of the death of the Emperor Charles VI the King set aside 200,000 thalers to purchase foreign rye to be stored in case there should be a war with Austria. Splitgerber and Daum were asked to secure the bulk of this grain but their efforts to buy rye in Russia met with unexpected difficulties since the Czar suddenly prohibited its export.[1] In both the War of the Austrian Succession and the Seven Years War Splitgerber and Daum provided the Prussian forces with arms and munitions both from the royal workshops and from foreign sources. Army contractors in Prussia faced many difficulties in wartime since prices were inflated, the coinage was debased and the King failed to pay his bills promptly.

Splitgerber and Daum continued to serve the Crown as bankers and financiers. They settled Frederick's accounts for English horses for the royal stables, for marble and paintings for the palace of Sans Souci, for lead and copper for the Berlin opera house, and for plants for the royal gardens. Voltaire received 16,000 livres from the King; a jeweller was given an advance in respect of a dinner service that he was making for the royal household; the silk merchant Stiphout received a loan of 4,000 thalers; and a sum of money was paid to free a certain Gottfried Brüderich from slavery in Algeria.

Many payments were made in connection with Frederick's campaigns. Splitgerber and Daum in association with F. W.

---

[1] W. Naudé and A. Skalweit (ed.), *Die Getreidehandelspolitik und Kreigsmagazinverwaltung Preussens 1740-1756. (Acta Borussica: Denkmäler der Preussischen Staatsverwaltung im 18en Jahrhundert)*, III, (1910), p. 61 and pp. 195-7 and documents on pp. 327, 343 and 353. The Prussian government made representations to the Russian government concerning its failure to allow grain to be sent to Prussia which had been ordered before the announcement of the embargo. Eventually in the summer of 1741 some Russian rye (3,000 *Wispel*) was delivered at Stettin. Many years later—between 1768 and 1771—the firm of Splitgerber again purchased grain in Bordeaux and Rotterdam for the royal warehouses.

Schütze handled the receipts of the English subsidies[1] and in 1757-8 funds were remitted to Frederick's forces in East Prussia and in Silesia. When the Austrians appeared before Berlin in October 1757 Splitgerber raised a fifth of the contribution which was paid to save the city from being plundered. Three years later the Russians occupied the city for a few days but on this occasion it was Gotzkowsky who took the lead in negotiating with the enemy on behalf of the Berlin merchants though Splitgerber raised 160,000 thalers towards the contribution. J. J. Schickler (of the firm of Splitgerber and Daum) joined with Gotzkowsky in underwriting the bills of the Berlin merchants which the Russians had accepted and, on this understanding, Frederick the Great accepted responsibility for the payment of the contribution.[2] After the Seven Years War Splitgerber and Daum held shares in the Royal Bank of Berlin (1765),[3] the Overseas Trading Corporation (1772),[4] the Tobacco Monopoly (1765), the Grain Commercial Company,[5] and other financial and commercial institutions established or fostered by the King.[6] The firm also invested in mortgage bonds issued by the newly established land mortgage banks.

[1] See L. Beutin, 'Die Wirkungen des Siebenjährigen Krieges auf die Volkswirtschaft' *Vierteljahrschrift fur Sozial-und Wirtschaftsgeschichte*, XXVI, (1933), p. 220. The subsidies were paid partly in specie and partly in bills of exchange on finance houses in Amsterdam and Hamburg.

[2] For this transaction see below, p. 18.

[3] For the Bank of Berlin see W. O. Henderson, *The State and the Industrial Revolution in Prussia*, (1958), pp. 140-143.

[4] For the Overseas Trading Corporation (*Seehandlung*) see W. O. Henderson, op. cit., pp. 119-148.

[5] For the Grain Commercial Company (*Getreidehandlungs-Compagnie*) see A. Skalweit (ed.), *Die Getreidehandelspolitik und Kriegmagazinverwaltung im 18en Jahrhundert (Acta Borussica: Denkmäler der Preussischen Staatsverwaltung im 18en Jahrhundert*), IV (1931), pp. 264-5. The house of Splitgerber and Daum held 50 shares. Schickler wrote that owing to ill-health he could not become a director of the company. His bookkeeper, Bauer (who owned ten shares) represented the firm on the board.

[6] The house of Splitgerber had 30 shares in Philip Clement's ill-fated Levant Company of 1766. See H. Rachel, *Die Handels-, Zoll- und Akzisenpolitik Preussens 1740-86 (Acta Borussica: Denkmäler der Preussischen Staatsverwaltung im 18en Jahrhundert*), III, Part 2 (1928), p. 598. The King hoped that Splitgerber and Daum would take over the management of the Silk Warehouse in Berlin (1749-54) but satisfactory terms could not be arranged. See G. Schmoller and O. Hintze, *Die Preussische Seidenindustrie im 18en Jahrhundert* (1892), I, p. 547 (letter from Fäsch to Splitgerber and Daum).

Splitgerber and Daum supported overseas trading enterprises in which the King took an interest. The firm had been engaged in foreign trade since the days of the Russia Commercial Company of Berlin and it had operated a small fleet of ships in the Baltic. When Prussia acquired Emden, Splitgerber advised the King to give the harbour the status of a free port and his firm was represented by J. J. Schickler in negotiations which led to the establishment of the Asiatic Commercial Company at Emden (1751).[1] The first ship to be fitted out by the Asiatic Commercial Company (the *König von Preussen*) left Emden in February 1751 and returned in July 1753 with a cargo of tea and silks which, when auctioned, fetched double what it had cost in Canton. The company traded successfully in the Far East for several years and at one time its shares were worth five times their nominal value. Its voyages ceased during the Seven Years War and subsequent efforts to revive them failed so that the enterprise had to be wound up in 1765.

Shortly after the founding of the Asiatic Commercial Company an Englishman named Harris came to Berlin and suggested that a company should be established to trade with India. The authorities referred him to Splitgerber who was recognised as the leading expert on enterprises of this kind. The Bengal Commercial Company of Emden was set up (1753) but misfortune dogged its attempts to open up trade with India. One vessel was seized by the British authorities at Gravesend[2] whilst another was lost in the Ganges.[3]

It was, however, in the management of metal works and arms factories that Splitgerber and Daum rendered their greatest services, since the production of guns and munitions was of vital importance to the nation during the wars of Frederick the

[1] Splitgerber and Daum invested 54,500 thalers in the enterprise.
[2] This ship was eventually purchased by the British Government.
[3] For Prussian trading voyages in Frederick the Great's reign see V. Ring, *Asiatische Handelskompagnien Friedrichs der Grossen* (1890); H. Berger, *Überseeische Handelsbestrebungen und Koloniale Pläne unter Friedrich dem Grossen* (1899); R. Koser, 'Der Grosse Kurfürst und Friedrich der Grosse in ihrer Stellung zu Marine und Seehandel' *Marine Rundschau*, 1904; E. Schultz-Ewerth, 'Überseeische Bestrebungen aus Preussens Vergangenheit', *Süddeutsche Monatshefte*, XVII, 1920, pp. 427-32; and A. Berney, 'Die Anfänge der Frederizianischen Seehandelspolitik', *Vierteljahrschrift für Sozial-und Wirtschaftsgeschichte*, XXII, 1929, pp. 16-31.

Great's reign. The fortunes of the metalworks operated by Splitgerber and Daum varied from time to time. In 1743 Splitgerber declined to continue the management of the Neustadt-Eberswalde rolling and slitting mill unless the rent was reduced. The lease was given up in 1750 but the establishment was again under Splitgerber's management between 1768 and 1780. The Neustadt-Eberswalde copperworks ran at a profit until they were damaged by Russian troops. The Hegermühle brassworks were a profitable concern for many years but after 1768 these works were mismanaged and output declined.[1] In 1780 the King agreed to take over the ironworks, brass works and copper works, but he did so with some reluctance and declared that in his experience manufacturing establishments did not prosper under State management.[2] In 1766 Splitgerber gave up the lease of the Zehdenick furnace which had been seriously damaged by Swedish troops during the Seven Years War.

The small arms workshops at Potsdam and Spandau received large orders during the War of the Austrian Succession, but it was difficult to maintain output since some of the workers were called up for military service while others were sent to the front to repair guns damaged in action. In 1753-4 the King arranged for the construction of a new boring mill and an additional warehouse at Spandau and more skilled workers were secured from Liège and Suhl. During the Seven Years War there was again a heavy demand for small arms and munitions and again the labour force was depleted when some of the workers were called up.[3]

In 1760 when the Russians occupied Potsdam they threw guns and equipment from the royal workshops into a canal and it was nearly two years before production could be resumed. The losses suffered by Splitgerber owing to the destruction of

[1] A former scullion of the Splitgerber household was in charge of them for a time.

[2] H. Rachel, op. cit., III, Part i, p. 649.

[3] Suhl, one of the greatest centres in Germany for the manufacture of armaments, lay in the County of Henneberg in Electoral Saxony. Although Prussia and Saxony were at war the Elector of Saxony allowed 20,000 small arms to be exported to Prussia between 1757 and 1762. See R. Forberger, *Die Manufaktur in Sachsen vom Ende des 16en bis zum Anfang 19en Jahrhunderts*, (1958), p. 191.

royal workshops at Potsdam and Neustadt-Eberswalde amounted to 26,000 thalers and compensation was eventually paid by the Chamber of the Mark Brandenburg. Nevertheless as armament manufacturers and as army contractors the firm made substantial profits in both the War of the Austrian Succession and the Seven Years War.[1]

Frederick the Great was responsible for the establishment of the cutlery industry in Neustadt-Eberswalde.[2] Soon after he came to the throne he issued an edict establishing the industry but at first no experts were available to give the new venture a start. In 1743 some skilled workers settled in Neustadt-Eberswalde but it was nearly ten years later before 130 master cutlers and their families came from Ruhla (Thuringia), Solingen (Berg) and other towns.[3] They drew their raw materials from a royal warehouse and made knives, scissors, locks and files in their own workshops. The finished articles were brought to the warehouse and the cutlers were then paid for their work.

The value of the cutlery made at Neustadt-Eberswalde soon amounted to 14,000 thalers a year. Frederick decided to hand over the warehouse to a private entrepreneur and Gotzkowsky found a master cutler at Iserlohn who was willing to migrate to Prussia though he was unable to come immediately. In 1753 the King turned to Splitgerber and Daum who agreed to manage the warehouse for twenty years. The new industry was fostered by the King in various ways—by supplying metal from the royal ironworks at Neustadt-Eberswalde and timber from the royal forests; by giving the firm a monopoly of the home market;[4] by giving Splitgerber and Daum an assured supply of horns to turn into knife-handles; and by remitting all export duties payable on the cutlery which they sold abroad.

[1] The turnover of the firm rose from 97,000 thalers to 882,000 thalers between 1756 and 1762. In the period 1759-62 profits of about 1 million thalers were made.

[2] R. Schmidt, 'Die Stahl- und Eisenwarenfabrik zu Eberswalde und ihre Schicksale', *Mitteilungen des Vereins für Heimatkunde zu Eberswalde*, Jahrgang II-III, p. 203.

[3] According to L. Beck, *Die Geschichte des Eisens*, III (1897), p. 911, some 200 cutlers and their families migrated from Ruhla to Neustadt-Eberswalde.

[4] The import of cutlery was forbidden and no knives might be sold in Prussia unless they bore the stamp of an eagle which was the mark of the Neustadt-Eberswalde warehouse.

At first Splitgerber was unable to sell all the cutlery which he made but by 1760 the initial difficulties appear to have been overcome. At that time the value of the output of the workshops was about 60,000 thalers a year and there was a considerable demand for cutlery in Mecklenburg and Poland. In the summer of 1765 the cutlery workshops became Splitgerber's property on condition that the premises were extended and that full employment was maintained. The trading results were not very satisfactory in the 1770's and 1780's and towards the end of Frederick's reign Heinitz made an unfavourable report on the workshops. Splitgerber thought that this was due to the poor location of the factory, to the demands of the workers for wage increases, and to the failure of the authorities to prevent the smuggling of foreign cutlery into Prussia. But Splitgerber's critics argued that his goods were poor in quality and high in price. The firm offered to relinquish the works to the Crown but the King would not agree to this. Two other workshops operated by the house of Splitgerber in the 1770's were the Crown copperworks at Radich (1771) and a factory at Potsdam for the manufacture of ivory combs (1771).[1] Johann Jacob Schickler established an independent firm—called Schickler and Splitgerber—which took over the Crown mirror factory at Neustadt an der Dosse.[2]

Another of Splitgerber's achievements was the introduction of sugar refining to Berlin. In the 1740's nearly all the sugar consumed in the Mark Brandenburg and the County of Magdeburg came from the sugar refineries of Hamburg. Frederick was determined to introduce the refining of sugar into his dominions and Splitgerber, ever ready to fall in with the King's wishes, stated that he was prepared to finance the establishment of sugar refining in Berlin. Frederick provided him with the land on which to build a factory; granted him a monopoly of the sale of refined sugar in Brandenburg, the New Mark and Pomerania;[3] and raised to 12 per cent the import duty on sugar refined abroad. Splitgerber's first refinery was

[1] The comb workshops were soon transferred to Neustadt-Eberswalde. The government encouraged the export of ivory combs made at these workshops by the grant of a bounty and by the remission of export duty.
[2] The establishment employed 145 workers in 1788.
[3] This monopoly was subsequently extended to Silesia and Glatz.

opened in 1749 and this was followed by the establishment of a second and a third in Berlin (in the 1750's) and a fourth in Bromberg in West Prussia (in 1774). A sugar refinery, which had been set up at Minden (Westphalia) by Harten and Möller, was acquired in 1774 and the firm was then given a monopoly of the sale of sugar in Ravensburg, Lingen and Tecklenburg.

The refineries prospered and brought large profits to the firm. In 1784 some 200 workers were employed and the value of the output was 286,254 thalers. There were complaints that the price of sugar was too high and after the Seven Years War the King told Splitgerber that he must bring his prices down to their pre-war level. In 1770 a group of merchants was allowed to set up a refinery in Breslau and shortly after Frederick's death the house of Splitgerber lost its sugar monopoly altogether but its refineries managed to compete successfully with those of its newly established rivals.[1]

David Splitgerber, having survived Daum by twenty-one years,[2] died in 1764. He had lived long enough to know that Schickler had brought the firm through the commercial crisis of 1762, although not without financial sacrifices.[3] Splitgerber's son took no active part in the management of the business and his nephew never secured a partnership.[4] The firm was now run by J. J. Schickler and F. H. Berendes. After the death of Berendes (1771) J. J. Schickler was left in full charge. When Schickler died (1775) the firm was managed by his sons David and Johann Ernst.[5] The many disputes between the

---

[1] *E.g.*, the sugar refineries set up by Henri Charles Jordan (1788), Johann Burchard Rönnenkamp (1792) and the Berlin Sugar Refining Company (1793).

[2] Daum's son Carl Friedrich Daum was not a member of the firm of Splitgerber and Daum. He set up a cotton factory in Brandenburg in 1753 but this was a costly failure. Daum's grandson, (Friedrich Adolph) was a banker in Danzig. He founded the New Insurance Company in Berlin in 1792.

[3] The losses amounted to 742,933 (revaluation of debased coins issued during the recent war) and 150,000 thalers (bad debts).

[4] David Splitgerber's nephew entered the firm in 1762 with a salary of 500 thalers a year and a share of the profits. In 1768 he gave up his share of the profits in return for a lump sum (20,000 thalers) and an increased salary (1,000 thalers). The house of Splitgerber and Daum paid higher salaries than many other Berlin firms.

[5] David Berendes (son of F. H. Berendes) was a partner in the firm for four years (1781-5).

Schicklers and David Splitgerber's son were eventually settled in 1795 and the firm was henceforth owned and run by the two Schicklers. They changed the name of the firm to Schickler Brothers.

By the end of the eighteenth century the character of the firm was changing. After Frederick's death the relations between the Crown and the firm were not so close as in David Splitgerber's day. The existence of the Bank of Berlin and the Overseas Trading Corporation meant that the King no longer needed the personal service of private merchants and financiers to handle his business affairs. The Schicklers—and their descendants—devoted themselves more to banking and less to commercial and industrial activities. In the nineteenth century the process of turning a merchant house into a bank was completed. The buying and selling of goods on commission gradually declined and this account was closed in 1850. Soon afterwards the arms factories at Spandau and Potsdam were taken over by the State. In 1860 the firm sold the last of its ships and in 1870-1 both the cutlery warehouse and the last of the sugar refineries were given up. Schickler Brothers were no longer merchants or manufacturers. They were 'the oldest bank in Berlin'.[1]

The kings of Prussia recognised the value of the services which the house of Splitgerber and Daum had rendered to the Crown. In the early days of the firm Frederick William I gave them 200 thalers towards the expense of building a house and a larger contribution came from the Fire Insurance Office. In 1755 at the time of the commercial crisis which followed the Lisbon earthquake Frederick the Great granted David Splitgerber a loan of 80,000 thalers to help him out of his financial difficulties. At the end of the Seven Years War the King presented the firm with a portrait of himself. Although Frederick despised the merchant class he realised that he could not do without men like Splitgerber and Schickler and that the task of raising Prussia to the status of a great power required the services of merchants, manufacturers and bankers as well as soldiers and civil servants.

[1] Hans Fürstenberg (ed.), *Carl Fürstenberg: Die Lebensgeschichte eines deutschen Bankiers, 1870-1914* (1931), p. 120. Elsewhere in these memoirs Carl Fürstenberg referred to Schickler Brothers as 'one of the oldest and most respected banks in Berlin' (p. 133).

CHAPTER II

The Rise of the Berlin Silk and Porcelain Industries

IN the autumn of 1760 Berlin was occupied for a few days by enemy troops for the second time during the Seven Years War. A Russian flying column, under General Tottleben,[1] suddenly appeared before the Halle Gate on 3 October. Prince Eugen of Württemberg marched forty miles to Berlin to assist in the defence of the city. Tottleben retired to Köpenick. But when Austrian troops under Count Lacy occupied Potsdam and Charlottenburg the defenders of Berlin decided to withdraw to Spandau. The Prussian capital was left to its fate. The municipal authorities decided to capitulate to the Russians and not to the Austrians. Tottleben entered Berlin on 9 October. The Austrians—ignored in the discussions between Tottleben and the Berlin city council—also forced their way into the city. At first the Russians demanded the large sum of 4,000,000 thalers in specie in return for a guarantee to respect the private property of the citizens.[2] Karl David Kircheisen, Burgomaster of Berlin,[3] was reduced to such a state of nervous prostration that the Russians believed him to be intoxicated and declined to negotiate with him.

A Berlin merchant named Gotzkowsky stepped into the breach.[4] Although he was only a private citizen and held no

[1] Czernichef was the Commander of this force. Tottleben was second in command. Carlyle describes him as 'a clever soldier who knows Berlin'. Tottleben had been born in Thuringia and had lived in Berlin before he entered the service of the Czarina.

[2] Frederick the Great stated that only the firm protests of Verelst, the Dutch Minister, saved parts of Berlin from destruction at this time. The royal palaces at Charlottenburg and Schönhausen were sacked by Cossack and Saxon troops (*Oeuvres historiques de Frédéric II*, Vol. IV, (1847), p. 81).

[3] Kircheisen was both the President of the City Council and the Director of the City Police.

[4] For Gotzkowsky's career see Johann Ernst Goztkowsky, *Geschichte eines patriotischen Kaufmanns*, (first German edn., 1768; French translation, 1769; new German edition edited by O. Hintze, 1873); Franz Otto (pen name for Otto Spamer), *Der Kaufmann zu allen Zeiten oder Buch berühmter Kaufleute*,

public office he had had previous dealings with the Russians[1] and he was able to persuade Tottleben to moderate his demands on the municipal authorities. Tottleben accepted 1,500,000 thalers instead of 4,000,000 thalers and only 500,000 thalers had to be paid at once.[2] The instalment of 500,000 thalers—and also 200,000 thalers (*Douceurgeld*) for distribution among the occupying force—were brought by the merchants to Gotzkowsky's house to be handed over to the Russians. The balance of 1,000,000 thalers was paid in commercial bills due in two months' time.

The occupation of Berlin lasted only four days (9-12 October). A rumour that Frederick the Great was on his way from Silesia to relieve his capital was sufficient to cause both Russians and Austrians to evacuate the city. Gotzkowsky subsequently paid three visits to the Russian headquarters to secure a postponement of the final date of payment of the war contribution—for which the King eventually accepted responsibility.[3] The Marquis d'Argens had these services in mind

Vol. II, (1869), pp. 213-236; Otto Hintze, 'Ein Berliner Kaufmann aus der Zeit Friedrichs des Grossen', *Schriften des Vereins für die Geschichte Berlins* Vol. XXX, (1893), pp. 1-18; and an article by T. Hirsch on Gotzkowsky in the *Allgemeine Deutsche Biographie*, Vol. IX, pp. 448-9. For Berlin merchants and bankers in the eighteenth century see Hugo Rachel and Paul Wallich, *Berliner Grosskaufleute und Kapitalisten*, Vol. II, 1648-1906, (Berlin, 1938), pp. 441-67; F. Lenz and O. Unholtz, *Die Geschichte des Bankhauses Gebrüder Schickler*, (Berlin 1912); Otto Wiedfeld, *Statistische Studien zur Entwicklungsgeschichte der Berliner Industrie in 1720 bis 1890*, (1898); and Wilhelm Treue, 'David Splitgerber . . . 1685-1764', *Vierteljahrschrift für Sozial-und Wirtschaftsgeschichte*, Vol. XLI (iii), pp. 253-67.

[1] Gotzkowsky explains in his memoirs that he had become friendly with the Russian Brigadier (later General) von Sievers who had been a prisoner of war in Berlin after the great defeat of the Russian army at Zorndorf in 1758. When a deputation of Berlin town councillors and merchants went to the Cottbus Gate to discuss terms of surrender with the Russians one of their officers (named Bachmann) asked if Gotzkowsky were among those present. He said that von Sievers had instructed him that every consideration was to be shown to Gotzkowsky during the occupation. Franz Otto (Otto Spamer) op. cit., p. 215, stated that Gotzkowsky had befriended a number of Russian officers after the Battle of Zorndorf.

[2] The 500,000 thalers war contribution (instalment) was paid in pre-war coins but the 200,000 thalers *Douceurgeld* was paid in the new depreciated coinage. A quarter of the *Douceurgeld* eventually went to the Austrian troops.

[3] Gotzkowsky in association with Schickler (of the firm of Splitgerber and Daum) agreed to underwrite the bills of the Berlin merchants. It was on this understanding that the King accepted responsibility for the payment of the

when he wrote to Frederick the Great on 28 November 1760 that 'Gotzkowsky is a splendid fellow and a fine citizen. I would wish that many such men were numbered among your subjects'.[1]

Historians of the Seven Years War have not failed to pay tribute to Gotzkowsky for his skill in negotiating with the Russians when the fate of Berlin hung in the balance. To the economic historian, however, his career is of interest for other reasons. He was a leading merchant, financier and entrepreneur in Berlin at a time when the first steps towards the industrialisation of Prussia were being taken. The development of the silk and porcelain industries in Berlin owed much to his initiative. Moreover, he gave a detailed account of his business activities in his autobiography[2] so that more is known about him than about many other entrepreneurs in Frederick the Great's reign.

Gotzkowsky's autobiography, however, must be used with caution. It was written when the author was bankrupt and harassed by his creditors. He considered that he had been unjustly treated and that the services which he had rendered

contribution. The transaction was handled by Splitgerber and Daum (550,000 thalers) and by F. W. Schütze (450,000 thalers). See F. Lenz and O. Unholtz, op. cit., p. 71. According to the editor of the *Oeuvres historiques de Frédéric II*, Vol. IV, (1847, p. 81 (note)) payment of the final instalment of Berlin's war contribution to the Russians was made on 7 April 1761. Carlyle wrote: 'Friedrich from his own distressed funds handed to Gotzkowsky the necessary million and a half, commanding only profound silence about it'. As late as 1764 the Berlin municipal authorities still owed over 100,000 thalers to persons who had subscribed to the war contribution. Annuities were issued to pay this sum.

[1] Quoted by Franz Otto (Otto Spamer), op. cit., p. 218 and by the *Allgemeine Deutsche Biographie*, Vol. IX, p. 447. See also J. G. Büsch's tribute to Gotzkowky after his death (quoted by O. Hintze in his essay on Gotzkowsky in the *Schriften des Vereins für die Geschichte Berlins*, Vol. XXX, 1893, p. 18).

[2] J. E. Gotzkowsky's autobiography, entitled *Geschichte eines patriotischen Kaufmanns*, was first published in 1768. Neither the author nor the editor was named on the title page. The editor did not print the whole of the manuscript and appendices mentioned in the text were omitted. The Berlin police banned the first edition probably because Gotzkowsky had attacked the Jewish financiers Ephraim and Itzig who held the mint concession in Prussia. Nevertheless a second edition appeared in 1769. Otto Hintze, after examining the original manuscript in the library of the Joachimsthal Gymnasium, brought out a new edition of Gotzkowsky's autobiography in 1873 (*Schriften des Vereins für die Geschichte Berlins*, Vol. III).

to the King and to the city of Berlin deserved some recompense. In the circumstances it is not surprising that Gotzkowsky sometimes exaggerated his achievements. His claims to have acted solely from motives of distinterested patriotism rather than from hopes of future financial advantage may also be regarded with some suspicion. His accounts of the activities of his rivals —such as Ephraim and Itzig—can hardly be taken at their face value.

Gotzkowsky states in his autobiography that he was born on 21 November 1710 in Konitz (Chojnice) in Poland.[1] His father, an impoverished nobleman, died shortly afterwards and Gotzkowsky was left an orphan at the age of five. He was brought up by relatives in Dresden. At the age of fourteen Gotzkowsky joined his older brother (Christian Ludwig) in Berlin and served his apprenticeship with the merchant house of Adrian Sprögel between 1724 and 1730. When Sprögel's business premises were destroyed by fire Gotzkowsky joined his brother who had established himself as a dealer in haberdashery, jewellery, ornaments and trinkets.[2] Before long Gotzkowsky appears to have been trading on his own account. He claimed that he quickly succeeded in building up a very successful business and that the goods which he exported earned substantial sums (in specie) for Prussia. His reputation as a dealer brought him to the notice of the future Frederick the Great. Gotzkowsky was summoned to the Crown Prince's castle at Rheinsberg and he was commissioned to make purchases at the Leipzig Fair on behalf of his royal patron.

When Frederick the Great ascended the throne in 1740 he immediately set up a Department of Commerce and Manufactures (the Fifth Department of the General Directory)[3] under Samuel von Marschall[4] to promote the industrial

---

[1] Annexed to Prussia in 1772 (West Prussia).

[2] Gotzkowsky described the goods he sold as *Galanteriewaren* and *Bijouterien*.

[3] Hans Hausherr, *Verwaltungseinheit und Ressorttrennung vom Ende des 17ten bis zum Beginn des 19ten Jahrhunderts*, (1953), pp. 125-7.

[4] Samuel von Marschall—who was also Postmaster General—was head of the 5th Department until his death in 1750. He was succeeded by Johann Rudolf Fäsch, a civil servant who did not have the status of a Minister of State. Fäsch was a Swiss merchant who had worked in Amsterdam (where he was Prussian Consul) before he settled in Berlin.

expansion of Prussia.[1] At this time Gotzkowsky was summoned to the royal palace at Charlottenburg. Frederick the Great told him that if new industries were to be established it would be necessary to attract skilled artisans to the country. The King asked Gotzkowsky to try to persuade foreign workers to settle in Prussia and he promised that the royal patronage would be extended to workshops in which such craftsmen were employed.

Gotzkowsky decided to further the King's plans by promoting the establishment of a large workshop for the manufacture of velvet.[2] Little success had attended earlier efforts to introduce into Prussia the manufacture of silk, lace, ribbons, stockings, velvet and gold and silver thread.[3] The trade depression of the late 1730's was aggravated in the early 1740's by the War of the Austrian Succession. Claude Pitra, for example, was using only six out of his thirty-two silk-looms in 1740. In the same year Charles Vigne, a well-known manufacturer of silk tapestries,

[1] For Frederick the Great's industrial policy see Gustav Schmoller, 'Studien über die Wirtschaftspolitik Friedrichs des Grossen . . .' (*Schmollers Jahrbuch*, Vol. VIII (1884), Vol. X (1886) and Vol. XI (1887) and *Umrisse und Untersuchungen zur Verfassungs-Verwaltungs- und Wirtschaftsgeschichte besonders des preussischen Staates im 17ten und 18ten Jahrhundert*, (1898)); T. Mommsen, 'Über die volkswirtschaftliche Politik Friedrichs des Grossen', (*Schmollers Jahrbuch*, Vol. XV, 1891); R. Koser, *Geschichte Friedrichs des Grossen* (2 vols., 1900-1901 and abridged edition, 1925); Otto Hintze, *Die Industrialisierungspolitik Friedrichs des Grossen*, (Danzig, 1903); C. Ergang, 'Friedrich der Grosse in seiner Stellung zum Maschinenproblem', *Beiträge zur Geschichte der Technik und Industrie*, edited by Conrad Matschoss, Vol. II, (1910); Conrad Matschoss, *Friedrich der Grosse als Beförderer des Gewerbefleisses* (1912); A. Zottmann, *Die Wirtschaftspolitik Friedrichs des Grossen*, (1937); and Eberhard Faden 'Das friderizianische Berlin—die Stadt der Soldaten und Manufacturen' in M. Arendt, Eberhard Faden and Otto-Friedrich Gaudert, *Geschichte der Stadt Berlin*, (1937), pp. 230-80.

[2] For the development of the Prussian silk industry in the eighteenth century see Gustav Schmoller and Otto Hintze, *Die preussische Seidenindustrie im 18ten Jahrhundert und ihre Begründung durch Friedrich den Grossen*, (*Acta Borussica*, 3 vols.; 1892: the first two volumes are a collection of documents edited by Schmoller and Hintze while the third volume is an account of the rise of the Prussian silk industry by Otto Hintze: cited as Schmoller and Hintze): see also Gustav Schmoller, *The Mercantile System*, (1931), Appendix 1, pp. 81-91.

[3] A few of the early attempts to set up silk works in Prussia deserve mention. In 1687 Jean Beat of Paris established a silk manufactory in Berlin but it survived for only a short time. In 1709 Bourguignon founded works in Berlin for the production of velvet while Delon set up a workshop for knitting silk stockings. In 1732 Claude Pitra of Lyons came to Berlin from Dresden and opened a workshop for the manufacture of silks.

was operating only seven of his looms. Cuissart, one of Pitra's apprentices who had set up silk-works of his own in 1742, was working only four of his looms five years later. The Department of Commerce and Manufactures reported in 1744 that the silk industry was moribund and that a new start would have to be made if it were to be revived.

Frederick the Great encouraged the silk industry in various ways. He persuaded foreign entrepreneurs to come to Berlin by giving them machines, subsidies, pensions and privileges and by reducing their tax liabilities. He paid the travelling expenses of many skilled workers who migrated to Prussia. The majority of the silk workers came from France and the French colony in Berlin—originally established by Huguenot refugees in the 1680's—was greatly strengthened. Frederick paid a monthly premium on the silk-looms which were in operation in some—but not all—Prussian silk-works. Shortly after the signing of the Treaty of Dresden (December 1745) the King set up the *Haupt-Manufacturkasse* (Central Industrial Fund)[1] with an initial grant of 100,000 thalers from the *Kurmärkische Landschaft*—a State credit institute—to promote the expansion of the silk industry.[2] The *Haupt-Manufacturkasse*, which was administered by the head of the Department of Commerce and Manufactures, had its own budget and was free from the control of the *Ober-Rechnungskammer* (Chamber of Finance).

While small silk-works of the type operated by Pitra and Cuissart were struggling to survive, David Hirsch's larger enterprises in Potsdam were in a relatively flourishing condition. Since 1730 this Jewish entrepreneur had enjoyed a monopoly of the sale of velvet in Prussia. An official report of 1744 stated that he was operating 144 looms. He had also assumed responsibility for organising the spinning and weaving of wool in the prison in Spandau. Since Hirsch was unable to supply the whole of the home demand, Frederick the Great suggested that

---

[1] Also known as the *Seidenmanufacturkasse*.

[2] Between 1746 and 1763 the fund had 122,000 thalers at its disposal. In addition to the 100,000 thalers from the *Kurmärkische Landschaft* it received 5,000 thalers from the profits of the Post Office (1749) and 12,891 thalers from the Excise Department (1760-1). Expenditure in 1746-63 amounted to 112,561 thalers. See balance sheet in Schmoller and Hintze, op. cit., Vol. 1, p. 426.

a new velvet manufactory should be established to supply the East Prussian market and the export trade from that province to Russia and Poland. Gotzkowsky persuaded Christian Friedrich Blume to set up velvet works in Berlin at his own expense. Blume secured the concession in July 1746[1] but he died before the workshop in the Königsstrasse was opened. Gotzkowsky, who had married Blume's daughter, Anna Louise, now took a partner (Johann Christian Streckfuss) into his jewellery business so as to be able to devote much of his time to the management of Blume's velvet workshop on behalf of the heirs.[2] Skilled foreign artisans were brought to Berlin to work in this factory. In January 1748 Gotzkowsky was operating 60 looms and employing 244 workers. He stated that the initial capital to start the works amounted to 30,000 thalers.

Gotzkowsky had to overcome many difficulties before his silk-works were firmly established. Considerable initial costs had to be incurred to set them up. Expensive equipment had to be purchased from abroad. Travelling expenses paid to skilled foreign workers who migrated to Berlin amounted to 1,000 thalers—sometimes even 1,500 thalers—for a single family. To attract these artisans to Prussia, high wages had to be offered. Even so, the quality of the work performed by foreigners was sometimes disappointing. In 1750, for example, it was reported that the brothers Druet (who had come to Gotzkowsky's works from Marseilles) had failed to give satisfaction. They left Gotzkowsky's employment, set up a workshop of their own and promptly petitioned the King for a pension. This was refused.

The cost of the raw material rose soon after Gotzkowsky established his works. In 1749 raw silk was in short supply and high prices had to be paid for imports from Italy. The King tried to alleviate the situation by establishing a state Silk Warehouse in Berlin.[3] Government agents purchased raw silk in

---

[1] Not 1743 as stated by Gotzkowsky in his autobiography.

[2] The firm was known as 'C. F. Blumes sel. Erben' (Executors of the late C. F. Blume). The heirs were Blume's widow, his two sons and the daughter who had married Gotzkowsky.

[3] The first Silk Warehouse (1749-54) was financed by loans from the Post Office (5,000 thalers) and the *Kurmärkische Landschaft* (20,000 thalers). In 1753 it received a grant of 30,000 thalers from the General Domains Fund (*General-Domänenkasse*). In his political testament of 1752 Frederick the

Italy and Prussian merchants were granted six months' credit when they made purchases at the warehouse.

Unfortunately for Gotzkowsky the public preferred foreign to Prussian silks and before long he had 20,000 thalers worth of unsold stocks on his hands. A series of Cabinet Orders—17 January 1748, 31 August 1749, 30 June 1753 and many more —forbade the importation of silks from abroad but despite these prohibitions substantial quantities of foreign silks continued to be sold in Prussia.[1]

Disputes arose between Gotzkowsky and the Jewish wholesalers who traded in silks. These merchants were well established and they complained that Gotzkowsky was not only making velvet and silks but was engaged in the wholesale trade as well. They considered this to be unfair competition. Gotzkowsky and the Jewish merchants each accused the other of defrauding the revenue by falsely representing as Prussian silks the foreign silks which they sold at the great fairs. Another difficulty which Gotzkowsky had to face was competition from entrepreneurs who followed his example and set up new silk-works. These competitors benefited from the work of men like Hirsch and Gotzkowsky and were able to establish their workshops with a relatively smaller capital outlay. Instead of paying the expenses of foreign skilled artisans who migrated to Prussia, they were often able to secure German workers who had been trained in existing establishments in Berlin or Potsdam.[2] Moreover, the newcomers paid their workers lower wages. When Gotzkowsky took over Blume's workshop he had to pay 1 thaler 8

Great stated that he hoped to make the warehouse a permanent institution with a capital of 100,000 thalers. But this plan was not carried out and the warehouse was closed in 1754. A second silk warehouse was established in Berlin in 1767.

[1] It was reported that between 1 August 1751 and 31 January 1752 the Berlin merchants (Christians and Jews) imported foreign silks to the value of 28,052 thalers but had purchased Prussian silks to the value of only 16,412 thalers. On 26 February 1753 Gotzkowsky complained that Jewish merchants were selling foreign silks in Prussia every year to the value of at least 150,000 thalers. See Schmoller and Hintze. op. cit., Vol. I, p. 257 (note) and p. 291.

[2] Gotzkowsky, in a letter of 23 June 1753, complained to the King that the merchant Lange of Breslau had enticed skilled workers from his own establishments and also from David Hirsch of Potsdam, (Schmoller and Hintze, op. cit., Vol. I, pp. 309-310.)

groschen for the winding of one pound of silk. But within a few years so many workers were proficient in winding that the piece-work rate dropped to only 12 groschen.

By August 1750 Gotzkowsky was in such a state of financial embarrassment that he asked Frederick the Great for help. The King at first rejected this appeal. He reproached Gotzkowsky for having ignored his advice. Gotzkowsky had set up a large and costly workshop in the centre of Berlin instead of being content with more modest and less expensive premises in the suburbs. But Frederick the Great helped Gotzkowsky in another way. Gotskowsky was given 10,000 thalers on condition that he took over Simond's silk-works which were not paying their way. Gotzkowsky was also presented with the workshop, the looms and a house in the Leipzigerstrasse. Only about ten workers were employed in 1750 but before long the number had been increased to eighty.

With additional capital and a second workshop at his disposal Gotzkowsky's business now made rapid progress. He succeeded in increasing his sales by improving the style of his silks. Every year he took his samples to the trade fair at Leipzig and his silks found a ready market in Russia and Poland. His annual output of velvet and silks at this time amounted to 100,000 thalers. He enjoyed the King's confidence and frequently acted as spokesman for all the silk merchants of Berlin and Potsdam. Numerous government measures to safeguard and to promote the industry were originally suggested by Gotzkowsky. He continued to support the King's policy of attracting new silk-works and skilled artisans to Berlin even though this increased the competition that his own works had to face. On 15 August 1752 Frederick the Great thanked him for persuading F. W. Schütze to set up his silk-works in Potsdam.[1] In the next year Gotzkowsky reported to the King that he had persuaded several foreign skilled workers to migrate to Prussia.[2] Early in 1754 the King once more showed his appreciation of Gotzkowsky's services by making him a loan of 18,500 thalers from the

[1] Schütze's silk-works were established in Berlin (and not in Potsdam as originally planned). In 1756 they were taken over by C. F. Treitschke who went bankrupt in 1766. (See Schmoller and Hintze, op. cit., Vol. I, p. 273 and p. 518). Schütze then devoted his attention to banking.

[2] Schmoller and Hintze, op. cit., Vol. I, p. 310.

funds of the silk warehouse. Eleven years later the King decided that the loan need not be repaid.[1]

In the following year Gotzkowsky's position at Court was strengthened when Frederick the Great gave him a commission to purchase paintings and ornaments on his behalf for the new palace at Sans Souci. A similar order was received from the Court of Saxony. Gotzkowsky's subsequent activities as an art dealer were independent of the business conducted by the firm of 'Gotzkowsky and Streckfuss'. Soon afterwards, however, Gotzkowsky was again in financial straits. The Lisbon earthquake had been followed by a severe commercial crisis and credit was very difficult to obtain. The Berlin banking firm of Splitgerber and Daum declared that 'the unfortunate disaster in Lisbon has had such repercussions on commerce that all the large merchant houses have closed their books and have called in their debts.'[2] Gotzkowsky informed the King in December 1755 that he was in urgent need of ready money. His establishments, which now employed over 1,000 workers, needed (a capital of) 400,000 thalers and nearly half of this sum had been borrowed from merchants in Amsterdam and Hamburg. Frederick the Great, who had lent Splitgerber and Daum 80,000 thalers free of interest, hesitated at first to help Gotzkowsky but eventually lent him 40,000 thalers from the *Kurmärkische Landschaft*.[3] The King insisted that the transaction must be kept secret. Gotzkowsky wrote in his autobiography: 'I was so affected by His Majesty's kindness and by this new mark of confidence in me that I went to see the King two days later. I clasped his knees and wept in gratitude and this showed better than words how much I appreciated his goodness'.[4] The King

---

[1] *Ibid.*, 329-30 and 453.

[2] F. Lenz and Otto Unholtz, op. cit., p. 49.

[3] At the King's request Ursinus and Kircheisen examined Gotzkowsky's books. They reported that Gotzkowsky was solvent.

[4] This passage was omitted from the first edition of Gotzkowsky's autobiography. It was printed by Schmoller and Hintze, op. cit., Vol. I, p. 376. On 1 November and on 16 November 1756 Gotzkowsky asked for more time to repay this loan as the Court of Saxony owed him 60,000 thalers and he had not yet been paid by the King of Prussia for paintings purchased on his behalf. Frederick the Great's reply is not known but the debt was probably paid to the King's satisfaction—though not within twelve months as Gotzkowsky claimed in his autobiography. See Schmoller and Hintze, op. cit., Vol. I, pp. 396-7.

told him that he hoped to make him a grant of 50,000 thalers but could not afford to do so just then.

Hardly had Gotzkowsky recovered from the shock of the commercial crisis of 1755 than new troubles loomed ahead. Industry and trade were soon adversely affected by the Seven Years War which broke out in 1756.[1] At the autumn fair at Leipzig in that year Gotzkowsky secured orders worth only 200 thalers which did not cover his travelling expenses. Prussian territory was invaded. The province of East Prussia was occupied by the Russians for most of the war. Berlin was twice seized by enemy troops. On the other hand Frederick the Great overran Saxony which became the base for his military operations and a source of additional revenue.[2] It was no longer possible to regulate manufactures as strictly as in peacetime. Foreign goods, which the King had long tried to keep out of his territories, were now smuggled into Prussia in large quantities. Frederick the Great's close supervision of the country's economy came to an end. Only five Cabinet Orders were sent to the Department of Commerce and Manufactures during the whole period of the war.

Above all, the debasement of the coinage—the only way by which Frederick the Great could pay his bills—caused prices to rise and inflicted untold harm on the country's economy.[3] In November 1757 the King ordered the silver plate from the royal palaces to be melted down and minted into 600,000 thalers. To do this 21 thalers—instead of the normal 14—had to be minted from every (Cologne) Mark of fine silver. This rate (or something like it) was maintained throughout the war years. The mints of Saxony, which were under Prussian control

---

[1] For the economic consequences of the Seven Years War in Prussia see Ludwig Beutin, 'Die Wirkungen des Siebenjährigen Krieges auf die Volkswirtschaft in Preussen', *Vierteljahrschrift für Sozial-und Wirtschaftsgeschichte*, Vol. XXII, (1929), pp. 16-31.

[2] The contributions in cash and kind paid by Saxony during the war were valued at 48 million thalers.

[3] See F. von Schrötter, *Das preussische Münzwesen im 18ten Jahrhundert*, (*Acta Borussica*, 3 vols., 1910) and 'Das preussiche Münzwesen im 18ten Jahrhundert', *Forschungen zur Brandenburgischen und Preussischen Geschichte*, Vol. XXII, (1909); R. Koser, 'Die preussische Finanzen im Siebenjährigen Kriege', *Forschungen zur brandenburgischen und preussischen Geschichte*, Vol. XIII, (1900).

during the war, also turned out depreciated coins. And the mints of both Prussia and Saxony supplied Poland—which did not mint its own coins at this time—with debased money.[1] Gotzkowsky soon found himself in serious difficulties. He was bound by law to accept debased coins from those who owed him money but he was in debt to foreigners who naturally insisted on being paid in sound currency. Gotzkowsky lost 200,000 thalers on these transactions.

The manufacture of silks in Prussia did not suffer as much as might have been expected during the war. This was because the King, despite heavy calls upon his purse, continued to subsidise the industry. Pensions for certain foreign workers were still paid at the rate of 3,000 thalers a year while subventions to manufacturers amounted to about 50,000 thalers between 1757 and 1762. The number of silk-looms at work in Berlin declined from 1,034 in 1754 to 1,001 in 1760 but early in 1761 Frederick the Great wrote that he was glad to learn that there had recently been an increase in the number of looms in operation. Gotzkowsky explains in his autobiography that he kept quiet about the heavy losses that he had suffered from the inflation. He took the risk of borrowing more money from the financiers in Hamburg and Amsterdam and these funds enabled him to keep his silk-works running. Indeed, in February 1759 he actually extended his interests by taking over Samuel Schwartze's small taffeta works which had 20 looms. The King gave him Schwartze's house and workshop at the Royal Gate in Berlin. Before long Gotzkowsky was operating 75 looms in this establishment.

It had been seen that when the Russians occupied Berlin, Gotzkowsky rendered important services to the city by conducting negotiations with General Tottleben concerning the war contribution to be paid by the city. He did more than this. When the Russians were approaching Berlin, Gotzkowsky and a few other merchants stored provisions in the opera house for the use of the relieving force. These stores, valued at 57,000 thalers, ultimately fell into Russian hands. Many merchants —both Christians and Jews—deposited their valuables in Gotz-

[1] The Polish coinage of this period had as many as thirty or even forty thalers to the mark of fine silver.

kowsky's house. Since Captain von Brinke (Tottleben's adjutant) was quartered there the property of the Berlin merchants was safe from looting. The Russians proposed to levy a special contribution on the Jews and to seize Ephraim and Itzig as hostages for its payment. Gotzkowsky explained to Tottleben that the Jews had full rights of citizenship and were paying their share of the general contribution of 1,500,000 thalers already agreed upon and the Russians waived their demand for a special payment. Gotzkowsky also interceded with the Russians on behalf of a group of Berlin journalists. But for his intervention they would have been flogged for criticising the Russians in their newspapers. Again, when Tottleben proposed to take three Berlin bankers with him as hostages for the payment of the war contribution Gotzkowsky persuaded him to take their cashiers instead.

Gotzkowsky saved some industrial establishments from destruction. Tottleben had received instructions to destroy all royal manufactories in Prussia that he could find. Gotzkowsky could not save the royal foundry, mint and powder mills from destruction but he did plead that the royal cloth warehouse and gold and silver works should be spared since their profits were set aside for the maintenance of the military orphanage at Potsdam. Gotzkowsky also saved the ironworks, cutlery workshops and brassworks at Neustadt-Eberswalde and Hegermühle. He was in Eberswalde[1] at the end of October 1760 shortly after the Russians had left Berlin. The burgomaster told him that the Russians were proposing to destroy not only these works but also the recently constructed Finow Canal. Gotzkowsky bribed a Russian officer to start a small fire in the works and then move his troops away quickly so that the conflagration could be put out before any serious damage was done. A little later he heard that Tottleben had learned that the works at Neustadt-Eberswalde were still standing and had sent two hundred Cossacks to destroy them. Gotzkowsky told Tottle-

[1] Eberswalde, a town of medieval origin, was situated on the Finow Canal, 27 miles from Berlin. It was extended in size in 1747 when a colony of Germans from Thuringia was established there. Between 1747 and 1877 the town was called 'Neustadt-Eberswalde'. For the 'royal' metal works of Eberswalde leased to Splitgerber and Daum see F. Lenz and O. Unholtz, op. cit., ch. 1.

ben that these works were not royal manufactories but belonged to Splitgerber and Daum. The Cossacks were recalled.[1]

Towards the end of the year 1760 Gotzkowsky travelled to Meissen, near Dresden, to report to Frederick the Great on his recent discussions with the Russians. The King undertook to pay Berlin's war contribution but told Gotzkowsky that this promise must be kept secret for the time being. A letter which Gotzkowsky had written to the Czarina was as yet unanswered and there was still a possibility that the contribution might be reduced. Gotzkowsky received 150,000 thalers from the King. He states that 100,000 thalers was due to him for pictures which he had purchased for Frederick the Great shortly before the outbreak of war. The remaining 50,000 thalers may have been the gift promised five years before or they may have been given to Gotzkowsky in recognition of his recent services in connection with Berlin's war contribution. Another possibility is that the King intended the money to be used for the establishment of a porcelain factory in Berlin.

In spite of the critical military situation, the King found time to discuss with his visitor the possibility of introducing the porcelain industry into Berlin. Meissen, now occupied by Prussian troops, was famous for its porcelain. On the last occasion that the Prussians had occupied the town—during the second Silesian War—Frederick the Great had sent sixty-five boxes of porcelain to Berlin and had persuaded some of the local workers to settle in Prussia. The new opportunity of learning the secrets of the manufacture of Meissen was too good to miss. Frederick the Great showed Gotzkowsky some samples of Meissen china and expressed the hope that Berlin would one day have its own porcelain factory.[2] The only porcelain works in

---

[1] Gotzkowsky's intervention was not entirely successful since Splitgerber subsequently estimated that the damage done to his industrial establishments outside Berlin in 1760 amounted to 26,000 thalers. These establishments included not only metal and cutlery works at Eberswalde and Hegermüle but also an arms factory at Potsdam and an iron furnace at Zehdenick. The Zehdenick works had been seriously damaged by Swedish troops in 1758. See F. Lenz and O. Unholtz, op. cit., p. 71 and p. 82.

[2] For the development of the porcelain industry in Berlin see '*Königliches Berlin*' *1763-1913. Gedenkblatt zum 150-jährigen Jubiläum der Königl. Porzellenmanufaktur Berlin*, (1914); G. Kolb, *Geschichte der Königlichen Porzellan-*

the Prussian capital—those founded by Wilhelm Casper Wegely in 1751—had been closed in 1757[1] and nothing had come of Frederick the Great's efforts to persuade H. K. Schimmelmann to establish porcelain works in the Prussian capital.

Gotzkowsky's financial position at the beginning of 1761 was far from secure. He had lost heavily over the depreciation of the coinage. He had incurred heavy expenses in connection with his negotiations with the Russians. He had neglected his velvet and silk-works for some months. Nevertheless he acted promptly to carry out the King's wishes. As soon as he returned to Berlin he got into touch with a porcelain expert who showed him samples of his skill. The workmanship was superior to that of Wegely. Gotzkowsky persuaded the expert to set up a workshop in the Leipzigerstrasse and paid him 10,000 thalers for his trade secrets. The craftsman also received an annual salary of 1,000 thalers and free accommodation. Gotzkowsky was soon employing seventy men and eighty apprentices in this workshop. He engaged a painter of miniatures named Clause at 2,000 thalers a year to teach painting to the apprentices. In January 1762 Gotzkowsky went to Leipzig to see Frederick the Great and showed him some pieces of porcelain which had been made at the new Berlin factory. The King expressed his astonishment and delight at the speed with which Gotzkowsky had acted and at the high quality of the samples which he had brought to Leipzig.

Although Gotzkowsky was now one of the most important entrepreneurs in Berlin, a large employer of labour and a man who enjoyed the confidence of the King, he was heavily in debt to Dutch and Hamburg merchants and his position was far from secure. He tried to improve matters by financial deals of a dubious character. When he was in Leipzig in 1761 mem-

---

manufaktur zu Berlin, (1863); Paul Seidel, 'Friedrich der Grosse und seine Porzellan Manufactur' *Hohenzollern Jahrbuch*, Vol. VI, (1902), pp. 175-206; reprints in an appendix Grieninger's account of the origin of the industry and *250 Jahre Staatliche Porzellan-Manufaktur Meissen* (1960).

[1] Wegely owned cloth works in Berlin and made silk ribbons in Potsdam. His porcelain works in the Friedrichstrasse (near the King's Gate) had been opened in 1752. Previously the only porcelain workshops in Prussia appear to have been those established at Plaue (on the River Havel) between 1714 and 1730. Plaue is in Kreis Westhavelland (Brandenburg).

bers of the City Council and representatives of the local merchants asked him to intercede on their behalf with the King of Prussia to secure a reduction of their war contribution for that year. Frederick the Great agreed to mitigate his demands on condition that Gotzkowsky gave his personal guarantee that the money would be paid. It appears that Gotzkowsky made no less than 500,000 thalers on the series of transactions which the payment of the contribution involved.[1] He stated in his memoirs: 'All that I did was to take the precaution of securing from the Leipzig merchants bills of exchange expressed in pre-war gold values while my payments to His Majesty were made in current coins which had fallen so much in value that I was able to make a thirty per cent profit on the deal'.

In the end, however, Gotzkowsky went too far. He tried to pay the King 400,000 thalers of Leipzig's war contribution in Holstein-Plön money which was one of the most debased currencies in Germany. A consignment of this money (50,000 thalers), on its way from Hamburg to Leipzig, was confiscated by the Prussian authorities at Minden (Westphalia). A complaint had been made by Ephraim and Itzig, the 'Mint Jews' who held concessions for both the Prussian and Saxon mints at this time. Gotzkowsky could consider himself fortunate in not being more severely punished for this attempt to evade the currency regulations.

Two transactions in 1762 and 1763 worsened Gotzkowsky's financial position. In September 1762 he visited Hamburg in order to get to know personally the merchants who had given him credit. He was told that there were rumours in Hamburg concerning the solvency of the Berlin firm of Adrian Sprögel. After enquiries had been made in Berlin Gotzkowsky agreed to underwrite Sprögel's bills because he feared that if Sprögel failed many other Berlin merchants would be unable to meet their obligations. But when he returned to Berlin and examined the books of the firm himself he discovered that there was a deficiency of 150,000 thalers that he had to meet. His action, however, did not save the Berlin merchants from the crisis which came in the following year.

[1] Ludwig Beutin, op. cit., 221. Gotzkowsky also handled similar transactions on behalf of Mecklenburg and the city of Nürnberg.

In 1763 when the war ended,[1] Gotzkowsky was given the opportunity of acquiring some Russian army grain which was stored at the Pomeranian port of Kolberg. In partnership with the merchants Leveaux and Stein and the Amsterdam financial house of de Neufville Brothers, he agreed to buy the grain, closing the deal himself with the Russian agent, Login Shuvesnikov. The purchase price of the grain was 1,170,000 Dutch guilders. Too late, Gotzkowsky discovered that the price at which he could sell the grain was much lower than he had at first supposed. His partners attempted to cancel the transaction but the Russians refused and he was involved in a serious loss.

One of Gotzkowsky's partners in this unfortunate affair was de Neufville, an Amsterdam merchant who had recently been invited to Berlin by the King. Frederick the Great had tried to persuade de Neufville to establish himself in Berlin, but the Jewish merchants were strongly opposed to the appearance of a new competitor and did their best to discredit him both in Amsterdam and in Berlin. De Neufville's creditors demanded their money back in cash and refused to accept bills. On 25 July 1762 the firm of de Neufville (Amsterdam) failed and 'a general crash took place on the Continent'.[2]

The crisis of 1763[3] was brought about by the collapse of an inherently unsound system of commercial credit which had developed during the war. For seven years wholly abnormal

[1] The Treaty of Paris was signed on 10 February 1763 and the Treaty of Hubertsburg was signed on 15 February 1763.

[2] The phrase 'a general crash' was used by the Englishman John Parish who was a merchant banker in Hamburg. See Richard Ehrenberg, *Das Haus Parish in Hamburg*, (second edn., 1925), p. 11.

[3] For the commercial crisis of 1763, which affected the main commercial centres of the Continent, see Johann Ernst Gotzkowsky, *Geschichte eines patriotischen Kaufmanns*, (1768), pp. 187-9; Johann Georg Büsch, *Versuch einer Geschichte der Hamburgische Handlung*, (Hamburg, 1797; reprinted in collected works); W. P. Santiju Kluit, *De Amsterdamsche Beors in 1763 en 1773*, (Amsterdam, 1865); Max Wirth, *Geschichte der Handelskrisen*, (1890), pp. 86-95; Mentor Bouniatian, *Geschichte der Handelskrisen im England*, (1908), pp. 130-4; A. Dietz, *Frankfurter Handelsgeschichte*, (5 vols., 1910-25), Vol. V, p. 440; Richard Ehrenberg, *Das Haus Parish in Hamburg*, (2nd edn., 1925), pp. 8-13; S. Skalweit, *Die Berliner Wirtschaftskrise von 1763 und ihre Hintergründe: Vierteljahrschrift für Sozial -und Wirtschaftsgeschichte*, supplementary volume XXXIV, (1937); and Spiethoff's article on 'Krise' in the *Handwörterbruch der Staatswissenschaften*, (4th edn.), Vol. VI, p. 46.

conditions had prevailed. Prices rose as rival army contractors competed for limited supplies of grain and cloth and the debasing of many German currencies aggravated the situation. Credit was everywhere in demand—from great cities like Leipzig which were trying to borrow specie to satisfy the insatiable demands of their conquerors to dealers who were attempting to raise money to speculate in scarce foodstuffs or manufactured goods that were being supplied to one or other of the many armies in the field.

The failure of de Neufville was quickly followed by the collapse of a number of firms in Amsterdam. The next commercial centre to be affected was Hamburg where ninety-five firms could not meet their obligations. In Berlin the most important failure was that of Gotzkowsky who had strained his resources to breaking point by underwriting the bills of other merchants in the hope of averting a general crash. The King purchased his porcelain works for 225,000 thalers and Gotzkowsky was able to come to an agreement with his creditors to pay fifty per cent of his debts. The transaction concerning the Russian grain was settled when he handed over 226 valuable paintings (including several old masters) to the Czarina of Russia. He still had his three silk-works and he was able to raise new credits. Before long he paid his creditors an additional 400,000 thalers.

Nevertheless Gotzkowsky's efforts to re-establish his position after the crisis of 1763 failed. His financial affairs were in a state of great confusion. It was no easy matter for his creditors to discover the exact financial position of the various enterprises in which he was concerned. These still included the textile works (C. F. Blume's heirs), the jewellery firm of Gotzkowsky and Streckfuss, as well as his business as an art dealer and his transactions as a financier and speculator. In the autumn of 1764 he informed the King that he would not be able to keep his silk-works in operation much longer. Frederick the Great declined to do anything further for him except to give him some good advice. He was urged to work hard and to pay strict attention to his business.[1] In 1765 Gotzkowsky sold his velvet

[1] See Resolution of the Cabinet of 22 October 1764 in Schmoller and Hintze, op. cit., Vol. I, pp. 440-2.

manufactory to Moses Riess.[1] The silk-works[2] and the taffeta works[3] were sold to Meyer Benjamin Levi who already owned a calico establishment. So two Jewish merchants took over the silk business that Gotzkowsky had built up over the past twenty years. In 1767 he went bankrupt for the second time.

Frederick the Great instituted an enquiry into the causes of the depression of trade in 1765-6. The report, compiled by Eduard Ursinus (of the Department of Manufactures and Commerce) criticised the King's policy concerning the silk industry with remarkable frankness. Ursinus blamed the silk entrepreneurs for their inefficiency and the artisans for their slovenly workmanship. He stated that the quality of Prussian silks was so poor that it was not surprising that five manufacturers had unsold goods valued at over 623,000 thalers on their hands.[4] Ursinus was sent to cool his heels in the fortress of Spandau while the King continued his policy of subsidising the silk industry.

After his second bankruptcy Gotzkowsky hoped to retrieve his fortunes by starting up a new business with the trust funds left by Blume to his daughter (Gotzkowsky's wife) and to his son. It appears, however, that Gotzkowsky's creditors stopped him from gaining control over this capital.[5] Plagued by his creditors to the end, he died in poverty in 1775. It was not without justification that he complained bitterly at the end of his memoirs of the ingratitude of those whom he had once befriended.[6] It is astonishing that neither the King nor the Berlin City Council granted a pension to the man who had saved their property during the Russian occupation of 1760. Hintze, the leading authority on the history of the Prussian

[1] Formerly Blume: 100 looms were in operation in these works when they were sold. For the sale see Schmoller and Hintze, op. cit., Vol. I, pp. 450-2.

[2] Formerly Simond: Levi paid 15,000 thalers for the house attached to the works.

[3] Formerly Schwartz: the purchase price was 14,800 thalers.

[4] For extracts from this report of the General Directory see Schmoller and Hintze, op. cit., Vol. I, pp. 526-8.

[5] For Gotzkowsky's bankruptcies see Hugo Rachel and Paul Wallich, *Berliner Grosskaufleute und Kapitalisten*, Vol. II, 1648-1806, (1938), pp. 458-467.

[6] Gotzkowsky wrote: 'Ich kann diese Geschichte mit Recht mit den Worten aus einer bekannten Fabel schliessen: "Mit Undank lohnet die Welt".'

35

4

silk industry in the eighteenth century, summed up Gotzkowsky's character as follows: 'He was a true patriot and a lover of mankind. But it must be admitted that he was also a confirmed gambler who rashly sacrificed thousands and tens of thousands of thalers in the hope of gaining hundreds of thousands'.[1]

The significance of Gotzkowsky's career lay less in the part that he played in the dramatic events of 1760 than in his efforts to develop the silk and porcelain industries of Berlin. The porcelain factory which he established was taken over by the King and had a long and successful life as a nationalised enterprise. The Berlin silk industry, however, eventually declined. Frederick the Great appears to have sunk about two million thalers in this industry. In 1783, towards the close of his reign, Berlin had 2,316 silk looms and the value of the industry's output amounted to 1,749,596 thalers.[2]

In the nineteenth century believers in the doctrine of *laissez-faire* criticised Frederick the Great for trying to establish 'artificial' industries in his dominions. Macaulay, for example, declared that 'neither the experience of other rulers, nor his own, could ever teach him that something more than an edict and a grant of money was required to create a Lyons, a Brussels, or a Birmingham'.[3] Schmoller's judgment, however, was probably sounder. He argued that Frederick's attempt to establish the silk industry in Berlin achieved a considerable measure of success. He observed that 'Berlin in 1780-1806 stood almost on a level with all other places where the silk industry was carried on. It was mainly through the silk industry that Berlin became an important factory town, and the town whose inhabitants were distinguished by the best taste in Germany . . . And the fact that in the sixties and seventies,[4] as living became dearer in Berlin, and the competition of Crefeld and of foreign countries became more intense, most of the Berlin men of business, capitalists and workmen, turned to other occupations—while some parts of the old industry, like

---

[1] Otto Hintze, *Die preussische Seidenindustrie im 18ten Jahrhundert . . .*, (*Acta Borussica*, 3 vols., 1892), Vol. III, p. 159.

[2] von Reden, 'Die Gewerbetätigheit Berlins in älterer und neuester Zeit', *Zeitschrift des Vereins für deutsche Statistik*, Vol. II, (1848), pp. 476-80.

[3] T. B. Macaulay, *Historical Essays*, Vol. II, (Everyman edition), p. 145.

[4] I.e. the 1860s and 1870s.

the business of dyeing, maintained themselves in an even more flourishing state—this fact is not proof that the Berlin silk industry of the eighteenth century was not in its place.'[1]

[1] Gustav Schmoller, *The Mercantile System*, (1931), pp. 86-7.

CHAPTER III

The Recovery of Prussia after the Seven Years War

(i) *Economic Consequences of the War*[1]

IN 1762 Peter III of Russia withdrew from the coalition which had opposed Frederick the Great during the Seven Years War. Russian troops left East Prussia and Pomerania.[2] Sweden came to terms with Prussia on the basis of no territorial changes and no indemnities. In 1763 the peace of Hubertusburg between Prussia on the one hand and Austria and Saxony on the other also provided for the re-establishment of the *status quo* and for no reparations. Frederick had to evacuate Saxony and secured neither territorial nor financial compensation for Prussia's losses during the war.

The economic effects of the Seven Years War upon Prussia were varied in character. On the one hand there was much devastation; the currency was depreciated; land, houses, foodstuffs and manufactured goods rose in price; agricultural and industrial output was disorganised; internal and foreign trade was interrupted. Yet certain branches of manufacture were stimulated, for the metal, armament and woollen industries worked at high pressure to fulfil orders for the army. Trading and financial practices changed to meet the new conditions created by a wartime economy and new figures came to the fore in industry, commerce, and finance.

Some parts of Prussia escaped the worst consequences of the war. Magdeburg, for example, actually profited from the war since it was never occupied by the enemy and became for a time

---

[1] L. Beutin, 'Die Wirkungen des Siebenjährigen Krieges auf die Volkswirtschaft in Preussen' (*Vierteljahrschrift für Sozial-und Wirtschaftsgeschichte*, XXVI, 1933, pp. 209-243 and S. Skalweit, *Die Berliner Wirtschaftskrise von 1763 und ihre Hintergründe* (Supplement XXXIV of the *Vierteljahrschrift für Sozial- und Wirtschaftsgeschichte*, Stuttgart and Berlin, 1937).

[2] A force of 20,000 Russians under Czernichef was stationed in Silesia to cooperate with the Prussians against the Austrians but it was withdrawn when Peter III of Russia was deposed.

the temporary home of the court and the centre of the administration. Its commerce expanded since it handled Prussian trade diverted from Stettin to Hamburg. This, however, was exceptional. The provinces east of the Elbe lost a population of 332,586[1] and suffered either from enemy occupation or from military operations which led to the destruction of towns, villages, manors, farms cottages, and barns. Farms were neglected, for able bodied men were conscripted, while women and children fled at the approach of hostile armies. Artisans migrated to regions less affected by the war. By 1763 land-owners, farmers and peasants were short of horses, cattle, sheep, fodder, and seed. Some regions were on the verge of famine and there was a danger that starvation would be followed by an epidemic. A number of factories, workshops and bleaching grounds had been destroyed. Some craftsmen suffered because government orders for public works and for house building had come to an end. In some parts of Prussia the civil administration had virtually collapsed since vacancies in the public service had rarely been filled and those who stayed at their posts had been overworked. The collection of taxes had fallen into arrears, smuggling was rampant, and the police and judiciary had failed to function with their normal efficiency.

The cost of the war to Prussia probably amounted to nearly 140 million thalers.[2] The money was not raised by levying additional taxation[3] or by borrowing.[4] It was raised in three ways. First, some 93 million thalers came from previous savings (13 million thalers), the war contributions paid by Saxony, Mecklenburg, and Swedish Pomerania (53 million thalers) and the English subsidy (27 million thalers). Secondly, money was raised by taxation but income from this source was much

[1] R. Koser, 'Zur Bevölkerungsstatistik des preussischen Staates 1756-86' (*Forschungen zur Brandenburgischen und Preussischen Geschichte*, XVI, 1903, pp. 583-9.

[2] R. Koser, 'Die preussische Finanzen im Siebenjährigen Kriege' (*Forschungen zur Brandenburgischen und Preussischen Geschichte*, XIII, 1900). Frederick's estimate of the cost of the war was 125 million thalers and this figure was accepted by Otto Hintze in his article on 'Friedrich der Grosse nach dem Siebenjährigen Kriege und das Politische Testament von 1768' (*Forschungen zur Brandenburgischen und Preussischen Geschichte*, XXXII, 1920, pp. 1-56).

[3] Except for a levy of 4 million thalers at the beginning of the war.

[4] Except for small sums borrowed from the *Kurmärkische Landschaft*.

less than in normal times. No revenue came from East Prussia during the Russian occupation. The annual receipts of the General Domains Fund fell far short of the 3·5 million thalers secured in peacetime. Only Silesia paid its usual contribution throughout the war. The income from customs, excise and tolls and from the profits of nationalised undertakings declined sharply. Thirdly, Frederick bridged the gap between income and expenditure by debasing the coinage.

Since Graumann's currency reform of 1750 14 thalers had been coined from a Mark of fine silver. In November 1757, when Frederick needed 600,000 thalers, he ordered the royal silverware to be melted down and coined at the ratio of 18 thalers to the Mark. But to produce the required sum 21 thalers were coined from each Mark. In April 1758 the mint was instructed to turn out coins with a ratio of 1 : 19 and in December 1758 there was a further depreciation to a ratio of 1 : 19¾.

When Frederick occupied Saxony he debased its currency to an even greater extent than the Prussian thaler. While approximately 20 Prussian silver thalers were being coined from a Mark 30 Saxon thalers were coined from a Mark in 1760. In 1761 the Saxon coinage was still further depreciated, the ratio being 1 : 50 instead of 1 : 14. Since Poland had no mint—her coins were minted in Saxony—the Prussian authorities were also able to debase the Polish currency. The Polish *Tympfe*—equal in value to a Prussian thaler—was minted at a ratio of 1 : 40 instead of a 1 : 14. Frederick purchased war supplies in Saxony and Poland with depreciated coins but before long the merchants raised their prices so as to avoid loss.

These events were followed by the issue of debased currencies in Holstein, Anhalt-Bernburg, and Mecklenburg while considerable quantities of paper money circulated in Swedish Pomerania. Since it was not uncommon for several national currencies to circulate in a single region Prussia suffered from the existence not only of her own debased coins but also of the depreciated coins and notes of her neighbours.

[1] For the Polish coinage see E. Hutten Czapski, *Catalogue de la collection des médailles et monnaies polonaises* (3 vols., Graz 1957: a reprint of an edition which appeared in 5 volumes between 1871 and 1916) and M. Gumowski, *Handbuch der pölnischen Numismatik* (Graz, 1960).

Currency depreciation led to inflation and all its attendant evils. Coins minted before the war disappeared from circulation and there was a sharp rise in prices. Despite the minting of large quantities of depreciated coins not enough of them were available. There was a flight from the thaler and people tried to secure property—land, houses and jewellery—which would keep its value in the future. The survival of luxury industries was largely due to this desire to turn depreciated money into goods.

Just before the war commerce had been adversely affected by the economic crisis which followed the Lisbon earthquake. In 1756 the harvest was exceptionally poor while the output of manufactured goods declined owing to the destruction of towns, factories and workshops. Commerce was soon disorganised, Prussia's Baltic ports being blockaded by the enemy. The Berlin merchant Gotzkowsky reported that very little business was done at the Leipzig fair of 1756.

In the first winter of the war the inflation and the harvest failure caused the prices of agricultural products to rise. Rye bread in Berlin cost twice as much as before the war. If this had occurred in peacetime the grain stored in royal warehouses would have been sold at controlled prices to check the rise in the cost of living. But in wartime the needs of the army came first and the warehouses could not be used to hold grain prices in check. In later campaigns the military authorities requisitioned cereals in the Duchy of Magdeburg and this left Berlin short of grain. The price of rye eventually rose to five times what it had been before 1756. Horses once worth 40 thalers cost 150 thalers in depreciated money in 1762. Landed estates, urban property, house rents, manufactured goods, and foodstuffs also cost much more than before the war. In one case a house in Berlin increased in value at this time from 3,000 thalers to 12,000 thalers and the tenant's rent was increased threefold.

Inflation caused great hardships particularly among those living on fixed salaries and pensions. The salaries of civil servants fell into arrears and minor officials (such as excisemen) were virtually forced to accept bribes while landlords and shopkeepers complained that the King's officials were no longer paying their rents or their bills. Frederick issued vouchers

(*Kassenscheine*) to civil servants which were cashed by money changers at a heavy discount.[1]

Creditors suffered in the early days of the war when the government tried to insist that depreciated thalers should be accepted on their face value. Gotzkowsky stated that money owing to him was paid in depreciated coins while his debts to foreigners had to be paid in hard currencies. In 1759-60 the government specified the currencies in which pre-war debts might be paid and further adjustments in the settlement of these claims were contemplated in the event of a subsequent re-valuation of the thaler.

This was an official admission that the wartime thalers had a lower value than the pre-war thaler. The government also realized that taxes could no longer be collected in Prussian currency. Although large quantities of depreciated coins had been minted there were not enough in circulation to meet the needs of the public. So the government decided to accept Saxon coins for payments other than customs duties.

While many people suffered from the inflation others bene-fited. Borrowers could liquidate pre-war debts in depreciated money. Fortunes were made by those who were able to take advantage of inflation. Ephraim and Sons, who held the concession for the mints, claimed that they were losing money on their contracts but the firm made substantial profits by coining more Saxon thalers to the silver Mark than the number stipulated by the King.[2] Gotzkowsky made a profit of 500,000 thalers in transactions concerned with the payment of Leipzig's war contribution for 1761.

Substantial profits were also made by army contractors and by manufacturers who secured army orders. H. K. Schimmel-mann[3] had been a bankrupt trader when war broke out but he made enough money to start a new career which culmin-ated in his appointment as a Minister of State in Denmark. Brenkenhof earned large sums by supplying the army with grain and horses. The expansion of the Berlin firm of Split-

---

[1] After the war the King redeemed these vouchers in depreciated currency.
[2] Ephraim subsequently secured the lease of the royal gold and silver manufactures in Berlin and left a fortune when he died in 1775.
[3] For Schimmelmann see article in the *Allgemeine Deutsche Biographie*.

gerber and Daum showed how a business could prosper in wartime. This firm, which was engaged in a variety of commercial, manufacturing and financial enterprises, lost some property owing to enemy action but it doubled its capital and increased its turnover from 97,000 thalers to 882,000 thalers.

Count Lehndorff, the Queen's Chamberlain, contrasted the austerity of the court and the poverty of the nobles with the wealth amassed by profiteers and speculators. He stated that when foreign ambassadors returned to the capital after the war they could not find suitable accommodation because the great mansions had all been acquired by merchants and financiers who had become rich in the last few years.[1] One of these envoys observed that 'le luxe a considérablement augmenté et ce qui n'est pas militaire rêve que du commerce'.[2] A focal point of Berlin society during the war years was the residence of Gotzkowsky, whose gardens and paintings were admired both by by old nobility and the new bourgeoisie.

Prussian burghers were not normally allowed to acquire land in the country districts. During the war, however, some impoverished nobles sold land to wealthy merchants and financiers and in 1762 this was officially permitted in Silesia. Much urban capital was invested in landed estates not only by purchase but by lending money on mortgages.

The effects of the war upon farming, industry and commerce varied from place to place and from year to year. In the summer, when campaigns were in full swing, the towns and villages lying in the path of armies on the march might suffer severely. In the winter the region near a large military camp might lose its cattle, grain, fodder and even its trees. But other districts might escape relatively unharmed.

In the eighteenth century foraging was a recognised method of providing an army with food, fodder and horses,[3] which

[1] K. E. Schmidt-Lötzen (ed.), *Dreissig Jahre am Hofe Friedrichs des Grossen* (aus den Tagebüchern des Reichsgrafen Ernst Ahasverus Lehndorff) (Gotha Vol. I 1907, Vol. II 1910). Lehndorff wrote in French and this translation is an abridgement of the diary.

[2] Report by von Stutternheim (Saxon ambassador), March 28, 1766, quoted by S. Skalweit, op. cit., p. 23.

[3] For foraging and contributions in the eighteenth century see Fritz Redlich, *De Praeda Militari. Looting and Booty 1500-1815* (Supplement XXXIX of the *Vierteljahrschrift für Sozial-und Wirtschaftsgeschichte*, 1956).

supplemented the supplies drawn from military stores. It was an alternative to the levying of a contribution in cash or in bills of exchange. Foraging and contributions often saved civilians from indiscriminate looting. But officers sometimes lost control over their men with the result that troops indulged in the type of looting that had been common in the seventeenth century. Irregular troops engaged in individual looting rather than in official foraging. Economic losses were also incurred when military commanders deliberately destroyed workshops so as to weaken the enemy's war effort.

There was some decline in Prussia's agricultural output during the war but the requisitioning of foodstuffs and timber from the territories occupied by Frederick's troops and considerable imports of grain and horses from Poland alleviated the most serious shortages.

Industrial production was well maintained. Several important branches of manufacture—such as the production of cloth and metal goods—normally supplied the home market and relied upon regular orders from the military authorities. In wartime the decline in civilian consumption was counterbalanced by additional army orders. Luxury industries survived partly because the king supported them financially and partly because those who made money during the war bought jewellery, paintings and furniture as an investment. Frederick encouraged Gotzkowsky to start a new luxury industry—the manufacture of porcelain—in Berlin at this time. Of course manufacturers might suffer heavy losses if their works lay in the path of invading armies. Some factories and workshops were destroyed and stocks were looted by the enemy.

Prussia's export industries were in greater danger than branches of manufacture which supplied the domestic consumer. Nevertheless the output and the export of Silesian linens survived the critical years of war, for although some markets were lost, exports to Poland increased. The manufacture of unfulled cloth (*Zeugmacherei*) at Schweidnitz and Reichenbach declined. The timber trade of East Prussia was lost during the Russian occupation of the province but a new export trade in timber from Saxony took its place.

The fact that Splitgerber and Daum prospered during the

war suggests that the metal and armament industries were expanding to meet the demands of the war economy. The output of the firm's sugar refineries was also well maintained although sugar was being smuggled from Hamburg on an unusually large scale.

Prussia's commerce was disrupted without being permanently weakened. To some extent the inability to use the blockaded Baltic ports was overcome by diverting trade to Hamburg. The Prussian mercantile marine practically disappeared from the high seas and the limited wartime trade of Königsberg, Memel, Stettin and Emden fell into the hands of foreign shippers. While interruptions to normal industry and trade affected output, there was an expansion of other commercial activities under the stimulus of wartime needs. A new class of financiers arose to meet the requirements of the king, the nobles, the merchants, and the manufacturers for cash in this era of currency devaluation and high prices. It is significant that in these years the Jewish financiers and manufacturers rose to a position of real importance in Berlin.[1] It is equally significant that—on the initiative of the silk merchant Platzmann—the activities of the Berlin Stock Exchange should have been considerably expanded[2] and that the financial links between Berlin, Amsterdam and Hamburg should have been greatly strengthened.

(ii) *The Berlin Commercial Crisis of 1763*

The rise of Berlin to the position of a financial centre and the speculation in both commodities and currencies were factors which contributed to the commercial crisis of 1763. The crisis originated in Holland. In the eighteenth century the great port

[1] For the history of the Jews in Berlin see L. Geiger, *Geschichte der Juden in Berlin* (2 vols., Berlin, 1871).

[2] The reorganised bourse was established at the Steckbahn. Berlin already had an embryo exchange which met at the *Lusthaus zur neuen Grotto* but its activities had been limited to collecting information concerning currency and share quotations on foreign exchanges. The premises had also been used as a meeting place for the Berlin gilds. For the history of the Berlin bourse see G. Buss, *Geschichte der Berliner Börse von 1689-1913* (Berlin 1913) and Michel Carsow, 'La Bourse de Berlin' (*Journal des Économistes*, November 15, 1930, pp. 263-274).

of Amsterdam[1] handled large quantities of grain, linens, and colonial products, and its merchants and shippers controlled a vast transit trade between Germany and Austria on the one hand and France, Spain, Russia and colonial territories on the other. Amsterdam was also the greatest European financial centre and Dutch capital penetrated into almost every corner of the continent. Large sums had been advanced to the Emperor on the security of the Idria mercury mines and the revenues of Silesia and heavy investments had been made in English funds. "There was a time in the eighteenth century when one third of the shares of the Bank of England, one third of those of the English East India Company, and one half of the English national debt bonds were in Dutch hands".[2] Amsterdam was an important market for dealings in gold and silver since—contrary to the policy adopted by many other countries—Holland did not restrict the export of bullion. The city was also the principal European market for dealings in commercial bills of exchange. The international transactions of the great private banking houses—Deutz, Clifford, de Smeth and Hope—were settled in bills valued in units of the "bank money" of the Bank of Amsterdam.[3]

Dutch bankers and merchants tried to extend their profitable dealings in foreign bills by developing a system of open credits to business associates in the leading commercial cities on the continent and this type of business brought in profits of about

[1] For Amsterdam in the eighteenth century see W. P. Sautijn Kluit *De Amsterdamsche Beurs in 1763 en 1773* (Amsterdam 1865); W. M. F. Mansvelt, 'Het Amsterdansche acceptbedrifj en credietwezen in de 18e euw' (*Tijdschrift vor Geschiednis*, XXXVII, 1922); J. G. van Dillen, 'De Beurscrisis te Amsterdam in 1763' (*Tijdschrift vor Geschiednis*, XXXVII, 1922); E. Baasch, *Holländische Wirtschaftsgeschichte* (1927), pp. 192-252, and E. E. de Jong-Keesing, *De economische Crisis van 1763 te Amsterdam* (1939). For the Dutch economy in the eighteenth century see C. H. Wilson, 'The economic decline of the Netherlands' (*Economic History Review*, IX, 1939.) For the economic relations between Holland and north west Germany in the eighteenth century see L. Beutin, 'Nordwestdeutschland und die Niederlande seit dem Dreissigjährigen Kriege' (*Vierteljahrschrift für Sozial- und Wirtschaftsgeschichte*, XXXII, 1939, pp. 105-147).

[2] Admiralty Geographical Handbook on the *Netherlands* (1944), p. 153.

[3] This 'bank money' appears not to have fluctuated to the same extent as national currencies. It was a credit on the Bank of Amsterdam for bullion deposited there. See Adam Smith, *An Inquiry into the Nature and Causes of the Wealth of Nations*, 1776 (Everyman edition, 1910), Vol. I, p. 422.

six million guilders a year. But since the Dutch bankers were operating on a total capital of only 30,000,000 guilders a vast structure of credit transactions had been erected on slender foundations. This system had inherent weaknesses and a continued increase in the volume of foreign bills handled by Dutch merchants and bankers might well have precipitated a crisis even if there had been no war.

The effects of the war, however, should not be underestimated. The worldwide conflict led to a great expansion in the demand for Dutch credit. Amsterdam finance houses handled the transfer of much of the English subsidy to Prussia. In 1759 the British government relied largely on Dutch and Anglo-Dutch banks for the raising of a substantial loan.[1] The purchase of grain, fodder and armaments by belligerents led to the issue of bills of exchange endorsed by Dutch financiers. When the Prussian and Swedish authorities issued debased coins they generally bought bullion in Amsterdam on credit and so more bills came into existence. Ephraim and Itzig probably secured mint concessions from Frederick because they had excellent contacts with the Amsterdam bullion market and bourse.

The more conservative Dutch bankers and bullion brokers exercised caution in accepting new business in wartime but the commissions they declined were handled by other firms which could not resist the chance of making quick profits. The de Neufville brothers, for example, a relatively unimportant mercantile and financial house in Amsterdam,[2] supplied the Duke of Brunswick's army with fodder and Frederick the Great's mints with silver. Other commissions—including some from Sweden and Russia—followed, and the business of the firm quickly expanded. The de Neufvilles speculated in depreciated currencies and endorsed an ever increasing number of foreign bills. Their success encouraged other finance houses to extend their business transactions by similar means.

---

[1] Sir John Clapham, *The Bank of England . . .*, Vol. I, (1944), p. 236 and C. H. Wilson, *Anglo-Dutch Commerce and Finance in the Eighteenth Century* (1941). It appears that 'Joshua van Neck & Co., an Anglo-Dutch firm, were Newcastle's most important loan contractors'.

[2] This firm (Gebroeders Neufville) was distinct from the old established firm of J. I. de Neufville & Co.

Meanwhile similar developments had occurred in Hamburg.[1] This was another great port with a substantial trade with colonial territories—through Amsterdam, Liverpool, Cadiz and Bordeaux—and with northern Germany and Scandinavia. Hamburg had its city bank with its own relatively stable bank money. Hamburg's commerce was stimulated by the war. Prussian merchants diverted much of their Polish trade from Stettin to Hamburg and incidentally avoided paying the Sound dues in doing so. The decline of Leipzig's fair was also to Hamburg's advantage. A new trade in timber developed because the Prussians exploited Saxony's forests and sent the timber down the Elbe.[2] The export of refined sugar to Prussia flourished since Frederick could not enforce his customs regulations as strictly as in peacetime. In Hamburg, too, the merchants supplied belligerents with grain, fodder and other supplies while the finance houses handled the payment of subsidies and contributions, dealt in inflated currencies, and endorsed bills of exchange. Büsch, one of the earliest historians of the city's commerce, declared that Hamburg had never been so prosperous as in 1759.

In 1763 many German merchants hoped that an increased demand for consumer goods would counterbalance a decline in army orders; that the circulation of depreciated money would keep prices high; and that their creditors would renew bills of exchange when they fell due. But events followed a different course largely because Frederick was determined to bring inflated prices down and to revalue the thaler. In May 1763 the King advised the Berlin wholesale corn merchants not to

[1] For Hamburg during and immediately after the Seven Years War see J. G. Büsch, *Versuch einer Geschichte der Hamburger Handel* (Hamburg, 1797: reprinted in 1816 as Vol. XII of Büsch's collected works) and the quotations from the memoirs of John Parish in R. Ehrenberg, *Das Haus Parish in Hamburg* (Jena 1925), pp. 8-13. See also Max Wirth, *Geschichte der Handelskrisen* (Frankfurt am Main 1890), ch. 6, 'Die Hamburger Handelskrise in den Jahren 1763 und 1799' (pp. 86-111).

[2] The Hamburg timber merchants soon extended this trade to Austria (Bohemia), Prussia, and Poland. They 'began to send large quantities of timber—particularly staves—to Hamburg by way of the Warthe, the Oder, the Mühlrose Canal, the Spree, the Havel and the Elbe' (Max Wirth, op. cit., p. 87).

hold on to their stocks. He gave or sold to his subjects the grain which had been stored for the next campaign so that grain prices fell and merchants who had ignored the King's advice suffered heavy losses. The Mint Edict of May 1763 fixed the rates at which various depreciated coins would be accepted and provided for the payment of taxes in coins of pre-war value. Frederick withdrew from circulation some of the depreciated money and ordered the minting of thalers at a 'transitional ratio' of 19¾ thalers to the Mark of fine silver. This was a substantial improvement on the depreciated coins of 30—even 40—thalers to the Mark. Since other rulers soon followed Frederick's example and reformed their currencies there was a shortage of ready cash. Profiteers and currency speculators suddenly saw their hopes of further financial gains disappear. Merchants could not secure enough coins to pay their debts and found that the rate for discounting bills of exchange was rising at an alarming rate.

Greatly increased credit transactions and continued speculation in land, commodities and currencies were the main causes of the commercial crisis of 1763. In Amsterdam the de Neufville brothers suspended payments on July 29.[1] The firm was unpopular in Amsterdam since it had been involved in negotiations for the revival of the Asiatic Company in Emden. Suggestions that the Amsterdam bankers should advance money to save the de Neufvilles were rejected. The leading Hamburg bankers wrote to their colleagues in Amsterdam to protest against a decision which would 'infallibly plunge all Europe in an abyss of distress',[2] and threatened to suspend their own payments for as long as might be necessary in the circumstances.

The gloomy forebodings of the Hamburg bankers were justified since all confidence in bills of exchange vanished overnight. In almost every commercial centre merchants refused to renew such bills and demanded payment in cash whenever bills fell due, while bankers generally refused to

[1] Their debts amounted to about £350,000. The firm eventually made an arrangement with its creditors to pay 60 per cent of its debts. For the crisis in Amsterdam see E. E. de Jong-Keesing, *De economische Crisis van 1763 te Amsterdam* (1939).

[2] *Gentleman's Magazine*, September 1763, p. 423.

advance money by discounting bills. The Bank of England adopted a different policy from the continental banks and advanced £1·6 millions in bullion in a week to support financial houses in Holland and Hamburg.[1] There were limits to the assistance that London could give and there were over 30 failures in Amsterdam and 95 in Hamburg. Contemporaries were baffled at the sudden panic and at the failure of so many firms.[2] To make matters worse the sudden demand for bullion and hard currencies led to a further decline in the value of depreciated coins.

In view of the close financial links recently forged between Berlin, Hamburg and Amsterdam it was inevitable that Berlin should quickly have felt the effects of the crisis.[3] The suspension of payments by many Amsterdam and Hamburg merchants and bankers was followed by similar failures in Berlin, the most serious being that of Gotzkowsky. He was an industrialist, a merchant and a financier who had quickly come to the fore during the war. He had undertaken numerous commissions for the King, had negotiated with the Russian commander when Berlin was occupied in 1760, and had made large sums in transactions concerning Leipzig's war contributions.

Gotzkowky's difficulties were due to the fact that he had neglected his silkworks and his jewellery business to make quick profits by financial speculations. He had accepted sole responsibility for the purchase of a consignment of Russian army grain and his partners[4] deserted him when a fall in prices jeopardised the success of the transaction. Gotzkowsky was

---

[1] Adam Smith, *An Inquiry into the Nature and Causes of the Wealth of Nations*, 1776 (Everyman edition), Vol. I, p. 285. But Adam Smith was not prepared 'to warrant either the greatness of the sum or the shortness of the time.' According to David Macpherson, *Annals of Commerce . . .*, 4 vols., (1805) Vol. III, pp. 372-3, the Bank of England and the chief London banks suspended payment of their own bills so as to keep funds available to assist finance houses on the continent.

[2] Frederick the Great, for example, wrote: 'D'où viennent donc toutes ces banqueroutes?' 'Depuis que je suis au monde, je n'ai entendu parler de rien de pareil'.

[3] For a contemporary account of the Berlin crisis see J. E. Gotzkowsky, *Geschichte eines patriotischen Kaufmanns* (1768), pp. 187-9. The best modern account is S. Skalweit, op. cit.

[4] The de Neufvilles were among Gotzkowsky's partners in this ill-starred affair.

also faced with demands from Hamburg bankers for the payment of his bills of exchange. And just when he was being pressed by his creditors, Gotzkowsky underwrote the bills of other Berlin firms, such as Adrian Sprögel, in the vain hope of averting a general crash. He might have ridden the storm had he not made so many enemies. Ephraim, Itzig,[1] Schütze, and Schickler[2] all welcomed the downfall of a powerful rival and did not raise a finger to save him.

Only a week after the de Neufvilles suspended payment, ten Berlin firms warned Frederick that local manufacturers might have to go out of business if the panic spread to Prussia and asked for a moratorium on the payment of bills of exchange. Frederick had probably not yet heard from his envoy in Amsterdam concerning the de Neufville failure and he refused to interfere with the normal processes of commercial law.

A few days later Gotzkowsky asked for a moratorium and Frederick realised that if a merchant of Gotzkowsky's standing could not honour his bills of exchange a serious situation had arisen. Although he rejected Gotzkowsky's application he tried to help the hard pressed financier in another way. He suggested that Gotzkowsky's payment of the next instalment of Saxony's contribution might be deferred. But Ephraim and Itzig had taken over responsibility for this debt and the King's proposal was of no assistance to Gotzkowsky.

On the following day (August 10) Frederick instructed von Jariges (the Grand Chancellor) to consult von Fürst as to how the merchants could be helped without infringing the sanctity of commercial law.[3] The King was still optimistic concerning Gotzkowsky's affairs. On August 12, he told von Finkenstein that Dolgorucki[4] should be informed that Gotzkowsky would doubtless be able to pay for the Russian army grain which he had purchased, provided that he was given a little time.

On the same day, however, Frederick learned that his efforts

---

[1] The Jewish mint entrepreneurs.

[2] Schickler was now virtually in control of the firm of Splitgerber and Daum.

[3] Frederick justified his proposal on the ground that the Hamburg authorities had granted a moratorium on the payment of bills of exchange. The King, however, had been misinformed on this matter.

[4] The Russian ambassador in Berlin.

to secure a private loan for Gotzkowsky had failed. He had suggested to Ephraim and Itzig that—on receipt of one million thalers due to them for the purchase of silver—they should advance Gotzkowsky 400,000 thalers. Ephraim and Itzig realised that the heyday of quick profits was over and that since the currency was being reformed it was unlikely that their mint contracts would be renewed. As they were unpopular in Berlin and their future was uncertain, they wanted to collect money due to them and did not propose to make fresh loans. Ephraim and Itzig argued that the proposed loan would not save Gotzkowsky who needed a much larger sum to avoid bankruptcy.

On August 12 Frederick followed up the instructions already given to von Jariges with further instructions to prepare a Moratorium Edict in the hope that this would save the Berlin merchants who were in difficulties. Von Jariges, however, had already acted on his initial instructions and had asked the Berlin City Council to call a meeting of merchants at which statements could be taken from both those who could not redeem their bills and from those who were solvent. Gotzkowsky was instructed to submit a financial statement to the City Council. In a report to von Jariges of August 13 the City Council argued that Gotzkowsky's inability to redeem his bills of exchange lay at the root of the crisis in Berlin. A loan of 500,000 thalers would save him from bankruptcy and since the solvent merchants were not prepared to raise the money, the King should be asked to provide the necessary funds.

The same point of view was expressed in a statement issued by the merchants who could not honour their bills of exchange. They claimed that 500,000 thalers was not too high a price to pay to prevent Gotzkowsky's silkworks and porcelain works from closing down. Schickler, Schütze and Scheel submitted no report because there had not been enough time to prepare a statement of Gotzkowsky's financial position. On the same day (August 13) von Jariges suggested that since detailed information concerning Gotzkowsky's financial affairs was not yet available and since the solvent merchants were unwilling to help Gotzkowsky neither a loan nor a moratorium would solve the problems of the merchants who were unable to redeem their bills of exchange. The King, exasperated by the delay in taking any action, ordered von Jariges to prepare a Moratorium Edict immediately, declaring that Gotzkowsky was 'un fol qui a follement administré ses affaires' but that 'il s'agit beaucoup dans cette malheureuse affaire de gagner du temps, pour que les manufactures ne tombent point'. He warned von Jariges not to be influenced too much by the views of Schickler 'qui est ennemi juré de Gotzkowsky'.

Von Jariges prepared the necessary document granting Gotzkowsky a three months' moratorium on bills of exchange and this was signed by the King (August 16). But von Jariges argued that the moratorium could not save Gotzkowsky and that Prussia should follow Hamburg's example and insist that merchants unable to redeem their bills of exchange, should come to an arrangement with their creditors. This would show that the government had no intention of tampering with the laws on bills of exchange. He believed that the disappearance of insolvent firms would strengthen the position of those who were able to meet their obligations.

These arguments appeared to be justified when Gotzkowsky submitted his statement of assets and liabilities (August 17). It might be doubted whether Gotzkowsky's figures were correct but it was clear that his liabilities were nearly all in bills of exchange which ought to be paid at once while his assets were fixed capital (the silkworks and the porcelain factory) which could not be turned into cash quickly.

Von Jariges submitted Gotzkowsky's balance sheet to Frederick with the comment that if Gotzkowsky were to preserve his industrial establishments it would be necessary for him to come to an understanding with his creditors. Frederick observed that it was 'une maudite affaire' but he realised that the moratorium would not save Gotzkowsky. The fate of the other insolvent Berlin merchants had also to be considered. Some were Gotzkowsky's creditors and they might be able to meet their obligations if they could collect money due to them from Gotzkowsky. On August 22, a fortnight's moratorium was granted to eight Berlin firms in the hope that this would give Gotzkowsky time to settle his affairs.[1]

[1] One of these firms (the cloth manufacturers Stöber and Schröder) drew

A special bankruptcy court was now set up to settle the affairs of the insolvent merchants. Firms which were in financial difficulties for any reason other than the recent failures in Amsterdam and Hamburg were referred to the normal bankruptcy courts. The new court was to some extent a conciliation tribunal which helped debtors and creditors to agree upon terms which would enable debtors to stay in business. The court was instructed to do everything in its power to ensure the survival of workshops belonging to merchants who applied for relief.

The most difficult case to be dealt with was that of Gotzkowsky. On August 24, the King offered to buy Gotzkowsky's porcelain works for 265,000 thalers and to lend Gotzkowsky 235,000 thalers for three years on the security of his silkworks. Frederick's willingness to advance half a million thalers made it possible for the court to secure a settlement between Gotzkowsky and his creditors.

Various obstacles delayed a settlement of Gotzkowsky's affairs. It was difficult to make an accurate valuation of Gotzkowsky's assets which included industrial establishments and numerous claims on merchants and financiers. Gotzkowsky was a manufacturer, a merchant, and a banker who was operating at least four separate enterprises[1] and several different sets of ledgers required investigation before his financial position could be ascertained. A committee,[2] which examined Gotzkowsky's affairs, informed the court that the old gentleman who kept some of Gotzkowsky's accounts was no longer able to perform his duties efficiently, and that certain accounts were in a state of disorder. This report damaged Gotzkowsky's reputation and gave rise to suspicions that he was trying to defraud his creditors. The authorities refused to allow Gotzkowsky to leave Berlin for the Leipzig fair where he had hoped to dispose

up a memorandum asking for a two months moratorium on bills of exchange. The memorandum observed that a strict application of the Prussian Law on Bills of Exchange was impracticable at a time of crisis because statements of assets and liabilities could not be drawn up since the value of assets (particularly bills of exchange issued by or endorsed by foreign firms) could not be ascertained.

[1] A silkworks, a porcelain factory, a jewellery business, and a commission agency.

[2] Rausleben and the bankers Gregori, Scheel and Schütze.

of the silks and velvets lying unsold in his Berlin warehouse.

The settlement of Gotzkowsky's affairs was also delayed because Brenkenhof and Dolgorucki demanded that money owing to them should be repaid before the claims of other creditors were considered. Gotzkowsky had been entrusted by Brenkenhof (acting for the New Mark Chamber) with the transfer of 27,000 thalers to Poland for the purchase of pedigree oxen. Owing to the crisis his bill of exchange had not been honoured in Poland and the New Mark Chamber wanted its money back. But as this was a claim by a civilian authority, and not by a military authority, it could not receive special consideration.

Meanwhile the Russian ambassador vigorously supported Shuvesnikov's demand for the prompt payment of money due to him for grain sold to Gotzkowsky and his partners. The court had to consider whether the transaction was a private one between Shuvesnikov and Gotzkowsky or whether Shuvesnikov was acting as an official Russian agent. Eventually the claim was settled by a cash payment and the transfer to the creditors of a number of valuable paintings.

Meanwhile progress was being made in the negotiations between the trustees of Gotzkowsky's undertaking and his creditors. On January 30, 1764 the trustees informed the King that it would not be necessary to accept his offer to take up a mortgage on Gotzkowsky's silkworks. On April 2, 1764 Gotzkowsky's offer of a payment of 50 per cent of his debts was accepted by 43 (out of 74) creditors. Von Jariges hoped that Gotzkowsky would be able to make a fresh start with new credits. This agreement helped to restore confidence in Berlin. With the money that they secured from Gotzkowsky some merchants either paid their debts in full or came to an arrangement with their creditors through the good offices of the special bankruptcy court.

While this court was endeavouring to promote settlements between debtors and creditors which would enable insolvent firms to stay in business, the King was trying to help the merchants in another way. He was determined to frustrate any attempts by the bankers of Amsterdam and Hamburg to get out of their difficulties, at the expense of Berlin merchants. It was alleged that bills of exchange, issued by (or endorsed by) solvent Berlin firms were not being honoured in Holland and in Hamburg simply because local bankers wished to keep specie in their vaults while the panic lasted. In such cases Frederick instructed his representatives to protest as energetically as possible. Frederick helped his subjects to secure assets which were held by their agents in Amsterdam and Hamburg. In September 1763 it was reported that 'the gold or silver, coined or in bars, deposited at Hamburg before the late bankruptcies were declared, have been reclaimed by his majesty's minister, under pain of military execution and a sum is demanded from the same city to make good deficiencies'.[1]

After the crisis of 1763-4 the King endeavoured to promote the revival of trade and industry in various ways. He continued to pursue a policy of deflation. By the Mint Edict of March 1764 the value of thalers coined in the ratio of 19¾ to the Mark was fixed at 40 per cent below that of pre-war thalers and this was in effect a return to the old valuation of 14 thalers to the Mark of fine silver. Frederick also tackled the problem of inflated property values and house rents in Berlin. First he gave every encouragement to the building industry in the hope that as more houses were built so the housing shortage would be met and the price of house property would fall. Secondly, the Rent Edict of April 1765[2] put an end to the principle that when a house changed hands the contract between the tenant and the former owner lapsed so that the purchaser could raise the rent immediately.[3] The new principle was that the purchaser of a house had to honour the obligations incurred in any contracts signed by the previous owner.[4] A tenant thus received a considerable measure of protection against a sudden increase in rent when there was a change in the ownership of the house in which he lived. Frederick succeeded in bringing down the price of urban property just as he had previously brought down the price of grain. There was, however, no general fall in prices at

[1] *Gentleman's Magazine*, September 1763, p. 460.
[2] For the Berlin Rent Edict of 1765 see Melle Klingenborg, 'Das Berliner Mietsedikt vom 15 April 1765' (in *Forschungen zur Brandenburgischen und Preussischen Geschichte*), XXV, 1912, pp. 179-189.
[3] This was the principle of *Kauf geht vor Miete*.
[4] This was the Dutch principle of *Huur gaet Koop*.

this time for while some prices sank others rose even beyond the inflated levels of wartime.

Frederick was disappointed at the incompetence of a number of firms (as revealed by the enquiries made by the special bankruptcy court) and at the inability of the Berlin merchants as a body to combat the crisis of 1763. He had no more confidence in Gotzkowsky and others who had been unable to weather the storm without his help. In the future he sought advice on commercial matters from men like J. J. Schickler whose firm had remained solvent during the crisis. Moreover, for a short time, he thought of employing highly unorthodox methods to promote Prussia's economic revival. He turned to the adventurer Calzabigi who wanted 'to organise the whole economy into a sort of giant trust'. Calzabigi's scheme was never put into operation but some of the new organisations established by the King—the Royal Bank of Berlin, the Tobacco Monopoly and the State lottery—owed their origin to some extent to Calzabigi's ideas.

The emergency measures taken by the Prussian government in the autumn of 1763 successfully allayed the panic. They enabled Gotzkowsky and other merchants to come to terms with their creditors and they preserved intact a number of workshops which might otherwise have been closed down. But Frederick's attempts to revive trade in the years following the crisis were less successful. The deflationary policy of the government and the shortage of coins checked the public demand for consumer goods. Fears that the recently established Royal Bank of Berlin might issue its own notes and so cause coins to lose their value again led some merchants to invest their savings abroad. Manufacturers and merchants found that the demand for goods was very sluggish. Although Gotzkowsky secured new credits he was in difficulties again in the autumn of 1764 and he had to sell his silkworks in the following year. By 1767 he was bankrupt again. A number of other Berlin firms went into liquidation in 1766-7, such as Stöber and Schröder, Wylich and de Roon, the Brothers Saltzmann and the silk manufacturer Treitschke. According to Lehndorff a number of nobles also went bankrupt at this time.

In June 1767 the Saxon minister reported on the 'pitoiable

état du commerce dans ce pays-ci, ou toutes les fabriques tombent et chaque jour annonce, pour ainsi dire, une nouvelle banqueroute'. The General Directory investigated the causes of the depression. Its report, drawn up by Ursinus, was surprisingly frank since important aspects of Frederick's economic policy were freely criticised. The report commented particularly upon the weakness of the silk industry which the King had done so much to foster. The King was furious and wrote to the General Directory: 'I am astounded at the impertinent report which you have submitted. I forgive the Ministers who know no better, but the malice and corruption of the actual author of the report must be punished in an exemplary manner for otherwise the rabble will never be brought to heel'. The events of 1763 caused Frederick to lose confidence in many of the Berlin merchants. The events of 1764-7 made him lose confidence in some of his ministers and senior officials.

It was not until 1768 that industrial production in Berlin expanded once more. In that year there were 330 silk looms at work in the capital as compared with 238 in 1766. In June 1769 the special bankruptcy court reported that 'owing to the completely changed state of affairs' it would now be possible to refer all future bankruptcy proceedings to the normal courts.

There is something to be said for Ziekursch's view that the earliest signs of an industrial revolution in Prussia may be detected in the economic changes that took place just before and just after the crisis of 1763.[1] Agriculture, industry and finance had all been stimulated by war demands and by inflation. Even luxury industries survived owing to the continued support of the King. The decline in demand for consumer goods coupled with the prompt deflation after the war proved to be only a temporary check to further expansion. The crisis swept away inefficient firms and brought men to the fore who were capable of meeting the challenge of a new age. New officials such as von Hagen, Brenkenhof, Roden and de Launay and new bankers and industrialists such as J. J. Schickler, F. W. Schütze and J. G. Sieburg made their mark in the 1760s. During the war itself and shortly afterwards several important institutions were established which were to serve the Prussian economy

[1] J. Ziekursch, *Hundert Jahre Schlesischer Agrargeschichte* (Breslau, 1915), p. 2.

well in the nineteenth century. They included the Berlin bourse, the Royal Bank of Berlin, the Overseas Trading Corporation, and new government departments such as the Mining Office and the Forestry Department.

(iii) *Administrative Reforms*[1]

To facilitate the reconstruction of Prussia after the Seven Years War Frederick not only introduced new policies but he established new organs of government and he sought new men to help him run the country. The administrative reforms of the 1760's were not entirely a new development since the King had been making changes in the machinery of government since 1740.

When Frederick came to the throne the central organ of government (as far as internal affairs were concerned) was the General Directory which had been established in 1723. The General Directory co-ordinated what had formerly been regarded as two entirely different things—control over a medley of provincial authorities and the administration of the private estates of the King. It dealt with a great variety of business such as the supervision of finance, public works, local government, the royal domains, welfare services, and the provision of grain, fodder and horses for the army.

The General Directory was composed of Ministers of State and Privy Councillors who worked together in one room in the Palace and were collectively responsible for the advice they gave to the King. It was divided into departments each of which administered a group of provinces. The General Directory was therefore an all-purpose organ of government based upon the two principles of the joint responsibility of Ministers to the King and the allocation of duties on a geographical—and not on a functional—basis.

[1] For the administration of Prussia when Frederick II came to the throne see R. A. Dorwart, *The Administrative Reforms of Frederick William I of Prussia* (1953). For the administrative reforms of Frederick the Great see Hans Haussherr, *Verwaltungseinheit und Ressorttrennung vom Ende des 17en bis zum Beginn des 19en Jahrhunderts* (1953) and W. L. Dorn, 'The Prussian Bureaucracy in the Eighteenth Century' (*Political Science Quarterly*, XLVI, 1931, pp. 403-423, XLVII, 1932, pp. 73-94 and pp. 259-273). Mme. de Staël wrote: 'Il faut louer Frédéric de sa probité dans le gouvernement intérieur de son pays; c'est un de ses premiers titres à l'admiration de la postérité.'

When Frederick came to the throne he complained that the General Directory was not doing its work properly. He said that only minor matters were settled and that important business was always referred to him for a decision. Important changes were soon made. In 1740 Frederick set up a new department of the General Directory which was responsible not for the general administration of a region but for the expansion of industry throughout the kingdom. The head of this Fifth Department—Samuel von Marschall—was told to promote the immigration of foreign entrepreneurs and skilled craftsmen. The other departments of the General Directory continued to supervise existing workshops and factories in their respective provinces. Marschall was instructed to devote himself entirely to his own department and he was not to concern himself with the other activities of the General Directory.

In 1746 a Sixth Department was established to organise on a national basis the supply of grain, fodder, horses, cloth and so forth for the army. The head of this department (Katt) was also expected to devote all his time to his new duties and was to take no part in the work of other departments. In 1750 the responsibility for the management of the mints was taken out of the hands of the General Directory. Graumann, the new director of the mints, had a seat in the General Directory but his work was not controlled by this body. He received his instructions from the King to whom he was directly responsible. In 1755 the management of the mints virtually passed out of public control for a time since they were leased to Jewish entrepreneurs.[1]

In 1742 Frederick made an even more drastic change in the structure of the central administration. When Silesia was conquered it was not placed under the authority of the General Directory in the same way as the older provinces but it was administered as a separate entity. A Minister of State, directly responsible to the King, was put in charge of the newly acquired territory.[2] Count Münchow, the first holder of this office, was

---

[1] Two Prussian mints had been leased to Jewish entrepreneurs prior to 1755. When Saxony was occupied by the Prussians during the Seven Years War Jewish financiers also secured leases for the mint in that country.

[2] The Ministers responsible for the administration of Silesia during the period of provincial autonomy (1741-1806) were Count Münchow (1742-

instructed to come to Berlin for only four days in each year to attend a meeting of the General Directory which would consider problems common to all parts of the kingdom. At this meeting, however, there was to be no discussion of matters concerning Silesia alone. These arrangements marked a decisive departure from the methods of administration employed by Frederick's father since the General Directory had lost some of its control over certain economic affairs and had no authority over Silesia at all. Moreover the old principle of the collective responsibility of all members of the General Directory for the advice offered to the King had been seriously weakened.

Frederick's early changes in the central administration were all concerned with economic activities—the promotion of industry and trade, the organisation of supplies for the army, and the management of the royal mints. Two of these departments enjoyed a considerable measure of freedom as parts of the General Directory while the third was an entirely independent body.

During the Seven Years War five senior Ministers died— Happe, the elder Blumenthal,[1] Katt, Boden and Gutier—and only one of them was immediately replaced. G. L. von Wedel succeeded Katt as head of the Sixth Department and received the title of Minister of War (1761). After the war Frederick's distrust of the depleted General Directory was shown in various ways. The emergency measures taken in 1763 to revive the economies of the devastated provinces were largely arranged by the King in consultation with the Presidents of the provincial Chambers and other senior officials. In Pomerania and the New Mark reconstruction was supervised by Brenkenhof, an official specially appointed for that purpose. In 1764 an application by members of the General Directory for an increase in salary to meet the rise in the cost of living was rejected by the King and in 1766 Ursinus was dismissed from his post and confined in the fortress of Spandau because he had drawn up a report criticising certain aspects of Frederick's economic policy.

53), von Massow (1753-1755), von Schlabrendorf (1755-69), and von Hoym (1770-1806). Legal affairs in Silesia were in charge of a special Minister of Justice.

[1] A. L. von Blumenthal.

61

After the war Massow, von Hagen, von der Horst, and the younger Blumenthal[1] were placed in charge of departments of the General Directory.[2] Although von Hagen[3] was the youngest he soon won the King's confidence and became the leading member of the General Directory. The Royal Bank of Berlin, the Mining Department, the Forestry Department, and the Overseas Trading Corporation all came under his control. This arrangement was contrary to the traditional idea of the General Directory as a body of equals jointly responsible for advising the King. Von der Horst's successor, Schulenburg-Kehnert[4] also exercised wide powers. Although he gave up the Mining Office to Heinitz[5] and the Overseas Trading Corporation to Struensee, he kept in his own hand the General Directory department responsible for the western provinces as well as the Forestry Department, the Coffee Monopoly, the Tobacco Monopoly, and the Royal Bank of Berlin.

One of the most difficult problems that Frederick had to solve in the period of reconstruction was the lack of men with the character, training, and experience that were needed for the running of a government department or public corporation. For one successful minister or senior official—a Hagen or a Brenkenhof—there were half a dozen men who proved to be incompetent or dishonest. The teething troubles of the Royal Bank of Berlin and the Overseas Trading Corporation (*Seehandlung*) were due largely to the failure of the King to find administrators of the necessary calibre to take charge of them.

[1] J. C. von Blumenthal.

[2] In 1766 the responsibility for the administration of the provinces was divided among the first three departments of the General Directory as follows:

> *First Department:* East Prussia, Pomerania, New Mark.
> *Second Department:* Mark Brandenburg, Magdeburg, Halberstadt.
> *Third Department:* Territories west of the River Elbe.

Other new appointments in the 1760's were Brenkenhof (reconstruction of Pomerania and the New Mark, 1762), Count von Reuss (Post Office 1762) and J. R. Roden (Audit Chamber, 1768). The Audit Chamber was no longer controlled by the General Directory.

[3] For Hagen see E. Posner, *Mitteldeutsche Lebensbilder*, Vol. III, (Magdeburg, 1928), pp. 46-63.

[4] For Schulenburg-Kehnert see B. Rosenmüller, *Schulenburg-Kehnert unter Friedrich dem Grossen* (1914).

[5] For Heinitz see A. Schwemann, *Friedrich Anton von Heinitz (Beiträge zur Geschichte der Technik und Industrie*, ed. by C. Matschoss, XII, 1922).

On the other hand the success of the Mining Office was assured when the King secured in Heinitz one of the leading mining experts in Germany—a man who was highly qualified himself and was able to find exceptionally competent assistants to run the local offices in the principal mining regions.

One way in which Frederick tried to overcome the shortage of skilled administrators was by appointing a number of French officials to important posts. The collection of indirect taxes was placed under the control of Frenchmen. Hitherto this had been done on a provincial basis under the supervision of the appropriate departments of the General Directory. In 1766 the King transferred the collection of customs and excise duties from the General Directory[1] to the *l'administration générale des droits du roi*. This *Regie*, as it was called, was run by a Frenchman (de Launay) with the help of a number of his countrymen. The business of the organisation was transacted in French. De Launay was directly responsible to the King for the collection of customs and excise duties.

The handing over of a major department of state to foreign officials was so extraordinary a proceeding that the significance of other aspects of this change were perhaps not fully appreciated at first. Since customs and excise duties were now levied on a national and not on a provincial basis a great step forward had been taken towards unifying the fiscal administration of the various Prussian territories. And since about $5\frac{1}{2}$ million thalers were paid annually to the General War Fund by the *Regie* in the late 1760's the General Directory had now very little influence in fiscal matters.[2] About one third of the total national revenue was collected by the *Regie* and most of it was paid directly into the General War Fund. The members of the

[1] The transfer of the collection of customs and excise duties from the provincial authorities (supervised by the General Directory) to the *Regie* was carried out by von der Horst, the member of the General Directory responsible for industry, commerce and customs and excise duties. Von der Horst's responsibilities concerning the customs and excise duties, however, were of a very limited character since de Launay exercised full authority in collecting these taxes. Von der Horst acted as chairman of a committee of officials which issued a report in 1768 recommending certain changes in the excise rates. See below, p. 69.

[2] The General Directory received only a fixed proportion of the customs and excise duties, based upon the revenues of 1765-66.

General Directory could only guess how much money was involved. The authority of the General Directory was seriously impaired.

The *Regie* was naturally very unpopular in Prussia. Its critics alleged that a large number of French officials were squeezing the last groschen out of the public. Mirabeau, for example, stated that 1,500 French officials were employed by the *Regie*, De Launay, on the other hand, claimed that fewer than 200 Frenchmen held posts at any one time in a service which employed some 2,000 officials. At first Frederick turned a deaf ear to the outcry caused by the establishment of the *Regie*. In the later years of his reign, however, he did make some concessions to public opinion. In April 1781 Frederick wrote to de Launay that his officials were 'rogues who steal whatever they can lay their hands on' and in a letter of February 28, 1783 he complained that 'most of the Frenchmen have come here because they have been chased out of their own country'. 'They secure posts in the *Regie*, plunder the provinces, and go home again when they have made their pile'. In the same year, after examining the estimates of the *Regie* Frederick reduced the staff, cut salaries, and forbade the appointment of any more French officials. In the following year Frederick, in a letter to von Werden, referred to the French officials as 'a pack of thorough scoundrels', and demanded the dismissal of one of the senior French officials. De Launay himself, however, retained the King's confidence until the end of the reign.

Frenchmen were also holding responsible positions in other official organisations such as the Post Office, the Overseas Trading Corporation and the Coffee Monopoly. Some of them did excellent work but the scandals associated with the dismissal of E. N. Moret and J. M. Bernard from the Post Office (1766-9), Delâtre from the Overseas Trading Corporation (1776), and Dubosque from the *Regie* (1781) provided ample ammunition for the critics of a king who allowed foreigners to hold important administrative posts. It was not only the senior foreign officials who were unpopular. The minor French officials who administered the tobacco and coffee monopolies were detested by the public.

By the end of his reign Frederick had greatly weakened the

all-purpose General Directory as established by his father. He had deprived it of virtually all influence over the finances since the collection of customs and excise duties and the auditing of accounts had been taken out of its hands. The General Directory had no control over the administration of Silesia. Frederick had set up a number of functional government departments and State corporations. There was a temporary reaction against Frederick's policy after his death. His successor abolished the *Regie*, the tobacco monopoly, and the coffee monopoly. But many of the institutions established by Frederick survived. The Mining Office, the Forestry Department, the Royal Bank of Berlin, and the Overseas Trading Corporation continued in the nineteenth century to foster the industrial and commercial development of the country.

(iv) *Financial Reforms*[1]

During the Seven Years War none of the Prussian provinces paid their taxes regularly except Silesia. Frederick levied no new taxes and raised hardly any loans. Apart from the English subsidy he paid his way by debasing the currency and by levying contributions upon Saxony and Mecklenburg. After the war Frederick was determined that the costs of reconstruction should not be financed by any further measures of devaluation. He realised that if the Prussian economy were to be revived a stable currency was necessary. He therefore initiated a policy of withdrawing depreciated coins from circulation. After a period of transition new coins of pre-war standard were minted again. All this may well have been done too quickly and, for a time, the country suffered from a shortage of currency.

It was clear that new sources of revenue would have to be found to help pay for the cost of reconstruction. Yet in 1763 the King had to remit tax payments in some provinces and two years later one of his ministers warned him that 'it was unthinkable that the rate of taxation should be increased since

[1] See R. Koser, 'Die preussische Finanzen von 1763 bis 1786' (*Forschungen zur Brandenburgischen und Preussischen Geschichte*, Vol. XVI, 1903, pp. 445-76) and Otto Hintze, 'Friedrich der Grosse nach dem Siebenjährigen Kriege und das Politische Testament von 1768' (*Forschungen zur Brandenburgischen und Preussischen Geschichte*, Vol. XXXII, 1920, pp. 1-56).

the country has been exhausted by the war.' It is not easy to discover exactly how much money was raised by old and new methods of taxation. There was no single government department responsible for the collection of taxes. Several distinct royal accounts existed such as the treasure, the Domains Fund, the General War Fund, the Silesian Account, and the Reserve Fund. Only the King could survey the whole income and expenditure of the kingdom.

Prussia's revenues rose from 13·8 million thalers in 1768 to 23·7 million thalers in 1786.[1] At the end of the Seven Years War the revenues of the King were derived mainly from the rents of the farms on his estates; from timber sold from his forests; and from the profits of the royal mint, manufactories, and salt-works; from the land tax and the 'occupation tax'; and from customs duties, excise duties and tolls of various kinds. Urban and rural districts were taxed in different ways. In the rural districts a land tax or 'contribution' was raised by the provincial authorities who kept part of the money they collected to defray local expenses and passed on the remainder to the King. The 'contribution' was usually paid by the farmers and

---

[1] (i) In 1776 Frederick wrote in his Political Testament: 'Since the war the revenues of the state have enormously increased—1,200,000 thalers by the acquisition of Pomerelia, 1 million thalers from tobacco, 1 million thalers from the bank, 50,000 thalers from timber, 400,000 thalers from the excise and tolls, 130,000 thalers from the Schönebeck saltworks, 56,000 thalers from the lottery, as well as 200,000 thalers from the new tax on the domains, so that the present total of the revenue amounts to 21,700,000 thalers from what, in addition to all other State expenses, an army of 87,000 soldiers is maintained'.

(ii) Benzenberg's estimate for 1778-9

Direct taxes	.	.	.	.	.	5	million thalers
Domains	.	.	.	.	.	9	,, ,,
Regie	.	.	.	.	.	6.2	,, ,,
Salt	.	.	.	.	.	1.3	,, ,,
Tobacco	.	.	.	.	.	1.3	,, ,,
						22.8	,, ,,

(iii) Koser's estimate for 1786

Domains	.	.	.	.	.	8.5	million thalers
War fund	.	.	.	.	.	5·3	,, ,,
Silesian fund	.	.	.	.	.	4.2	,, ,,
Reserve fund	.	.	.	.	.	5·7	,, ,,
						23·7	,, ,,

peasants while the nobles were generally exempted unless they were unable to perform their military duties. In Silesia the nobles were subject to the payment of 'contributions'[1]. Higher taxes were levied on the revenue of the church than on those of lay proprietors.[2]

The 'contribution' was a land tax which was assessed as a proportion of the value of the harvest. This proportion varied somewhat from province to province. J. R. Roden, the President of the Audit Chamber, pointed out that a 'contribution' might be so heavy as to make it impossible for the farmer to maintain himself and his family in a decent standard of comfort.[3] Since farmers and peasants had little chance of saving any money they faced ruin if the harvest failed or if their property were destroyed by storm, floods or fire.

Those who lived in the country districts but owned no land were not assessed for 'contributions'. They paid an 'occupation tax' instead. Those liable to this tax were, for the most part, the village domestic workers. It may be added that in Prussia in the eighteenth century only six types of artisans were allowed by law to exercise their crafts in the country districts. These were smiths, wheelwrights, carpenters, masons, flax weavers, and tailors.[4]

In the towns no direct taxes were levied. On the other hand excise duties had to be paid upon many consumer goods such as grain, leather, sugar, firewood, beer, spirits and wine. Nobles, clergy, officials and teachers paid no excise duties. The excise was paid at town gates by merchants when they brought

[1] In Silesia lands held by a noble tenure paid a rather higher tax than lands held by other tenures.

[2] Adam Smith, *An Inquiry into the Nature and Causes of the Wealth of Nations* 1776 (Everyman edition, 2 vols., 1927), Vol. II, pp. 316-7.

[3] J. R. Roden gave as an example a farm in the village of Tempelhof near Berlin. The farmers paid a 'contribution' of 8 thalers and 3 groschen on every *Hufe* (20 acres) of land. But the value of the surplus produce of 20 acres—i.e. after deducting what was consumed by the farmer and his family—was estimated at only 9 thalers and 18 groschen. What was left after paying the 'contribution'—a mere 1 thaler and 15 groschen—was not enough to pay other expenses such as feudal dues and tithes. See Franz Mehring, *Historische Aufsätze zur preussisch-deutschen Geschichte* (1952), pp. 138-9.

[4] It was not possible to enforce these regulations in the territories west of the Elbe.

67

dutiable goods into a town. But the excise duty was passed on to the consumer by raising the price of goods upon which the tax had been paid. The consumer included both burghers and villagers who purchased goods in the town markets. In 1764 the excise brought in 3·9 million thalers.[1] With the establishment of the *Regie* the collection of excise duties passed from the local authorities to the officials of a central authority.

From these revenues the King defrayed the expenses of his court (which were low by eighteenth century standards), the civil administration, and the army. Every year grants were made by the King to defray the cost of public works and to assist landowners and manufacturers. These subsidies and loans amounted to 4 or 5 million thalers a year. The King saved about 2 million thalers a year and this money was paid into the treasure (or war chest). The most striking change in the pattern of expenditure in Frederick's reign was the decline in the proportion of the revenue allocated to the upkeep of the army. It has been estimated that this proportion sank from 80 per cent in 1740 to just over 50 per cent in 1786.

At a meeting held on June 10, 1766 the King discussed with his ministers the financial estimates for the following year. He appears to have stated that the annual revenue would have to be increased by 2 million thalers to meet increased government spending. The fact that the collection of customs excise and tolls was being transferred from the local authorities to the *Regie*[2] at this time gave credence to the view that de Launay's administration had been set up with the express purpose of adding 2 million thalers a year to the revenue. But there is little evidence to support this view. When Frederick discussed the national finances in his Political Testament of 1768 he stated that the *Regie* had been set up because smuggling was so rife that Prussian manufacturers were denied the protection against foreign competition to which they were entitled. He declared that smuggling must be eradicated and that the excise must be collected in an orderly fashion. He mentioned a possible increase of 500,000 thalers in the revenues derived from the

---

[1] 3.4 million thalers after deducting costs of collection.
[2] For the history of the *Regie* see W. Schultze, *Geschichte der preussischen Regieverwaltung von 1766-86*, Vol. I (1887).

customs and excise. Although Prussia's revenues were increased by the *Regie* the fiscal aspect of the matter probably carried less weight with the King than some contemporaries imagined.[1]

In a letter to de Launay, dated March 16, 1766, Frederick recommended that customs and excise duties should be so arranged that wealthy landowners and merchants rather than peasants or craftsmen should shoulder most of the burden of indirect taxation. The King suggested that the luxuries of the rich should pay high duties while the necessities of the poor should pay low duties. He hoped to increase the revenue from customs and excise duties not so much by levying high duties as by reducing smuggling.

New excise duties, which were announced on April 14, 1766, applied for the first time to the whole kingdom. Duties on wine, beer, spirits and meat (except pork) were increased. The excise on beer was actually doubled. The grain excise was dropped but this made no difference to the price of the loaf since the bread tax was increased. A committee of civil servants was set up under von der Horst to examine the new rates. In 1768 this committee recommended certain reductions but in view of de Launay's protests the committee's report appears to have been shelved. Whatever may have been the King's intentions it seems clear that a high proportion of the money collected by the *Regie* came out of the pockets of the peasants, the soldiers, the artisans, the farmers and the shopkeepers and not from the nobles, the officers, the clergy or the merchants.

There was an increase in the revenues raised from indirect taxes in the last 20 years of Frederick's reign. When Prussia had recovered from the immediate effects of the war and the commercial crisis there was an expansion in agriculture, industry and commerce, except in 1770 and 1771 when the harvest failed. The expansion of foreign trade—fostered by the Overseas Trading Corporation—was particularly marked during the American War of Independence. The increased revenue from excise duties reflected increased consumption

---

[1] At the end of Frederick's reign it was estimated that an additional revenue of about 2 million thalers a year had been secured from the taxes collected by the *Regie*. But there is no evidence to suggest that this particular increase had been deliberately planned.

and an improvement in living standards. The additional revenue secured from West Prussia after 1772—including the valuable tolls on the Vistula—was an important factor in bringing about an expansion in the revenue from indirect taxes. The reduction in smuggling owing to the greater efficiency of the *Regie* also contributed to the improvement of the revenue. On the other hand costs of collection rose from 300,000 thalers to 800,000 thalers a year[1] and there was a strong suspicion that some of the French officials were lining their pockets at the expense of the taxpayers.

The *Regie* was extremely unpopular in Prussia. It was an anomalous organisation, quite different from other government departments. Its senior officials and some of the excisemen were Frenchmen who showed no mercy in putting down smuggling. In 1766 excisemen were attacked in Berlin and the King threatened to call out the troops if this occurred again. Mirabeau declared that 'an enormous number of poor wretches had been completely ruined—reduced from comfort to utter misery—by the damnable efficiency of the tax collectors'.[2] Dohm observed in his memoirs that Frederick was now looked upon not as the father of his people but as 'a tyrant who . . . was continually planning new conquests and was employing foreigners to screw out of his subjects the money needed to implement these plans.'[3] Heinitz—for a short time in charge of the fourth and fifth Departments of the General Directory—[4]

[1] Costs of collection were heavy because the French officials were highly paid and because a large staff was needed to collect the taxes. Each of the six *regisseurs*, appointed in 1766, drew a salary of 10,000 thalers a year—and a percentage of what was collected in excess of the revenue of 1765-6. This was far more than the salary of any Prussian Minister of State at that time. In 1781 forty excisemen were stationed in Berlin and the Mark Brandenburg and they collected 1.1 million thalers. On the other hand in 1816 in Berlin alone, only 15 officials were required to collect 2.2 million thalers.

[2] For Mirabeau's criticism of the *Regie* see *De la monarchie prussienne sous Frédéric le Grand* (4 vols., 1788; appendix to Vol. II). For de Launay's reply see *Justification du systéme d'économie politique et financière du Frédéric II, roi de Prusse* (1789).

[3] Quoted by H. Krüger, *Zur Geschichte der Manufakturen und der Manufakturarbeiter in Preussen* (1958), p. 111.

[4] Heinitz's criticisms of the *Regie* appeared in a report which was probably written in June 1784 immediately after he had relinquished the post of head of the fourth and fifth Departments of the General Directory (Manufactures and Commerce). It is unlikely that the report was submitted

attacked de Launay's fiscal policy and the harsh methods adopted by the *Regie* in collecting the excise. In his opinion the
high rates of duty were retarding the industrial expansion of
Prussia while the commercial treaty with Poland (1775) was
restricting commercial expansion, particularly in Silesia.
Frederick was impressed by these reports and he began to
realise how heavy a price he was paying for any additional
revenues that de Launay was able to raise.[1]

Although there was an increase in revenue from existing
direct and indirect taxes the King was anxious to find new
sources of income. The most important were the tobacco and
coffee monopolies. Frederick tried to farm out the tobacco
monopoly to private entrepreneurs but they all failed to raise
the necessary capital.[2] So the King took over the assets of the
last of these companies and set up a General Tobacco Administration of his own in July 1766.[3] It was linked with de Launay's
Regie for a short time and then became an independent organisation. It had the exclusive right to import, process and sell
tobacco and snuff. When the Overseas Trading Company was
established, it took over responsibility for the importing of
tobacco leaf. A preventive force, largely staffed by French
officials, was established to stop both smuggling and other
infringements of the monopoly. There were complaints con-

to Frederick the Great. Probably a copy was sent to the Crown Prince.
The report was printed in 1788 but it was not published. See W. Schultze,
'Ein Angriff des Ministers von Heinitz gegen die französische Regie in
Preussen' (*Forschungen zur Brandenburgischen und Preussischen Geschichte,* Vol. V,
1892, pp. 191-202) and Otto Steinecke, 'Des Ministers von Heinitz
mémoire sur ma gestion du 4e et 5e departement' (*Forschungen zur Brandenburgischen und Preussischen Geschichte,* Vol. XXII, 1909, pp. 183-191).

[1] De Launay claimed that in 20 years he had collected 42 million thalers
more than would have been raised by the method of collection used before
he took office in 1766. Several writers accept this estimate and state the
average annual increase in revenue from the excise was about 2 million
thalers. Preuss, however, gives a much lower figure (857,000 thalers). It
may be that the higher estimates include the revenues derived from the
tobacco and coffee monopolies. Heinitz in a report of January 17, 1783
argued that any increase in the revenues of the *Regie* was due to the annexation of West Prussia. He estimated that the revenues of 1780-1 were less
than those of 1765-6 if West Prussia were excluded.

[2] They were (i) F. L. Roubaud (of Marseilles), (ii) a group of Prussian
merchants (mainly from Berlin), and (iii) J. A. Calzabigi (of Leghorn).

[3] See E. P. Reimann, *Das Tabaksmonopol Friedrichs des Grossen* (1913).

cerning the high price of tobacco products and the strict methods employed by the officials of the Tobacco Administration. In 1776 the King stated that the tobacco monopoly was bringing in one million thalers a year and by the end of the reign this income had risen to 1,286,000 thalers.

The financial success of the tobacco monopoly encouraged Frederick to set up a coffee monopoly. Coffee was already heavily taxed and the high duties were unpopular. When the Estates of Pomerania complained about them in 1779 the King replied that coffee was heavily taxed not so much to increase the revenue as to reduce the imports of coffee so that the drain upon specie might be reduced. Frederick disapproved of the increased popularity of coffee and considered the beer soup which he had drunk in his youth to be a much healthier beverage than coffee. Two years later the King set up a coffee monopoly. The import of coffee—mainly from French colonies —was placed in the hands of the Overseas Trading Corporation. The annual cost of these imports was between 700,000 and one million thalers. In each province a coffee warehouse was set up from which privileged persons (nobles, clergy and army officers) might obtain supplies of relatively cheap unroasted coffee (at 9 groschen per lb.) provided that they purchased at least 20 lbs. a year. The majority of the people had to pay 1 thaler for a 10 ounce tin of coffee. The high cost of coffee[1] encouraged smuggling, unauthorised roasting, and the production of substitutes such as chicory. The efforts of the 'coffee smellers' to check smuggling and illegal roasting were only partially successful and in 1783 the King reduced the price of coffee. Owing to the excessive zeal with which the 'coffee smellers' carried out their duties the coffee monopoly was just as unpopular as the Tobacco Administration.

The fact that Frederick was able to add to his income by establishing monopolies in tobacco and in coffee suggests that the standard of living in Prussia was rising at this time. Tobacco and coffee, once the luxuries of the rich, were now being consumed by a larger section of the population than before. Since tobacco and coffee cost more than before there were protests

[1] In Hamburg coffee could be bought for 4 or 5 groschen per lb.

against the increase in price. This suggests that more people were acquiring a taste for tobacco and coffee.

Another monopoly was that on salt. In the seventeenth century the Mark Brandenburg secured some of its salt from sea-water while some was imported from Lüneburg (Hanover). The Great Elector had monopolised the trade in imported salt. When the Duchy of Magdeburg was annexed in 1680 the saltworks of Halle an der Saale (in the Saalkreis) fell to Brandenburg which now became self-sufficient as far as salt was concerned. New royal saltworks were opened in 1705 at Schönebeck (by Magdeburg) and in 1735 at Königsborn (by Unna) in the County of Mark. The royal salt works were generally leased to private entrepreneurs though sometimes they were operated by the state.[1] In 1773 it was reported that the revenue from the salt monopoly fell far short of what Frederick had expected[2] and in the following year he ordered his subjects to purchase at least one peck (*Metze*)[3] of salt in every year. The revenue derived from the salt monopoly was estimated at 1·3 million thalers in 1778-9. According to Mirabeau the cost of salt in Prussia was four times as high as the world price and this led to smuggling on a large scale. After 1772 the transit trade in salt destined for Poland was monopolised by the Overseas Trading Corporation.

Other sources of revenue were of relatively minor importance compared with the income derived from the royal domains, the 'contributions', customs and excise, and the salt and tobacco monopolies. The attempt to reorganise the post office with the aid of French officials after the war achieved little success and it was not until von Derschau took charge of it in 1769 that an improvement took place. The revenues derived from the mint, the royal forests, mines, ironworks and factories were hardly of vital significance at this time. The Overseas

[1] Schönebeck from 1705 to 1722; Königsborn in 1745-50 and again after 1774. There were some privately owned salt-works in Prussia but their output was controlled by the State.

[2] Lord Malmesbury (ed.), *Diaries and Correspondence of James Harris, first Earl of Malmesbury*, Vol. 1 (1845), p. 85 (letter of January 12, 1773).

[3] 3.44 litres to be purchased by everyone over the age of nine. The amount of salt to be purchased by farmers for their cows and sheep was also fixed.

Trading Corporation at first suffered heavy losses owing to the mismanagement of its affairs by Görne and Delâtre and it was some time before the financial returns from its trading and financial activities could be regarded as satisfactory. The profits of the Royal Bank of Berlin rose from about 22,000 thalers in 1767-8 to 216,000 thalers in 1785-6.

An important feature of Prussia's national finances in Frederick's reign was the accumulation of a reserve of bullion in readiness for war. In peacetime the army was maintained from the General War Fund but if mobilisation were necessary or if hostilities broke out, additional costs would be incurred and it was to meet these expenses that a permanent treasure existed. This reserve included the 'Great Treasure' at Potsdam and a number of supplementary funds such as the Silesian treasure (for the defence of Silesia), the Magdeburg Forage Fund (for the army of the Elbe), and the balance held by the General War Fund. At the end of the Seven Years War Frederick still had nearly 14·5 million thalers in his 'Great Treasure' but much of it was in depreciated money. Frederick aimed at raising the 'Great Treasure' to 20 million thalers[1] and he was determined to replace the debased coins by coins of pre-war value.

Every year 700,000 thalers were paid into the 'Great Treasure' from the General Domains Fund and this was increased to 1·1 million thalers after the annexation of West Prussia. By 1782 Prussia's balance of international payments was sufficiently favourable for Frederick to contemplate saving 3 million thalers for defence purposes. Between 1764 and 1773 the 'Great Treasure' grew from 14·5 to 19·25 million thalers. In the same period 7·7 million thalers of depreciated coins were withdrawn from the treasure and were replaced by coins of pre-war value. In 1786 the 'Great Treasure' was only a little larger than it had been in 1773 but the subsidiary funds available in wartime amounted to about 30 million thalers. According to Koser the total reserves kept in readiness for war amounted to 50 million thalers.

Frederick's critics condemned his policy of amassing a large treasure in bullion. Mirabeau, for example, declared that the

[1] This figure was mentioned in Frederick's Political Testament of 1768.

money lying in the war chest was 'absolutely dead and useless'. It was argued that the coins should have been put into circulation to stimulate commercial and industrial enterprise. The King, however, was unrepentant. He considered that it was essential to have immediately available the cash necessary to finance the first campaigns of a war. Wealthier countries might be able to raise large loans quickly if they were involved in war. Prussia, on the other hand, was hardly in a position to borrow either at home or abroad. Although the King may have appreciated the force of the arguments against permanently withdrawing from circulation large quantities of silver, he considered that the needs of national defence made it essential that a substantial sum of money should be kept in reserve in case a war should break out.

Frederick's financial policy was successful inasmuch as he 'contrived to produce on the economic resources of what was then the least prosperous section of Germany, a public revenue which was greater than that of Russia on the accession of Catherine II, with a *per capita* burden of taxation no greater than of Austria, and considerably less than that of France'. Moreover Frederick 'managed to support the army of a first-rate power on the resources of a third-rate state and at the same time accumulated a large reserve in the public treasury'.[1]

(v) *Reconstruction of the devastated Provinces*

The reconstruction of the devastated provinces was an urgent problem in 1763. East Prussia had been in the hands of the Russians between 1758 and 1762. The province had been administered for four years as if it were already a Russian province and the inhabitants had sworn fealty to the Czarina. The fortress of Marienburg had been the Russian headquarters from which the campaigns in Prussia's Baltic provinces had been directed. Except for the campaign of Gross Jägersdorf hostilities had caused little damage but the exploitation of the forests and the interruption of the transit trade with Poland had injured the East Prussian economy. Since the Russians

[1] W. L. Dorn, 'The Prussian Bureaucracy in the Eighteenth Century' (*Political Science Quarterly*, Vol. XLVI, 1931, p. 404).

had hoped to annex the province—and had secured the collaboration of some of the local gentry—they had treated East Prussia with less severity than other Prussian provinces which they had occupied during the war.[1]

The scattered Prussian territories between the Elbe and the Rhine had suffered from French attacks and had been occupied by French forces at various times. Much property had been destroyed in Halberstadt, Minden, Bielefeld, Hamm, Soest, Lünen and Wesel. The French occupation of Emden had brought the activities of the Asiatic Company to an end. In Cleves the population had declined from 72,447 to 62,412. Frederick visited this part of his dominions in the summer of 1763 and he ordered J. R. Roden to prepare a report on the extent of the damage sustained by the towns. A grant of 250,000 thalers was made towards their reconstruction. The owners of landed estates appear to have received no compensation. Mirabeau stated that the landed proprietors in Westphalia 'se sont relevés de leurs pertes sans caisse de crédit, sans dons, sans largesses, et ils sont moins redués que la noblesse des pays où l'on a tout prodigué'.[2]

Silesia had been the scene of several hard fought campaigns and had suffered from the depredations of Maria Theresa's Croat troops. When hostilities ceased Frederick visited the province even before he returned to his capital.[3] Some 6,000 dwellings and 3,700 farm buildings had been destroyed. Yet the production of flax and wool and the output and export of linens and woollens had not declined as much as might have been expected. Indeed Silesia was the only Prussian province

---

[1] It may be added that immediately after the war Königsberg suffered serious damage from a great fire in which many of its warehouses went up in flames.

[2] Mirabeau, *De la monarchie prussiene sous Frédéric le Grand* (4 vols., 1788), Vol. I, p. 324. Mirabeau pointed out that—in comparison with the main provinces of Prussia—the scattered territories west of the Elbe supplied fewer troops and horses, paid lower taxes, and were not subject to the same monopolies. He wrote: 'Les provinces Westphaliennes sont les plus florissantes des états prussiens, les plus peuplées à proportion de leur étendue, les plus riches, les plus heureusses; et cependant leurs habitans sont généralement peu industrieux. Voila ce que peut la liberté'.

[3] For Frederick's tours of inspection in Silesia see E. Pfeiffer, *Devuereisen Friedrichs des Grossen, besonders die schlesischen nach 1763 und der Zustand Schlesiens von 1763-1786* (1904).

which paid its taxes regularly throughout the war. After the war Frederick remitted taxes for six months and sent 17,000 horses as well as supplies of seed corn to Silesia. The financial difficulties of the feudal landlords were alleviated by royal grants and loans and by the establishment of a provincial land mortgage bank. The rich monasteries were ordered to establish industrial workshops. The decline in the population was remedied by the settlement of new immigrants. In 1773 it was stated that 72 villages had been built in Silesia in the last thirty years and an edict of that year provided for the establishment of a further 200 new settlements. Over 60,000 colonists came to the province between its annexation by Prussia and the death of Frederick the Great.[1]

Pomerania[2] and the New Mark[3] had been attacked by the Russians and the Swedes and had suffered from the depredations of irregular Cossack and Tartar troops. Kolberg,[4] Küstrin,[5] and Driesen[6] had been almost entirely destroyed while Stettin had suffered from the blockade and from the destruction of the embankments of the Swine channel. In the rural

[1] For colonisation in the Silesian villages of Horst and Finkenstein (in Kreis Oppeln) see Georg Stumpfe, *Betrachtungen zur Siedlungstätigkeit Friedrichs des Grossen, dargestellt an den Dörfern Horst und Finkenstein, Kreis Oppeln* (1941).

[2] East Pomerania (*Hinterpommern*) and that part of West Pomerania lying between the Oder and the Peene (*Preussisch-Vorpommern*) were Prussian territories at this time. The remainder of Pomerania (*Schwedisch-Vorpommern*) was held by the Swedes while Pomerelia (Polish Pomerania) belonged to Poland (until 1772). For the reconstruction of Pomerania see Hertzberg, *Receuil des déductions, manifestes, déclarations, traités et autres actes et écrits . . . depuis l'année 1778 jusqu'a l'année 1789* (2 vols., 1789).

[3] For the reconstruction of the New Mark see P. Schwartz. 'Die neumärkische Städte nach dem Siebenjährigen Krieg' (*Schriften des Vereins für die Geschichte der Neumark*, Vol. VIII, 1899) and H. Moegelin, 'Das Rettablissement des adlingen Grundbesitzes in der Neumark durch Friedrich den Grossen' (*Forschungen zur Brandenburgischen und Preussischen Geschichte*, Vol. XLVI, pp. 28-69 and pp. 233-74.) In the New Mark the districts of Schievelbein, Dramburg and Sternberg had been seriously damaged. On the other hand the districts of Cottbus, Krossen and Königsberg had been less affected by the war. The loss of population in the New Mark during the war was about 57,000.

[4] Kolberg (Pomerania) was a fortress on the Baltic coast.

[5] Küstrin (New Mark) was a fortress at the junction of the Oder and the Warthe.

[6] Driesen (New Mark) was a small town near the Polish frontier (Netze District).

districts of the two provinces over 3,000 dwellings had been destroyed. The New Mark was virtually denuded of cattle. The debts of its nobles amounted to 2,262,000 thalers which was nearly as much as the value of their estates. Pomerania had special claims upon the King's generosity since it was a province which supplied him with some of his crack regiments. When Frederick lost the battle of Kolin in Bohemia in 1757 the Estates of Pomerania raised 5,000 volunteers to defend Stettin where a tiny garrison faced a force of 20,000 men. The first steps towards the reconstruction of Pomerania and the New Mark began immediately after peace had been made with Russia in April 1762.

In the Mark Brandenburg the losses suffered during the war amounted to over 6 million thalers. Berlin had twice been occupied and over 2 million thalers had been paid to save the city from being plundered. By 1761 thirty thousand persons were drawing poor relief. Several manufacturing establishments —such as the Potsdam armament works, a blast furnace at Zehdenick, copperworks at Neustadt-Eberswalde and a paper mill at Wolfswinkel—had been destroyed or damaged. In April 1763 Frederick discussed with senior officials the immediate needs of the province and gave financial assistance both to the towns and the rural districts.[1]

Particular attention was paid to the needs of the capital. The King repaid the contribution exacted by the Russians and gave money and timber for the reconstruction of Berlin. Some of the rebuilding was done by direct labour through the Royal Building Office. Mirabeau remarked that 'c'est ainsi que Berlin est devenu une ville bien construit, bien percée, abondante en logemens sains et commodes. Les rues sont passablement pavées et souvent embellies de trottoirs'. He added that Frederick 'a fait de Berlin et de Potsdam deux villes fort imposantes, malgré le mélange disparate et quelquefois grotesque des genres d'architecture'. The erection of a new palace and of army barracks at Potsdam gave employment to masons, joiners and other artisans. An English visitor later declared that Potsdam was a beautiful town where Frederick had provided

---

[1] Mirabeau declared that the Mark Brandenburg 'a reçu les plus grands bienfaits de son souverain'.

accommodation for everybody—even the humblest mechanic —who had a poor or a small house.[1] Orders from the Berlin Wool Warehouse for military cloth stimulated the demand for local woollens and the danger of a shortage of labour was averted by settling some 400 spinners and their families in the Wollup district. The development of the textile, metallurgical and porcelain industries of the Mark Brandenburg was encouraged. Agriculture was fostered by royal grants to landowners, by the drainage of marshes, and by the establishment of new settlements in the valleys of the Havel, the Finow and the Rhin.

So serious was the situation in Pomerania and the New Mark that a special official was appointed to supervise the reconstruction of these provinces. This was Franz von Brenkenhof[2] who was described by Mirabeau as 'un ... homme aussi recommandable que singulier'. Brenkenhof had made a fortune during the war as a horse-dealer and army contractor and had impressed the King by the efficient manner in which he had supplied the army with horses and grain during the forced marches preceding the battle of Torgau. In 1762 Brenkenhof was appointed a member of the General Directory with the title of Finance Councillor and a salary of 2,000 thalers (£300) a year. He held office for eighteen years.

Brenkenhof promptly introduced emergency measures to revive agriculture and industry in Pomerania and the New Mark. Taxes were remitted for two years. Grants and loans

[1] H. S. Conway to the Marquis of Hertford, July 17, 1774 (in Thomas Carlyle, *History of Frederick II of Prussia*, Vol. III, Book 21. p. 134).

[2] Brenkenhof was born at Reideberg, near Halle an der Saale, in 1723. He entered the household of Prince Leopold of Anhalt-Dessau as a boy. His formal education was neglected and he was hardly able to read or write when he grew up. But he gained practical experience as a surveyor from a Prussian surveyor named Materne who was living in exile at the court of Anhalt-Dessau. For Brenkenhof see A. G. Meissner, *Leben Franz Balthsar Schönberg von Brenkenhof* (1782), Spude, *Franz Balthasar Schönberg von Brenkenhof* (1880: reprinted from the *Brandenburgisches Provinzialblatt*); Rehmann, 'Kleine Beiträge zur Charakteristik Brenkenhofs' (*Schriften des Vereins für Geschichte der Neumark*, Vol. XXII, 1908) and P. Schwartz, 'Brenkenhofs Berichte über seine Tätigkeit in der Neumark' (*Schriften des Vereins für Geschichte der Neumark*, Vol. X, 1907). Although most of Brenkenhof's work was done in Pomerania, the New Mark, and the Netze district, his services were occasionally used elsewhere. He was, for example, responsible for the establishment of the 'spinning villages' in the Wollup district.

were made to landowners to enable them to settle their most pressing debts and to put their ruined estates in order. Small-holders and peasants were supplied with cattle, sheep, and seed, and with timber to rebuild cottages and barns. Surplus army horses, fodder, and grain were distributed to landowners and farmers. Pedigree oxen were introduced from Poland. Brenken-hof secured money and building materials for the reconstruction of ruined towns. New settlers from other parts of Germany and from foreign countries replaced farmers and craftsmen who had disappeared during the war.

Pomerania had been occupied by Russian troops for practic-ally the whole of the war. Some 1,300 buildings had been destroyed and the population had declined by nearly 60,000. The district around Kolberg had no farms, no outhouses, and no cottages. Even the trees had disappeared. But when he visited the province in 1763 Frederick took an optimistic view of the situation. He declared that, although there had been much devastation, the damage was less than reports had led him to believe. He considered that 'in two years Pomerania will have a larger population and a more flourishing economy than before the war'.

A cabinet decree of 1763 ordered the abolition of serfdom in Pomerania 'implicitly and without argument'. But the re-sistance of the nobles was so strong that the edict remained a dead letter. In other respects Frederick was more successful in reviving the sorely tried province. In two years (1763-4) he spent 1·3 million thalers on the rebuilding of property; 444,000 thalers on supplying horses and grain; and 22,000 thalers to settle 250 new families of wool spinners in Pomerania. He set up a military boarding school at Stolpe for the sons of im-poverished noblemen. Brenkenhof persuaded a number of immigrants to come to Pomerania. He settled over 1,000 people on land belonging to small royal farms (*Vorwerke*).

Four important schemes of land reclamation and settlement were carried out during the period of reconstruction. These were the drainage of the marshes near Lake Madü (1769), on Usedom Island (the *Thurbruch* scheme, 1771), in the valley of the River Plöne (the *Damm* scheme, 1774), and at Schmölein (1777). The Lake Madü scheme cost the King 36,000 thalers and provided 700 settlers with a livelihood. The *Thurbruch* scheme (280 settlers) cost 10,000 thalers. The reclamation of the Plöne valley cost 40,000 thalers and 150 families were settled there.

In the New Mark the population had declined by 57,000 since 1756 and 1,900 houses had been destroyed in the rural districts. Several workshops had been burned down by the Russians. Georg Zimmermann's glassworks at Rohrbach, for example, had been destroyed. The worst devastation was in the district between Küstrin and Driesen. As in Pomerania so in the New Mark the King gave prompt assistance both in cash and in kind. He paid 768,000 thalers towards the reconstruction of farms, cottages and outhouses (1763); 684,000 thalers for the rebuilding of Küstrin after the Russian bombardment; grain and horses to the value of 300,000 thalers; and many grants and loans to the great landowners. On former royal farms (*Vorwerke*) Brenkenhof established settlers who brought with them 9,000 thalers in cash, 271 horses, 1,000 head of cattle, and 4,400 sheep.

Brenkenhof's most spectacular achievements in the New Mark were the reconstruction of Driesen and the inauguration of a great scheme for the drainage of the marshes in the valleys of the Warthe and the Netze. He planned not only to rebuild Driesen but to turn it from an unimportant frontier town to a great commercial centre. He hoped that the woollen cloth of the New Mark might find a market in Poland and that some of the trade between Prussia and Poland might be diverted from Danzig to the Stettin-Driesen route. Moreover, with the full support of the King, Brenkenhof made Driesen the centre of Prussian intrigue in the neighbouring Netze district which Frederick coveted and which he eventually seized in the first partition of Poland.

In 1763 Brenkenhof persuaded the King to exempt Driesen's trade from customs and excise duties for six years. The financial loss was made good by requiring Polish Jews to pay for permits to trade in Driesen. The town was rebuilt and a new market was laid out which was surrounded by imposing houses. Among the first immigrants after the war were a number of Protestants from Czarnikow. These Polish refugees were provided with temporary accommodation in the local barracks. A prosperous merchant from Posen, named Treppmacher, was persuaded to settle in Driesen. He started his business in the old garrison chapel and powder magazine and he soon built himself a mansion. He had a capital of 100,000 thalers and every year he brought to Driesen from Stettin goods to the value of 6,000 thalers. Not all Brenkenhof's schemes for the expansion of Driesen's trade were successful. He tried to control the export of salt to Poland but the King eventually rejected his plan in favour of a proposal of the influential Jewish firm of Ephraim and Sons to import salt for this purpose from Liverpool and from Cadiz.

Brenkenhof's efforts to promote trade with Poland were closely linked with his master's plans for the annexation of the Netze District. It was not only Protestants and Jews who were welcomed in Driesen. Emigré nobles who left Poland in the troubled times of the Confederation of Bar were also received with open arms. Their most influential representative was Countess Skorzewska from whom Brenkenhof secured valuable information concerning the intrigues of the various factions in Warsaw.

Two important land reclamation schemes, for which Brenkenhof was largely responsible, were launched in the New Mark. These were the drainage of the great marshes in the valleys of the Warthe and the Netze. In 1765 Lieutenant Colonel Petri, who had already had experience of land reclamation in the Oder valley, examined the Warthe marshes between Küstrin and Landsberg and reported that it would be possible to drain them. Brenkenhof submitted Petri's plans to the King and in December 1766 an initial grant of 350,000 thalers was made to start work on the project. Brenkenhof was in charge of operations and in nine years he settled 690 families (7,436 persons) on reclaimed land. He had to face some criticism concerning the way in which the scheme had been carried out. It was alleged that some of the new houses were jerry built and that some of the immigrants were idle and dissolute.

Frederick also advanced 150,000 thalers to initiate a scheme for draining the marshes in the valley of the Netze. Brenkenhof was responsible for carrying out this project. The first phase of the scheme involved the reclamation of the land between

Landsberg and Driesen. The Mielitz Winkel was drained and the villages of Mielitz Winkel and Neu Ulm were subsequently incorporated in Driesen to increase its revenues. The next phase of the Netze project involved the drainage of swamps to the east of Driesen right on the Polish frontier. In 1773-4, immediately after the first partition of Poland, Brenkenhof, acting upon Frederick's instructions, three times forced the Poles to agree to new frontier adjustments in the Netze District so that as large an area of land for reclamation as possible might come under Prussian control.[1] Seventeen villages in the *Netze-bruch* received new settlers and 19 completely new villages were established.

Since Brenkenhof had many contacts with the Netze District —the Polish territory adjacent to the New Mark—the King used his services at the time of the first partition of Poland (1772) to bring this region under Prussian control. He carried out this mission successfully although he had only a junior officer and a dozen dragoons at his disposal. It has been seen that in connection with the Netze land reclamation scheme Brenkenhof subsequently extended somewhat the area annexed by Prussia.

He also played an important part in the work of improving the communications and expanding industry and agriculture in the newly acquired Polish territories. Immediately after the first partition Frederick decided that the Netze and the Brahe should be joined by a canal. Brenkenhof was responsible for the prompt construction of this new waterway (the Bromberg Canal) and it was opened in 1775.

The way in which a temporary exemption from customs and excise dues had fostered the expansion of Driesen suggested to Brenkenhof that similar measures might be applied on a larger scale to Prussia's newly acquired territories. He asked Frederick to postpone for 12 years the introduction of these duties so as to give the Netze District an opportunity to recover from years of neglect. At first it seemed as if the King would be willing to

---

[1] Frederick's excuse for making these encroachments was that under the Russo-Prussian treaty of August 5, 1772 concerning the partition of Poland the new frontier was to be drawn in such a way that 'la Netze fasse la frontière des Etats de S.M. le Roi de Prusse, et que cette rivière lui appartienne en entier'. Frederick took full advantage of the fact that the wording of the agreement was vague.

83

agree to this proposal. In the circumstances Brenkenhof persuaded a merchant from Stettin named Friesner to establish a warehouse in Bromberg. Owing to the opposition of the customs administration, however, the King decided that normal customs and excise duties must be collected in the Netze District. The unlucky Friesner went bankrupt while Brenkenhof himself lost money in trading ventures upon which he had embarked.

Brenkenhof not only promoted the economic development of Pomerania, the New Mark and the Netze district by official schemes sponsored by the King and the local authorities but he invested some of his private fortune in farming and in commercial enterprises. Although his trading ventures in the Netze District were unsuccessful his work as a landowner and a farmer had an important influence upon the economic development of the provinces in which he served. When it appeared that the completion of the scheme to reclaim the Netze marshes might be delayed owing to the difficulty of acquiring von Unfried's estate at Breitenwerder, Brenkenhof purchased the property himself. His work on this estate—and on others—deservedly earned for him the reputation of being one of the most progressive farmers in this part of Prussia. Before he became an official he had made money by dealing in horses. Now he became the owner of more than one stud and he was a horse-breeder of some note. He brought Frisian cattle and Westphalian pigs to the Netze District. He experimented with rye from Archangel and with oats and peas from England. The value of the Breitenwerder estates increased considerably under Brenkenhof's enlightened management. His neighbours profited from his example. Mirabeau declared that farming standards in the New Mark had greatly improved as a result of Brenkenhof's work. 'Il a su répandre parmi les cultivateurs de cette province les lumières et l'esprit de spéculation'.[1]

---

[1] Mirabeau, *De la monarchie prussienne sous Frédéric le Grand* (4 vols., 1788), Vol. I, p. 384.

CHAPTER IV

Commercial Policy of Frederick the Great

REDERICK THE GREAT'S commercial relations with Poland, Austria and Saxony were an important factor in promoting the expansion of the Prussian economy. In 1740 Prussia was not one of the major economic regions of Germany, being an underdeveloped country with poor soil, a harsh climate, few minerals, inadequate communications and a small population. By 1786 Prussia was one of the leading agrarian and manufacturing countries on the Continent and this change had, to some extent, been achieved at the expense of Poland, Austria and Saxony. Owing to Poland's political weakness Frederick was able to exploit its economic resources for his own benefit and at the first partition of the republic he seized sufficient territory to secure control of the trade of the Vistula valley. By filching Silesia from the Habsburgs Frederick acquired a great linen industry, so that Prussia for the first time became an exporter, on a large scale, of linen cloth. Silesia also produced large quantities of raw wool and had important mineral resources. Saxony, a small but economically advanced state, was twice occupied by Prussian troops in Frederick's reign. He appropriated the revenues of Saxony and levied additional contributions in cash and in kind for the upkeep of his forces. He exploited the forests of Saxony and he tried to secure the secret of the manufacture of porcelain in order to establish this industry in Berlin.

(i) *Poland and Danzig*[1]

In 1770 Poland was one of the larger European states with an area of about 730,000 square kilometres and a population

[1] (i) For Poland in the early eighteenth century see C. Gurlitt, *Warschauer Bauten aus der zeit der sächischen Könige* (1917); C. Gurlitt, *August der Starke ...* (2 vols., 1924); P. Haake, 'Polen am Ausgang des 17en Jahrhunderts'

estimated by various authorities at between 12 millions and 20 millions.[1] The population was largely concentrated in the districts to the west of the Vistula and the Bug and was not racially homogeneous since it included not only Poles, but also Lithuanians, White Russians, Germans and Jews. Poland's territories included the plains, plateaus, forests, and marshes lying between the Baltic and the Carpathians. The Dvina and the Dnieper were Poland's eastern frontiers while in the west Poland's territories extended to within a few miles of the River Oder. The Polish lands were compact except for the Hohenzollern enclave of East Prussia which divided Pomerelia (Polish Pomerania) from Courland.

Poland's wealth lay in her farms and forests. Rye and wheat were grown in the basin of the Vistula and on the loess soil of the Podolian plateau. Cattle and horses were reared on the steppes between the Dnieper and the Dniester. Oxen were reared for use as beasts of burden or for their meat and hides. Sheep were pastured on the Podolian plateau, while flax and hemp were grown in Lithuania. The great forests of north east Poland provided timber, charcoal, tar, honey, wax, and the skins of wild beasts. The rich salt deposits of Wieliczka near

---

(*Neue Jahrbücher zur das klassische Altertum, Geschichte und deutsche Literatur*, Vol. VIII, 1905, pp. 723-6); P. Haake, 'Die Problematik Augusts des Starken' (*Neue Jahrbücher für Wissenschaft und Jugendbildung* Vol. VII, 1931, pp. 141-153); and J. Kalisch and J. Gierowski (ed.), *Um die polnische Krone . . . 1700-21* (1962).

(ii) For the relations between Poland and Prussia in the reign of Frederick the Great see J. Ziehkursch, *Sachsen und Preussen um die Mitte des achtzehnten Johrhunderts . . .* (1904); Margot Herzfeld, 'Der polnische Handelsvertrag von 1775' (*Forschungen zu Brandenburgischen und Preussischen Geschichte*, Vol. XXXII, 1920, pp. 57-107 and Vol. XXV, 1923, pp. 58-82); R. Damus, 'Die Stadt Danzig gegenüber der Politik Friedrichs des Grossen und Friedrich Wilhelms II' (*Zeitschrift des Westpreussischen Geschichtsvereins*, Vol. XX, 1887, pp. 1-213); S. Askenazy, *Danzig and Poland* (1921); Jean-Paul Garnier, *La Tragédie de Dantzig* (1935); and W. Sobieski, *Der Kampf um die Ostsee* (1933). See also Anderson's 'Observations on the distressed situation of the trade of Danzig' received by the Home Office on January 16, 1774 (*Calendar of Home Office Papers in the Reign of George III, 1773-75* (1899), No. 458).

(iii) For the first partition of Poland see A. Sorel, *La Question d'Orient au XVIIIe siècle* (2nd edn., Paris, 1889); A. Beer, *Die erste Teilung Polens* (3 vols., 1873), and three articles by G. B. Volz in the *Forschungen zur Brandenburgischen und Preussischen Geschichte*, (Vol. XVIII, 1905; Vol. XXIII, 1910: and Vol. XXXV, 1923).

[1] Archdeacon Coxe's estimate was 14 millions.

Cracow were among the most important in central Europe and brought the king of Poland an annual revenue of £100,000.[1] There were a few fairly large industrial enterprises—saltworks, ironworks, glassworks, saw mills and papermills—but, on the whole, manufactures were not highly developed in Poland in the eighteenth century. Craft industries existed in towns and villages to supply local needs.[2] Here and there technical progress had been made as when manual power was replaced by waterpower in a few sawmills and bleachworks.

The pattern of Poland's foreign trade was that of a relatively underdeveloped country. Poland exported raw materials and foodstuffs and imported manufactured articles, colonial goods and luxury products. Her main exports were cereals and timber. Grain accounted for half of the country's exports. Other exports were metals, salt, flax, linseed, hemp, wool, skins, honey, wax, tallow and potash. The chief manufactured articles to be exported were coarse linens and leather. Poland imported woollens, calicoes, metal goods and luxuries such as wines, spices, tapestries and silks. Some of these imports passed through her own port of Danzig while others were handled by Prussian ports (Stettin and Königsberg) and various inland commercial centres such as Frankfurt an der Oder, Breslau and Leipzig. Archdeacon Coxe reported that 'as the Poles are obliged to draw from foreign countries the greatest part of the manufactured goods necessary for their interior consumption, the specie which is exported exceeds the (specie) imported (by) more than £550,000'.[3]

Poland's central location in eastern Europe favoured the development of transit trade between Russia and Turkey in the east and Germany and Austria in the west. Routes from the interior to the Baltic followed the valleys of the Vistula, the Niemen and their tributaries. Much of the commercial traffic of western and central Poland was concentrated in the basins of the Vistula and the Bug and this river system was linked to

[1] For a description of the Wieliczka salt mines see W. Coxe, *Travels into Poland, Russia, Sweden, and Denmark* (3 vols., 1784-90), Vol. I, pp. 163-7.
[2] In the eighteenth century no attempt was made to exploit Poland's resources of coal, lignite, iron ore, and petroleum. Only after the Napoleonic wars did Warsaw and Lodz develop as great manufacturing centres.
[3] W. Coxe, op. cit., Vol. I, p. 414.

routes serving the Pripet, the Niemen and the Oder. Trade routes from east to west ran across the Polish plain, avoiding the great forests (such as Bialowieza forest) and the vast expanses of marshland (such as the Pripet marshes). Two of these routes were of particular importance. One ran from Moscow to Warsaw and then to Berlin by way of either the Thorn-Eberswalde or the Warsaw-Berlin glacial valleys. The second linked Odessa and Kiev with Lemberg, Cracow and Leipzig. Warsaw, Cracow, Vilna and Lemberg were important trading centres while Danzig was the chief port. Since the Poles had 'a settled aversion to commerce'[1] much of the country's trade was controlled by German merchants in Danzig and by Jewish or Armenian merchants in other centres of trade.

The personal union between Poland and Saxony, which lasted from 1697 to 1764, might have stimulated the industrial and commercial expansion of Poland since at that time the Saxon economy was one of the most advanced in Germany. There had long been a well-established trade between the two countries—an exchange of Saxon manufactures for Polish raw materials and foodstuffs—and Augustus the Strong hoped to extend this profitable commerce. His economic adviser P. J. Marperger[2] hoped to stimulate commerce on the great trade routes across Eastern Europe which ran through Poland and Saxony. He believed that the continued prosperity of Leipzig's fairs depended upon the expansion of this commerce between Western Europe, Russia and Turkey. But the territories of Poland and Saxony were not contiguous and the weakness of the crown in Poland, the jealousy of the Polish nobles and merchants, and the opposition of Austria and Prussia, prevented Augustus from carrying out his ambitious plans.

Nevertheless the economic links between Poland and Saxony were strengthened in the first half of the eighteenth century. Saxony took over the minting of Poland's coins. Her cloth-makers (such as Langguth of Torgau) and her arms manufacturers (e.g. at Suhl) appear to have secured new markets in

---

[1] Statement by the King of Poland to Archdeacon Coxe in 1778 (W. Coxe, op. cit., Vol. I, p. 183).

[2] Paul Jacob Marperger (1656-1730) was a prolific writer of commercial text books who popularised cameralist views.

Poland, particularly in time of war. Some Saxon artisans settled in Poland. But Saxony's efforts to obtained additional supplies of raw wool from Poland and to import salt from the Wieliczka mines do not seem to have had much success, and although the Leipzig fair generally attracted a considerable number of Jewish merchants from Poland, the Electors of Saxony were unable to divert to their dominions the Polish trade that was handled by Danzig, Breslau and Frankfurt an der Oder. When Frederick the Great seized Silesia the direct route between Saxony and Poland was cut and some of the trade between the two countries had to be diverted through Bohemia and Moravia.[1]

A contemporary observer, writing on Poland in 1772, remarked that 'had the form of its government been as perfect as its situation was compact, it might have been one of the most powerful kingdoms in the universe'.[2] But the Poles could not take advantage of their economic resources, their favourable location and their links with Saxony. The country had been ravaged during the Northern war and the War of the Polish Succession and the elective monarchy and parliamentary *liberum veto* were insuperable barriers to political stability. The Crown had neither the political power nor the financial resources to follow the example of other European monarchs who stimulated industrial expansion in the eighteenth century. The structure of Polish society was unbalanced. The nobles were a personal caste who formed an unusually large proportion of the population since eight out of every hundred Poles were nobles as compared with one out of every hundred Frenchmen. The nobility included wealthy magnates, landed gentry and relatively poor yeomen (*szlachta*).[3] The feudal magnates who owned great estates were wealthy men and they often left the management of their properties in the hands of agents. Moreover Poland was overrun with priests who contributed little to the economic development of the country. The majority of the

[1] Rudolf Forberger, 'Zur wirtschaftsgeschichtlichen Neueinschätzung der sächsisch-polnischen Union' in J. Kalisch and J. Gierowski, *Um die polnische Krone. Sachsen und Polen während des Nordischen Krieges 1700-21* (1962).

[2] *Gentleman's Magazine*, November 1772, p. 502.

[3] J. F. Baumann, *Darstellungen aus dem Leben . . .* (Königsberg, 1803), ch. 21.

Poles were serfs who were completely under the authority of their lords. In the early eighteenth century their position had been superior to that of serfs in Russia and other parts of eastern Europe and there had been a migration of peasants to Poland.[1] But in the second half of the eighteenth century the Polish serfs were generally oppressed by their lords and suffered from the effects of wars and civil disorders. The urban middle classes in Poland were small in number and had little influence in politics or in commercial affairs. This gap in the social structure was, to some extent, filled by about two million Polish Jews who enjoyed 'privileges which they scarcely possess in any other country excepting England and Holland'. They dominated the country's trade and commerce, acted as stewards to the landed gentry, and kept many of the taverns.[2]

The death first of Augustus III (1763) and then of his son (1764) was the end of the personal union between Saxony and Poland. France and Austria hoped that the union would continue but Catherine II of Russia, supported by her new Prussian ally, secured the election of her former lover Stanislaus Poniatowski to the throne.[3] Civil war broke out in Poland in 1768. It was partly a struggle between rival feudal clans—the Czartoryskis (the 'Family') and the nobles united in the Confederation of Bar—and partly a conflict between the Dissenters[4] and the Catholics. Both sides appealed to foreign powers for help. The Russians supported the Czartoryskis and the Greek Orthodox Dissenters, while the Turks assisted the Confederation. In the autumn of 1768 Turkey followed up a demand that Russian

[1] In 1708 and again ten years later it was reported that large numbers of peasants had migrated from East Prussia and Pomerania to Poland.

[2] W. Coxe, *Travels into Poland, Russia, Sweden and Denmark* (three volumes, 1784-90), Vol. I, p. 136. He wrote of Lithuania: 'If you ask for an interpreter they bring you a Jew; if you come to an inn the landlord is a Jew; if you want post-horses, a Jew procures them; if you wish to purchase, a Jew is your agent; this perhaps is the only country in Europe where Jews cultivate the ground; in passing through Lithuania, we frequently saw them engaged in sowing, reaping, mowing and other works of husbandry' (*ibid.*, Vol. I, p. 226).

[3] It may be added that in April 1763 the Duke of Courland, a son of the former King of Poland, had been ejected from Poland by Russian troops.

[4] There were about 1,000,000 Dissenters in Poland. About half of them were Protestants (many of them Germans) and half were Greek Orthodox (mainly in Lithuania).

troops should be withdrawn from Poland by declaring war upon Catherine II. In accordance with the terms of the Russo-Prussian alliance of 1764 Frederick paid Catherine a subsidy of 480,000 thalers a year.[1] In 1770 the horrors of famine and plague were added to the evils of civil strife and about a quarter of a million Poles perished. Frederick took advantage of the crisis. He claimed to be alarmed at the possibility of epidemics or cattle plague reaching his own dominions and he ordered his troops to establish a *cordon sanitaire* to cut off Danzig, Pomerelia and the Netze District from the rest of Poland. When Roskowski's forces threatened Konitz (Chojnice) a detachment of Prussian hussars was set to protect the town. Prussian troops, commanded by General Thadden and General Belling, were engaged in several skirmishes with the forces of the Confederation. Civil war, religious bigotry, political ineptitude, famine, plague, and foreign intervention paved the way for the first partition of Poland.[2]

Neither the central nor the local authorities functioned effectively. The feudal magnates and their armed retainers terrorised the countryside while the Dissenters were deprived of their religious and political liberties. The Lutherans looked to Frederick for aid, the Greek Orthodox to Catherine the Great. The country's economic and financial affairs were regulated in the laxest manner since taxes were no longer collected regularly, smuggling was rife, and roads, bridges, and towpaths were seldom repaired. Public institutions, such as

[1] Normally Frederick would have supplied 10,000 foot soldiers and 2,000 cavalry under the terms of the Russo-Prussian alliance but in the case of a Russo-Turkish war he paid his ally a subsidy instead of sending troops.

[2] Frederick wrote in his Political Testament of 1768: 'It is hardly possible to regard Poland as a European Power. The country is thinly populated because the great nobles treat their subjects like slaves. That is a weakness of this republic. Many other evils contribute to the dismal state of a country where the finances are in ruins and the army consists of only a handful of troops . . . In short all the faults of the old feudal system have survived in Poland to our own day—the royal elections which are followed by civil wars, the stormy parliaments which all have to be dissolved, and the failure of the courts to dispense justice'. He added that 'Poland would have fallen long ago, had it not been for the armed intervention of jealous neighbours which has prevented greedy princes from conquering the country.'

hospitals and schools, were neglected.[1] When Archdeacon Coxe travelled from Bielitz to Cracow in 1778 he found that 'the roads were bad, the villages few and wretched beyond description; the hovels all built of wood seemed full of filth and misery and everything wore the appearance of extreme poverty'. On the highway between Cracow and Warsaw he observed that 'the natives were poorer, humbler and more miserable than any people we had yet observed in the course of our travels'. Between Warsaw and Bialystok the Archdeacon passed through a district where 'the peasants were perfect slaves, and their habitations and appearance correspond with their miserable situation: I could scarcely have figured to myself such objects of poverty and misery'.[2]

When Frederick's officials took over the administration of West Prussia[3] they found that in some towns many of the inhabitants were living in the cellars of houses that had fallen into decay.[4] Bromberg lay in ruins. Kulm, which had once had 800 houses, now had only 100 and in its market place only 28 out of 40 houses were habitable. Some towns had still not recovered from the plague of 1709. In the country districts some of the nobles lived in luxury but the standard of living of the yeoman and the peasants was very poor.[5] The condition of the Wends, who lived on the frontier of Pomerania, was particularly

[1] Archdeacon Coxe wrote that Poland 'has few manufactures, scarcely any commerce; a king almost without authority; the nobles in a state of uncontrolled anarchy; the peasants groaning under the yoke of feudal despotism far worse than the tyranny of an absolute monarch. I never before observed such an inequality of fortune, such sudden transition from extreme riches to extreme poverty; wherever I turned my eyes, luxury and wretchedness were constant neighbours' (W. Coxe, op. cit., Vol. I, p. 122).

[2] W. Coxe, op. cit., Vol. I, pp. 141, 169 and 208.

[3] For the state of the territories acquired by Prussia by the first partition of Poland see Ernst Lippe-Weissenfeld, *Westpreussen unter Friedrich dem Grossen* (Thorn, 1866): Conrad Rethwisch, *Westpreussens Wiederaufleben unter Friedrich dem Grossen* (1872); Christian Meyer, *Friedrich der Grosse und der Netzedistrict* (1883); A. C. Holsche, *Der Netzedistrikt, ein Beitrag zür Länder- und Völkerkunde* (Königsberg, 1793); G. Markull, *Westpreussen unter Friedrich dem Grossen* (1886); and Gustav Freytag, *Bilder aus der deutschen Vergangenheit*, Vol. IV (edn. of 1893), pp. 272-277.

[4] In 1764 a leading Polish churchman declared that 'there are towns without burghers . . . every street a field, and every market place a desert'.

[5] For the rural population of Pomerelia (Polish Pomerania) in the 1770's see G. Dabinius, *Die ländliche Bevölkerung Pomerellens im Jahre 1772 mit Einschluss des Danziger Landesgebietes im Jahre 1793* (Marburg, 1953).

wretched. Frederick stated that in his Polish territories 'tout s'y ressentait de l'anarchie, de la confusion, et du désordre d'un peuple barbare qui croupissait dans l'ignorance et dans la stupidité'. Yet he may have exaggerated the extent to which West Prussia had decayed so as to claim that he had secured no great benefit from his share of the partition[1] and to heighten the contrast between the condition of the province before and after annexation. Since West Prussia paid 1·7 million thalers in taxes in the first year after the annexation its economic condition may not have been quite so deplorable as Frederick pretended.

Frederick took advantage of his neighbour's weakness to strengthen the Prussian economy at Poland's expense. He tried to attract Poland's transit trade from Danzig to Stettin and from Leipzig to Frankfurt an der Oder or Breslau in the hope of increasing his revenues from customs duties and from road, river and harbour tolls. The Prussian economy would benefit by providing goods and services to those who used Prussia's ports, highways and inland waterways. Transit trade would stimulate the transport industry and the manufacturers located in the ports. Frederick hoped that Prussian merchants, commission agents and bankers would be able to control and to finance the transit trade hitherto handled largely by Jewish merchants and by the shippers of Danzig, Hamburg, London and Amsterdam. The trade between Poland and Prussia consisted of an exchange of raw materials and foodstuffs for manufactured goods and luxuries. Economic backwardness and political instability made it impossible for Poland to foster her own industrial development. She fell into a state of economic dependence upon Prussia, selling the produce of her soil and her forests cheaply and buying manufactured goods at a high cost. Smuggling on a large scale across the frontiers represented a financial loss to the Polish treasury.

Prussia's economic penetration of the territory which divided Pomerania from East Prussia was facilitated by the fact that there was an estimated population of 1·6 million Germans in

[1] On July 12, 1772 Frederick wrote to his brother Henry that he had just returned from a visit to his new Polish territory. He declared that 'it is an excellent and very advantageous acquisition . . . But to avoid arousing the envy (of others) I tell anyone who is prepared to listen that on my travels I have seen only sand, heaths, fir trees and Jews'.

Poland at this time. In West Prussia the towns of Danzig, Marienburg, Elbing and Konitz—to some extent also Kulm, Bromberg, Marienwerder, Graudenz and Thorn—had largely retained their German character since the days of the Teutonic Knights and the Hanseatic League. Their citizens had not been assimilated by the Poles and had held fast to their own language and to the Lutheran faith despite the persecution which they sometimes had to endure. Even in an age of violence Europe was shocked at the beheading of the mayor of Thorn and nine leading citizens after the sacking of the local Jesuit college in 1724. German villages were generally of more recent origin than German towns. Those in the Warthe valley were inhabited by the descendants of German refugees from Silesia who had come to Poland during the Thirty Years War. Much of the Vistula valley from Thorn to Danzig as well as part of Pomerelia was inhabited by Germans. Some of them were colonists who had been settled there in the first half of the eighteenth century by the Saxon kings of Poland. The inhabitants of certain rural settlements—Oliva and Ermland for example—were Catholics. Archdeacon Coxe observed that because the German settlers enjoyed 'several privileges not possessed by the generality of Polish peasants . . . their villages are better built; and their fields are better cultivated than those which belong to the native Poles; they possess more cattle; pay their quit-rents to their lords with greater exactness; and, when compared with the others, are cleaner and neater in their persons.'[1]

Danzig (the second largest city in Poland) and its immediate hinterland were the most important centres of German life and culture in that country. Although it was part of Poland, Danzig enjoyed a considerable measure of self-government. Its prosperity in the sixteenth and seventeenth century had been due largely to two circumstances. First, the port had free access to a great hinterland in the basin of the Vistula, a region which supplied grain and timber and was a market for manufactured articles and colonial produce. Secondly, Danzig shippers had

[1] W. Coxe, *Travels into Poland, Russia, Sweden and Denmark* (3 vols., 1784–90), Vol. I, p. 129. Probably the most prosperous Germans in Poland at this time were those living in (i) Danzig, (ii) estates of the Cistercians at Oliva and Peplin, and (iii) Heilberg, Braunsberg and the villages controlled by the Catholic Bishop of Ermland.

built up a world-wide network of trade which survived from the days of the Hanseatic League. But by the second half of the eighteenth century Danzig had begun to decline. The shift in the balance of power in eastern Europe—the rise of Russia and Prussia and the decline of Poland—was greatly to Danzig's disadvantage. The city suffered severely from the wars of the first half of the eighteenth century. When Danzig supported Leszcynski's cause during the War of the Polish Succession the port was besieged by Russian and Saxon troops (1734) and about 1,800 houses were destroyed. Afterwards Danzig had to pay heavy contributions to Catherine the Great and to Augustus III (the new King of Poland). By 1763 the port had fallen on evil days. In comparison with the seventeenth century its grain exports had fallen sharply and there had been a marked decline in local revenues.[1] The patrician families who dominated the city's commerce failed to adapt themselves to a new situation. A number of them left the port and established themselves in Prussia or in other parts of Germany.

Frederick's policy of economic penetration in Poland began in the 1740's. The annexation of Silesia made him master of the valley of the Oder and enabled him to cut the most direct routes which linked Lemberg, Cracow and Leipzig. He tried to divert this commerce to his own markets and ports. The economic links between Saxony and Poland, forged in the days of the Saxon kings of Poland, were weakened in the second half of the eighteenth century, though some carriers used longer routes through Moravia and Bohemia rather than pay the Prussian transit dues.[2]

[1] Danzig's grain exports were only 57,500 tons a year in 1773-85 as compared with 117,500 tons a year in 1764-72. It may be added that Danzig was also important as a manufacturing centre. It had various industries connected with the activities of the port. Its distilleries produced an excellent schnapps. The Danzig craftsmen were well known for the high quality of their products which included church bells, enamelled stoves, clocks, furniture and amber trinkets. Moreover in the immediate vicinity of the city—in the region known as the Danzig *Niederung*—there were old established flourishing German farmers and peasants.

[2] Evidence was collected by the Breslau Chamber of Commerce in 1765-6 and in 1771, concerning this traffic between Poland and Saxony by way of Bohemia and Moravia. The traders took various routes. One, for example, was: Lemberg-Cracow-Bielitz-Teschen-Olmütz-Brünn-Iglau-Kolin-Brandeis-Chemnitz-Leipzig.

During the Seven Years War Frederick took advantage of Poland's political and economic weakness in another way. When his troops occupied Saxony Frederick gained control over the Saxon mint which supplied Poland with coins. The remount horses, the grain, and other supplies that the agents of the Prussian military authorities purchased in Poland were paid for in depreciated money. Frederick secured the supplies that he needed while the Poles suffered from the inconveniences of inflation.[1]

In 1764 the Polish government tried to increase its revenues by introducing a revised tariff. The new import duties varied from 6 per cent *ad valorem* on necessities to 12 per cent on luxuries. Tolls levied on the highways and bridges and taxes on goods stored in warehouses had to be paid in addition to customs duties. Export duties were also increased. Not only were rates of duty raised but the valuation placed on goods for purposes of calculating duties was also increased.

Frederick strongly objected to any attempt by the Poles to pursue an independent economic policy which might place obstacles in the way of the expansion of Prussian trade in eastern Europe. He was particularly annoyed at the threatened increase in the cost of Polish horses purchased by the Prussian military authorities. Frederick promptly retaliated by taxing the traffic on Poland's most important trade route. The territories of East Prussia extended to the River Vistula at Marienwerder and in 1765 Frederick set up a toll station to collect transit dues both on upstream and on downstream traffic. Troops were sent to Marienwerder to enforce the collection of these transit dues. The basic rate of duty was 10 per cent but luxuries, such as coffee, paid 30 per cent. The Polish government, under pressure from both Russia and Prussia, withdrew the new tariff in 1766 and the Marienwerder transit toll was dropped at the same time.

It has been seen that in 1769-70 Frederick had occupied much of West Prussia and the Netze District on the pretence

---

[1] For the Polish coinage see E. Hutten Czapski, *Catalogue de la collection des médailles et monnaies polonaises* (3 vols., Graz, 1957: a reprint of an edition which appeared in 5 volumes between 1871 and 1916) and M. Gumowski, *Handbuch der pölnischen Numismatik* (Graz, 1960).

that this was necessary to protect his dominions from a threatened epidemic.[1] In 1772 Poland's Baltic provinces, lying between Pomerania and East Prussia, were annexed. These territories had an area of 36,000 square kilometres.[2] Between 1772 and 1775 Frederick secured several rectifications of the new frontiers to his own advantage by seizing a number of villages near Danzig and in the valley of the Netze. The annexations ended the isolation of East Prussia and gave Frederick control over all the territories between Memel and Magdeburg. He had increased the population of his dominions by nearly 600,000 and the revenues of the state by 1·7 million thalers a year. He had acquired an agricultural region of great potentialities, though farming standards were low except in specially favoured districts such as the lands lying between the two branches of the Vistula. West Prussia's craft industries included the production of cloth and leather. Frederick was the master of the Vistula and Prussia controlled the grain and timber which were moved to the Baltic along this route. Prussia was now insured against the danger of famine. By seizing Neufahrwasser and a number of villages near Danzig he throttled the trade of

[1] Archdeacon Coxe stated that Frederick 'under pretence of forming lines to prevent the spreading of the infection, advanced his troops into Polish Prussia and occupied that whole district' (W. Coxe, *Travels into Poland, Russia, Sweden and Denmark* (3 vols., 1784-90), Vol. I, p. 46).

[2] The territories to be ceded to Prussia were defined as follows in the Russo-Prussian treaty of 25 July 1772: "Sa dite Majesté se mettra en possession, lesquels consistent en toute la Pomérellie, la ville de Danzig, avec son territorie excepté, de même que dans les districts de la grande Pologne en decà de la Netze, en longéant cette rivière depuis la frontière de la Nouvelle Marche jusqu'a la Vistule près de Fordon et de Solitz; de sorte que la Netze fasse la frontière des états de S.M.le Roi de Prusse, et que cette rivière lue appartienne en entier; et aussi pareillement en ce que Sa dite Majesté ne voulant pas faire valoir ses autres prétentions sur plusieurs autres districts de la Pologne limitrophes de la Silésie et de la Prusse, qu'elle pourroit reclamer avec justice, en se désistant en même tems de toutes prétentions sur la ville de Danzig et de son territoire, prendra en guise d'équivalent, le reste de la Prusse polonoise, nommément le palatinat de Marienbourg, la ville d'Elbing y comprise, avec l'évêché de Warmie et le palatinat de Culm, sans en rien excepter que la ville de Thorn, laquelle ville sera conservée avec tout son territoire à la domination de la république de Pologne" (G. F. de Martens, *Recueil de Traités* . . . Vol. II, 1771-1779 (Göttingen, 1817), p. 95). The territories allocated to Prussia therefore included Pomerelia (Polish Pomerania), the Netze District, Marienburg (including Elbing and Ermland) and Culm but not Danzig and Thorn (and their outlying territories).

this great harbour and directed some of its commerce to his own ports.

The first partition of Poland was not, however, wholly to Prussia's advantage. The fact that some Polish provinces now belonged to Russia and Austria had certain drawbacks for Prussia. The Russians tried to divert to Riga the grain and timber which had hitherto been exported from Königsberg. The merchants of East Prussia complained that their transit trade was reduced and that their export of salt to Lithuania was restricted. Austria took advantage of her possession of Galicia to try to monopolise the salt trade in Poland and to divert to Austrian routes the traffic between southern Poland and Saxony which had once passed through Silesia.

Frederick introduced many reforms in his new territories. He abolished serfdom, allowed freedom of worship, and established law and order. He stimulated agriculture and industry by the settlement of German peasants and artisans.[1] Some 12,000 Germans colonists were brought to Pomerelia and the Netze District. Several Polish villages were completely Germanised.[2] Frederick encouraged commerce by setting up the Overseas Trading Corporation at Marienwerder, the administrative centre of the new territory. The corporation secured a monopoly of the export of salt to Poland and the sale of wax imported from Poland. There was a market for salt in Poland since the Austrians had raised the price of salt obtained from the Wieliczka mines. A programme of public works was inaugurated which included the drainage of the Netze marshes and the building of the Bromberg Canal. But the introduction of Prussian taxes and of conscription was very unpopular and some 10,000 persons migrated from Pomerelia to Poland between 1772 and 1786.

After the first partition the Poles tried to put their house in order but Frederick was determined that no Polish reforms should injure Prussia's economic interests. He was alarmed at a

---

[1] M. Bär, *Westpreussen und Friedrich der Grosse* (2 vols., 1909) and K. Zimmermann, *Fryderyk Wielki i jego Kolonizacia na siemiach polskieh* (*Frederick the Great's Colonisation of Polish Territory*) (2 vols., 1915).

[2] E.g. Garschau, Schiwialken and Klempin in the Kreis Dirschau. A number of the new settlers in West Prussia came from Danzig and from Württemberg.

proposal that the Polish nobles should no longer be exempted from paying import duties. He would not allow the Poles to restrict the importation of Prussian goods or of foreign goods handled by Prussian merchants. Nor would he permit any restriction of the transit of goods from Prussia to Russia through Polish territory. He regarded Poland as a great open market for Prussian manufactured goods and his object was to control that part of Poland's foreign trade which went through Prussia. To achieve these aims he insisted upon the Poles signing a commercial treaty with Prussia. Backed by a powerful army he was able to get his way without difficulty. Agreement was reached at Warsaw in 1775.

The basis of the treaty had been suggested by de Launay and his colleagues in the *Regie* and the details of the new customs duties were virtually dictated to the Poles by Benoit, who was the chief Prussian delegate at the conference.[1] The commercial treaty was a supplementary convention to the first partition treaty and it was known as the *Acte separé*.[2] It was agreed that the exchange of Prussian and Polish goods should be virtually free. Prussian goods exported to Poland and Polish goods exported to Prussia paid only 2 per cent in duty. The same duty was levied on Prussian goods passing through Poland on their way to Russia. On the other hand when the Poles traded with countries other than Prussia a duty of 12 per cent had to be paid if the goods passed through Prussia. Thus direct Prussian-Polish and Prussian-Russian commerce was favoured, while Poland's trade with states other than Prussia was penalised.

There were also special provisions concerning particular commodities and particular trading centres. Raw materials—such as cotton—which were used by Prussian manufacturers were prohibited from passing through Prussia to Poland. Frederick hoped that this would prevent the Poles from developing a cotton industry of their own. Certain goods could be purchased by Polish merchants only at Königsberg or at the fairs held at Frankfurt an der Oder. To protect Splitgerber's

[1] The terms of the Prussian-Polish commercial treaty of 1775 closely followed the tariff for West Prussia which had recently been promulgated (December 1774).

[2] The full text of the Prussian-Polish commercial treaty of 1775 was not published until 1792.

99

refinery at Bromberg a duty was levied on sugar sent from Elbing to Poland. Poland undertook to admit foreign salt free of duty and to refrain from establishing a salt monopoly. It would therefore not be possible for the Poles to give a preference to salt imported from the Wieliczka mines in Galicia which now belonged to Austria. In this way Frederick hoped to make good the loss of salt exports from Königsberg and Memel to Lithuania which had been annexed by Russia in 1772.

The Polish commercial treaty of 1775 was vigorously attacked both at home and abroad. There was a storm of protest in foreign newspapers. It was asserted that old-established trades would be sacrificed to Frederick's ambition to dominate the commerce of the hinterland of Germany's Baltic coast. The citizens of Danzig argued that their port and its industries would be ruined. Frederick instructed de Launay to write an anonymous article to reply to foreign criticisms of the Polish treaty and this appeared in a number of Prussian newspapers in May 1775. At home too, there were several attacks on the Polish commercial agreement. The merchants of Königsberg and Breslau complained that they were losing commissions on goods in transit because the high Prussian tolls encouraged Polish and Jewish merchants to seek alternative routes. These merchants took their wares to the Leipzig fairs by routes running through Bohemia and Moravia rather than by those running through Silesia.[1] Well informed contemporaries—Mirabeau, Heinitz and Leonhardi—argued that Prussian merchants, shippers, and commission agents lost business because of the restrictions imposed upon Poland's foreign trade by the agreement of 1775. On the other hand the expansion of the business done at the fairs of Frankfurt an der Oder[2] may well have been partly due

[1] In 1776, the year after the signing of the Prussian-Polish commercial treaty five Polish wholesale merchants visited the Leipzig fair and did business there on a large scale.

[2] Three fairs were held annually at Frankfurt an der Oder in March, July and November. The Prussian goods sold there came mainly from the Mark Brandenburg and the New Mark. Silesian linens and woollens were generally sold at Breslau. The tariffs fixed by the Prussian-Polish commercial treaty of 1775 did not apply to the fairs held at Frankfurt an der Oder. At these fairs foreign goods, if sold by a Prussian merchant for export, paid only 2 per cent duty and if sold by a foreign merchant 4 per cent. Prussian goods sold at the Frankfurt fairs for export paid no duty.

to the encouragement given to Polish and Jewish merchants to bring their goods to Frankfurt rather than to Leipzig. Between 1773 and 1783 the value of Prussian textiles[1] and leather goods sold at these fairs rose from 1·4 million thalers to 1·7 million thalers while the sale of foreign woollens and cottons showed only a slight increase in this period.

Frederick was disappointed that he had been unable to annex Danzig in 1772. There had been occasions when the citizens of the port had opposed the Polish Crown in the past and their staunch adherence to the Lutheran faith had been a barrier to co-operation with the Polish Catholics. But they greatly preferred their status of a self-governing city loosely linked with Poland to that of a Prussian provincial town. In September 1770 some five thousand Prussian troops entered Danzig territory and camped within a few miles of the city. They claimed to be searching for army deserters. The municipal authorities had to defray the cost of the expedition and to promise not to harbour Prussian deserters in the future. In the following year when Frederick established a *cordon sanitaire* in Pomerelia his troops again entered Danzig territory and levied a further contribution on the city. Frederick did not seize the city itself since the Russo-Prussian agreement concerning the first partition of Poland provided that Danzig should not be annexed. But Frederick's troops occupied several districts lying outside the city walls on the pretext that they belonged to Oliva monastery and were therefore a part of Pomerelia and not of Danzig. These territories included Neufahrwasser, Holm Island, Alt-Schottland, Neu-Schottland, Langfuhr, Schidlitz and St. Albrecht. By annexing Neufahrwasser and the Westerplatte on the Vistula below Danzig the Prussians gained control over Danzig's trade by sea. A Prussian harbour commission was set up at Neufahrwasser to collect pilotage and other dues. Further up the river the Prussians levied tolls at Fordon (by Bromberg) and set up the Overseas Trading Corporation (*Seehandlung*) at Marienwerder in the hope of controlling the trade between Poland and Danzig.

Frederick tried to divert Danzig's trade with Poland in grain, flax, linen, hemp, potash, timber, salt and other com-

[1] Except silk.

modities to Prussia's Baltic ports and he expected that when Danzig's commerce declined the city would ask to be incorporated in Prussia. By levying tolls on the Vistula at Neufahrwasser and Fordon, by setting up the Overseas Trading Corporation (*Seehandlung*) at Marienwerder, and by constructing the Bromberg Canal to link the Vistula with the Netze and the Oder Frederick hoped to control much of the transit trade between Poland and the Baltic ports. Prussian troops and officials of the *Regie* threw a cordon round Danzig and restricted the city's trade. Even when travelling to the seaside the Danzigers were liable to have their luggage examined by de Launay's excisemen. Eventually the city paid a lump sum to the *Regie* every year to enable holidaymakers to travel to and from Danzig without being molested.

Several villages outside the city walls were joined together to form a new Prussian town called the 'Danzig Suburbs' or the 'United City'. Frederick tried to infuse life into the new town by giving privileges to its merchants and by establishing a fair, a *Seehandlung* agency, a garrison, a post office and a lottery. But the attempt to turn the 'United City' into a flourishing commercial centre by trying to force the Danzigers to buy grain there was not a success and its population fell from 9,600 in 1773 to 5,600 in 1796.

Relations between Prussia and Danzig rapidly deteriorated. The Danzigers declared that the Prussians had no right to tax their goods at Neufahrwasser and Fordon. Frederick objected when the city continued to levy its own dues at the junction of the Vistula and the Mottlau. He also alleged that Danzig was providing a haven for Prussian army deserters and for men who had absconded to evade military service. The Danzig authorities declared that insolvent debtors from the city were allowed to start new businesses in Frederick's 'United City'. It appears that at the height of the conflict Frederick actually threatened to cut off Danzig's supply of drinking water.

Danzig's trade declined while that of Prussia's Baltic ports increased. The number of ships entering Danzig fell from nearly 2,000 in 1770 to 145 in 1782. The climax of the long struggle between Prussia and Danzig was reached in October 1783 when Frederick blockaded the port. Two months later

Catherine the Great intervened on behalf of the sorely tried city and informed Frederick that Russia had an interest in the maintenance of the political independence and the commercial freedom of Danzig. Frederick now realised that, in spite of all his bullying, the Danzigers were still determined to resist his demands and that the prospect of annexing the city was as remote as ever. He gave way and raised the blockade on January 22, 1784.

After prolonged negotiations, in which Russia and Poland acted as mediators, an agreement was at last reached between Prussia and Danzig on February 22, 1785. Frederick agreed that Danzig merchants should have the sole right to export Polish goods by sea while Prussian and Danzig merchants were to enjoy equal rights with regard to the trade in goods arriving by sea at Danzig or Neufahrwasser. Goods imported by the Prussian State were to pass through Danzig without payment of import duty or transit toll.[1]

Frederick had made some concessions to Danzig because various measures that he had previously taken to injure the port could not be repeated without breaking the convention. It may be doubted whether the King seriously intended to leave Danzig in peace. Six months after the signing of the convention Frederick died. Johanna Schopenauer wrote: 'One day the news "Old Fritz is dead, at last, at last!" spread through the city like wildfire. The citizens happily passed on the goods news as if the passing of the great King had put an end to all their sorrows and as if the heavy burdens under which they had groaned for so long would at last be lifted from their backs. Now it seemed as if conditions must change—and must change for the better—in comparison with what they had been before'.[2]

[1] The goods included salt, tobacco, iron, gunpowder, uniforms and porcelains.

[2] Johanna Schopenhauer, *Jugendleben und Wanderbild* (edited by W. Cosack, 1884), p. 130. In these memoirs, written in 1837, the mother of the philosopher Schopenhauer bitterly attacked the policy of Frederick the Great towards her native city. She declared that Frederick 'fell upon my unhappy city like a vampire bent upon its destruction'. A French translation of parts of these memoirs appeared in an article entitled 'Fragments du "Journal" de Johanna Schopenhauer' in the *Cahiers Pologne-Allemagne* (No. 2, April-June 1961, pp. 79-89). When Prussia annexed Danzig in 1793 Schopenhauer's parents migrated to Hamburg.

(ii) *Austria*[1]

Austria, the largest and most important German state in the eighteenth century, had compact territories lying in the Danube basin between the Alps, the Sudeten mountains, the Carpathians and the Balkans.[2] Beyond these limits the Habsburgs ruled over the Austrian Netherlands, Milan, Mantua, the Breisgau, Galicia and Bukowina. The total population of their territories in 1770 was about 19·5 millions.

Diversities of soil and climate made it possible to grow a variety of agricultural products. The extensive conifer forests of the Alps, the Riesengebirge and the Carpathians provided large quantities of timber. Cereals—wheat, oats and rye—were grown in the Vienna basin, the Bohemian lowlands, and the plain of Hungary. Hungary was one of the most important areas of grain production in central Europe. Her cereal exports were valued at nearly 1·5 million florins in 1780. Maize, vines and mulberry trees were grown in the Adige valley. Flax was grown in Bohemia, Moravia and Styria; hemp in Galicia; and

---

[1] For the economic development of the Habsburg territories in the eighteenth century see A. Beer, 'Studien zur Geschichte der Österreichischen Volkswirtschaft unter Maria Theresia'. (1) Die österreichische Industriepolitik' (*Archiv für österreichische Geschichte*, Vol. LXXXI, 1894, pp. 1-133) and (ii) 'Die österreichische Handelspolitik unter Maria Theresia' (*ibid.*, Vol. LXXXVI, 1899, pp. 1-204); K. Pribram, *Geschichte der österreichischen Gewerbepolitik, 1740-1860*, Vol. I (1907); Heinrich Ritter von Srbik, *Der staatliche Exporthandel Osterreichs von Leopold I bis Maria Theresia* (1907); Fournier, *Maria Theresia und die Anfänge ihrer Industrie- und Handelspolitik* (1908); Heinrich Ritter von Srbik, *Studien zur Geschichte des österreichischen Salzwesens* (1917); A. Salz, *Geschichte der böhmischen Industrie in der Neuzeit* (1911); H. Marczali, *Hungary in the Eighteenth Century* (1910), pp. 17-99; V. Hofmann, *Beiträge zur neueren österreichischen Wirtschaftsgeschichte*, Vol. I (1919), Vol. II (1926), Vol. III (in two parts 1932 and 1936); M. Hainich, 'Das österreichische Tabaksmonopol im 18en Jahrhundert' (*Vierteljahrschrift für Sozial- und Wirtschaftsgeschichte*, Vol. VIII, 1910, pp. 394-444); P. Kandler, *Emporio e portofranco* (Trieste, 1861); and F. Cusin, *Appunti alla storia di Trieste* (Trieste, 1930).

[2] This region included the Grand Duchy of Austria (divided into the territories east and west of the Enns), the Duchies of Tirol, Styria, Carinthia, Carniola and Moravia and the kingdoms of Bohemia and Hungary (including Transylvania and the Banat). Silesia was lost in 1742. Zips was annexed in 1771, Galicia in 1772, Bukowina in 1775 and the Innviertel in 1779. Salzburg and the Trentino were ecclesiastical territories.

hops in Bohemia. Considerable quantities of fish were caught in the lakes and rivers, particularly in Bohemia. Cattle, horses, sheep and pigs were raised both in the Bohemian and Hungarian lowlands and in the meadows of the Alps and the Carpathians. Magyar horses had been crossed with Arab horses during the Turkish wars but the breed had degenerated somewhat in the eighteenth century.

There were large estates owned by the Crown, the Church and the great feudal magnates which were cultivated by serfs.[1] Medium-sized farms and smallholdings, cultivated by peasants, were also to be found in Austria. The farming of arable land in scattered strips in open fields followed a traditional pattern. The large estates, the farms, the fisheries, and the forests produced not only foodstuffs for a large and growing population but also raw materials for industry such as wool, flax, silk, hides and timber.

The Habsburg dominions were rich in minerals. The Alpine regions of Austria were 'undoubtedly the classical home of ironworking in central Europe'. The rich iron ores of the Erzberg and the Vordernberg in Styria and of Hüttenberg in Carinthia had been worked since Roman times. In the eighteenth century the iron and steel products of Austria maintained their high reputation and a variety of metalwares—such as scythes and sickles—were exported. By this time there was often a shortage of timber in the vicinity of the ironworks so that charcoal had to be brought from considerable distances. Technical advances in the eighteenth century included the erection of many blast furnaces. The largest and most important ironworks in Styria were the *Innernberger Hauptgewerkschaft*. Ironworks were also to be found in other Austrian provinces such as Bohemia, Moravia and the Tirol.[2]

---

[1] For the great estates in Bohemia in the seventeenth and eighteenth centuries see Werner Stark, 'Die Abhängichkeitsverhältnisse der gutsherrlichen Bauern Böhmens im 17en und 18en Jahrhundert' (*Jahrbücher für Nationalökonomie und Statistik*, Vol. 164, 1952, Heft 4-5, pp. 270-425) and 'Der Ackerbau der böhmischen Gutswirtschaft im 17en und 18en Jahrhundert' (*Zeitschrift für die Agrargeschichte*, Vol. V, No. i, 1957). For the emancipation of the serfs in the Habsburg dominions see Karl Grünberg, *Die Bauernbefreiung und die Auflösung des gutsherrlich-bäuerlichen Verhältnisses in Böhmen, Mähren, und Schlesien* (2 vols., 1894) and E. Murr Link, *The Emancipation of the Austrian Peasants 1740-98* (New York, 1949).

[2] L. Beck, *Die Geschichte des Eisens*, Vol. III (1897), pp. 789-826; Gabriel

Silver was mined at Joachimstal and Pribram in Bohemia as well as in Transylvania;[1] copper was produced at Neusohl and Schmölnitz in Hungary and at Majanpek and Oravica in the Banat; while mercury ore was mined at Idria (Carniola). There were numerous saltworks in the Habsburg territories, the most important being those at Hallstadt, Ischl, Hallein, Hall and Wieliczka. In the production of silver and copper the Habsburg dominions held a dominant position on the Continent.

The location and the geographical structure of the Habsburg dominions favoured the development of internal commerce and international transit trade. Vienna, with a population of over a quarter of a million at the end of the eighteenth century, was a focal point for home and foreign commerce. The Danube route-way—the great link between Germany, Austria, Hungary and the Balkans—passed through the Austrian capital. Shipping was restricted owing to the powerful current and the existence of the rapids at the Iron Gate but there was a considerable movement of passengers and goods along the roads in the Danube valley. From Vienna a route ran south across the Semmering pass to the port of Trieste. To the north of Vienna the valley of the March gave access to the Moravian gap (between the Sudeten and Carpathian mountain ranges) and so to Silesia and Poland. In the Tirol the Brenner pass carried traffic between northern Europe and Italy. A new road across the Brenner was built in 1772 and this enabled the Alps to be crossed by a route which did not rise more than 4,500 feet above sea level.

Although the Habsburg dominions had great economic potentialities their development was retarded in the eighteenth century. Craft industries were generally confined to the towns and their expansion was checked by the excessive powers wielded by the gilds. The Crown, however, did attempt to

Jars, *Voyages métallurgiques* (3 vols., 1774-81), Vol. I, pp. 58-63 (report by Dangenoux and de Wendel on ironworks and steelworks in Styria and Carinthia); Rambourg, 'Sur la fabrication du fer et de l'acier dans les forges de Styrie' (*Journal des Mines*, Vol. XV, 1803-4, pp. 271-85, 380-96, 436-45), N. G. J. Pounds and W. N. Parker, *Coal and Steel in Western Europe* (1957), pp. 49-50.

[1] At the end of the eighteenth century the Habsburg dominions produced over 80,000 lb. of silver a year. This was half of Europe's total output.

weaken the stranglehold of the gilds upon industry by establishing both public and private monopolies for the manufacture of particular commodities and by subsidising the establishment of new workshops and manufactories. The state owned valuable deposits of quicksilver and copper and it monopolised the production and sale of salt and tobacco. In the first half of the eighteenth century the Crown subsidised the establishment of a number of industrial workshops on the estates of great nobles. This proved to be so expensive that after about 1750 the available funds were used to encourage entrepreneurs and artisans to set up new workshops in the towns. After the loss of Silesia special efforts were made to promote the expansion of the linen industry in Bohemia and Moravia.

Overseas trade was somewhat restricted. Antwerp, once a great commercial centre, had been ruined by the closing of the Scheldt after the Thirty Years War. Ostend was the headquarters of the Austrian East India Company which was founded in 1772. The enterprise failed after only nine years, largely owing to the implacable hostility of Britain. Trieste was made a free port in 1719 and the Austrian Levant Company of Vienna was established in the same year. This company, which acquired a cloth factory at Linz and exported textile goods from Trieste to the Near East, flourished for a time but went bankrupt in 1740. The city was considerably enlarged in Maria Theresa's reign and its trade expanded somewhat after 1776 (when Count Zinzendorf was its governor) but the absence of adequate communications with the main part of the Habsburg dominions made it difficult for Trieste to compete successfully with Genoa or Venice. With only limited access to the sea and lacking colonies, Austria traded mainly across her land frontiers.[1]

Industry and commerce were hampered by numerous national and provincial customs and excise duties, transit tolls, consumption duties and local taxes of various kinds. Public and private river, road and bridge tolls accounted for a further

---

[1] For the state exports of the Habsburg dominions see H. R. von Srbik, *Der staatliche Exporthandel Österreichs von Leopold I bis Maria Theresia* (1907). For attempts in the 1770's to revive Austria's trade with India and the East Indies see H. Fechner, *Die handelspolitischen Beziehungen Preussens zu Österreich ... 1741-1806* (1886), pp. 743-5.

increase in the cost of goods. In the early eighteenth century customs duties were levied simply to raise revenue. Charles VI and Maria Theresa, however, gradually modified the tariff so as to protect agriculture and industry from foreign competition. The Habsburg dominions came to be divided into large regions within which goods could be freely moved.[1] In 1749 it was laid down that goods which had already paid consumption duty in one of the hereditary territories should be exempt from paying another duty of this kind in any other hereditary territory. Unified tariffs were introduced first into Bohemia and Moravia (1753) and then into Styria, Carinthia, Carniola, Görz and Gradiska (1766). In 1775 Austria[2] and Hungary[3] became independent tariff regions.

Austria's finances were disorganised and the state was in debt. To raise foreign loans valuable national assets—the mercury of Idria and the copper of Hungary—were pledged for a time to Dutch financiers. Lack of funds prevented the Habsburgs from exploiting Crown monopolies profitably, from giving adequate aid to private industry, and from improving the country's system of communications. Even busy and important routes, such as the Salt Road from Linz to Freistadt, were allowed to fall into decay. The heavy cost of the wars in which the country was involved in the eighteenth century added to the financial difficulties of the Habsburgs.

When Frederick the Great came to the throne it seemed most unlikely that Prussia would be able to secure any economic advantage at the expense of so large and so powerful a country as Austria. Yet within a few months, the death of the Emperor Charles VI gave Frederick the opportunity of seizing one of Austria's richest provinces. Lacking a male heir, the Emperor had secured from most of the European Powers a guarantee of a

[1] In 1740, on the completion of Charles VI's reorganisation of customs and excise duties, the Habsburg dominions were divided into the following tariff regions—(i) Upper and Lower Austria, (ii) Central Austria, Styria, Carinthia, Carniola and the Dalmatian coast, (iii) Bohemia and Glatz, (iv) Silesia, (v) Tirol, (vi) Hungary proper, (vii) Banat, (viii) Croatia, (ix) Trieste, (x) Fiume.

[2] Except Galicia, Pilsen and Eger (incorporated 1784), Tirol, Vorarlberg, Trieste and Fiume. The Austrian Netherlands and the Habsburg territories in Italy had their own tariffs.

[3] The Austro-Hungarian customs frontier survived until 1850.

new law of succession (the Pragmatic Sanction) by which his eldest daughter Maria Theresa was to succeed to his hereditary dominions. He would have been better employed in strengthening his army and in putting his finances in order. Shortly after the Emperor's death Frederick suddenly attacked Silesia and the Prussian victory at the Battle of Mollwitz encouraged those who had claims on Maria Theresa's inheritance to attempt to partition her empire. Far from securing any help from the guarantors of the Pragmatic Sanction she had to face the armies not only of Prussia but of France, Spain, Bavaria, Saxony and Sardinia as well. Britain alone upheld the Pragmatic Sanction. Maria Theresa failed to turn the Prussians out of Silesia and by the Treaty of Berlin (1742)[1] the province was ceded to Prussia. In the autumn of 1744 Frederick, alarmed at Austria's military successes against France and Bavaria, entered the war again. He overran Saxony and Bohemia but was unable to secure any new territories for himself when the war was over. The Treaty of Dresden (1745), however, left him in possession of Silesia.

Silesia was a valuable acquisition.[2] The province lay in the valley of the River Oder between the Sudeten Mountains and the Polish Jura. Its location attracted a considerable transit traffic. Breslau, the capital, had an important fair and the city was the focus of routes running north to Hamburg[3] and Stettin, south to Moravia and Galicia, west to Bohemia and Saxony, and east to Poland. Silesia had substantial agricultural, forestry and mineral resources as well as flourishing craft

[1] Two Austro-Prussian agreements concerning Silesia had been signed before the Treaty of Berlin (July 1742): (i) The agreement signed at Klein Schnellendorf in October 1741 by which Lower Silesia was ceded to Prussia. The English mediator Lord Hyndford took an important part in these negotiations. (ii) The preliminary Treaty of Breslau of June 1742.

[2] For Silesia in 1740 see T. Schönborn, 'Die Wirtschaftspolitik Österreichs in Schlesien im 17en und am Anfang des 18en Jahrhunderts' (*Jahrbücher für Nationalökonomie und Statistik*, New Series, Vol. IX, 1884, pp. 293-340 and H. Fechner, 'Der Zustand des schlesischen Handels vor der Besitzgreifung des Landes durch Friedrich den Grossen' (*Jahrbücher für Nationalökonomie und Statistik*, New Series, Vol. X, 1885, pp. 209-236.

[3] The construction of the Friedrich Wilhelm Canal (*Neuer Graben*) by the Great Elector (1668) facilitated trade between the Oder and the Spree and led to an expansion of Breslau's commerce with Hamburg. The merchants of Breslau paid lower tolls at Krossen than the merchants of Brandenburg.

industries. Cereals were grown on the rich soils south of the River Katsbach and north of the River Stober. Large flocks of sheep produced more wool than local cloth makers could use and there was a considerable surplus for export. Silesian flax was the raw material for the manufacture of linens in many villages on the Bohemian frontier. The four 'mountain towns'—Greifenberg, Schmiedeberg, Hirschberg and Landeshut—were centres of linen manufacture and markets for the sale of linen yarn and cloths. Silesian linens were exported to many parts of the world. Iron, silver, lead and zinc were mined but the coalfield of Upper Silesia was not yet exploited. In the middle of the eighteenth century Silesia's exports were valued at 9·2 million thalers and her imports at 6·7 million thalers.[1] The population of the province was estimated to be about 1 million in 1740. On the large feudal estates of Upper Silesia most of the serfs were Poles. The fertile farm lands and the industrial villages of Lower Silesia, on the other hand, were inhabited by the descendants of German immigrants.

Frederick had to pay a heavy price for his new province. He wrote that Maria Theresa became his 'vindictive and implacable enemy'. The aim of Maria Theresa's foreign policy was to crush Prussia and to recover Silesia. The object of her commercial policy was to injure the Prussian economy and to prevent Frederick from profiting from the annexation of Silesia.[2] The King of Prussia wished to prevent any contraction in the output of Silesia's farms and workshops or any interruption of the transit trade of the province. The preliminary peace terms (Treaty of Breslau, June 1742) provided that 'tout ce qui regarde le commerce entre les états et sujets réciproques sera réglé dans le futur traité de paix ou par une commission à établir de part et d'autre, les choses restant sur le pied où elles étaient avant la présente guerre jusqu' à qu'on en soit convenu autrement' (Article ix).

---

[1] The figures are for 1750-51.

[2] For Austro-Prussian commercial relations in the second half of the eighteenth century see Hermann Fechner, *Die handelspolitischen Beziehungen Preussens zu Österreich während der provinziellen Selbstständigkeit Schlesiens 1741-1806* (1886). See also Dr. Croon's criticism of this book in the *Zeitschrift des Vereins für Geschichte Schlesiens* (Vol. 42) and Dr. Fechner's reply in the *Vierteljahrschrift für Sozial- und Wirtschaftsgeschichte*, Vol. VII (1909), pp. 315-323.

Since the final peace treaty was signed only a month later there was no time to appoint commissioners to discuss Austro-Prussian economic relations. It was laid down in the Treaty of Berlin 1 July 1742 that 'pour mieux consolider l'amitié entre les états et sujets réciproques, les choses restant sur le pied où elles étaient avant la présent guerre, jusqu'a ce qu'on en soit convenu autrement, et les anciens accords au sujet du commerce et de tout ce qui y a du rapport seront religieusement observés et executés de part et d'autre' (Article VIII). This article proved to be a worthless guarantee of the *status quo commercii*. Since he had treated the Pragmatic Sanction as a scrap of paper Frederick can hardly have been surprised that Maria Theresa was not over-scrupulous in carrying out her obligations under the Treaty of Berlin. It was useless for the Prussians to appeal to 'les anciens accords' since no one knew what these agreements were.[1]

By the Treaty of Dresden, signed in December 1745 after the second Silesian War, Austria and Prussia pledged themselves 'de favoriser réciproquement autant qu'il est possible le commerce entre leurs états, pays et sujets respectifs et de ne point souffrir, qu'on y mette des entraves ou chicanes, mais elles tâcheront plutot de l'encourager et de l'avencer de part et d'autre fidèlement pour le plus grand bien de leurs états et sujets réciproques' (Article VI). This provision too was of no practical value to Frederick since it did not prevent the Austrians from imposing high duties on Silesia's exports and from taking measures to harm Silesia's transit trade.

In the peace settlement of 1742 Frederick had accepted responsibility for certain Austrian debts. These included the repayment of loans raised by Charles VI in England (£250,000) and Holland (over 2·5 million thalers) on the security of Silesia's revenues.[2] In addition Frederick agreed to pay to

[1] The Emperor had refused to ratify a draft Austro-Prussian trade agreement of 1710. Subsequent commercial negotiations in 1728-32 had been unsuccessful.

[2] Frederick delayed repaying the Silesian loan to Britain in the hope of securing satisfaction for his demand for compensation for the losses incurred by Prussian merchants whose ships had been seized as prizes during the war of 1740-48. Henry Legge, the British envoy in Berlin in 1748, admitted to Lord Newcastle that the conduct of British cruisers had been 'little short of downright piracy'. But the dispute was not settled until the signing of the

Silesian creditors various debts due to them from the Silesian Tax Office, the Silesian Bank (*Bancalität*) of Breslau and the Domains Administration. The division of responsibility for meeting the claims of Austrian and foreign creditors[1] was left to future negotiations between Prussia and Austria. Frederick delayed the payment of those Silesian debts which were due to Austria in the hope of forcing Maria Theresa to accept the *status quo* concerning the duties levied on trade between Silesia and the Habsburg dominions. But nothing came of discussions on these matters between Austria and Prussia in 1751 and subsequent negotiations for a commercial treaty were also abortive.

Maria Theresa was determined to foster Austria's economic development by surrounding her territories with a high tariff wall even if this resulted in the extinction of the flourishing trade between Silesia, Bohemia and Moravia. In 1753 a new regional tariff for Bohemia, Moravia and Austrian Silesia was promulgated. High duties—some of a prohibitive character— were levied. Maria Theresa hoped to prevent textiles and other manufactured goods from Silesia from competing with those made in Austria; to divert Polish-Saxon transit traffic from Silesia to Bohemia and Moravia; and to divert Austrian trade from Baltic and North Sea ports to Trieste and Fiume. The value of Silesia's trade with Austria sank from 3·7 million thalers in 1752-3 to 2·6 million thalers in 1755-6. Much Austro-Prussian trade was driven underground and the smuggling of Silesian manufactured goods across the frontier increased. Neither Austria nor Prussia had an efficient organisation for collecting customs duties and sometimes troops were sent to the frontiers to check smuggling.

In February 1754 Frederick replied to the new Austrian tariff by imposing upon Austrian wines sent to Silesia the same rates of import duty as those imposed by the Austrian govern-

Anglo-Prussian Treaty of Westminster in January 1756. Prussia agreed to pay off the Silesian loan while Britain paid £20,000 in compensation for injuries to Prussian shipping. Frederick refused to repay the Dutch Silesian loan because Holland would not accept his demands concerning the Meuse tolls.

[1] And also the claims of Prussian creditors on the Vienna Bank (*Bancalität*) and the Vienna City Bank.

ment upon Silesian manufactures. In April 1754 Prussia increased her duties upon a variety of manufactured goods imported from Austria and an export tax was imposed upon Silesian wool. To avoid paying this export duty Austrian merchants obtained Silesian wool which had first been sent to Poland or to Saxony. Frederick retaliated by imposing export duties on Silesian wool sent to Poland and to Saxony. Moreover a special tax was imposed on goods from Electoral Saxony which were sent to the fair at Frankfurt an der Oder. Prussia also increased the transit duties payable at Magdeburg on traffic using the Elbe route between Austria, Saxony and Hamburg. Thus the disputes over Silesia's trade had developed into a general tariff war between Prussia and Austria in which Saxony and Poland were also involved. Since Prussia's measures were to some extent being defeated by smugglers Frederick prohibited the export both of wool and of linen yarn from Silesia. Negotiations concerning a commercial treaty and the settlement of various Silesian debts continued until the outbreak of the Seven Years War but no results were achieved. In May 1756 Austria once more increased her import duties on Silesia products.

In the peace negotiations after the Seven Years War which were begun at Leipzig and concluded at Hubertusburg (1763), the vexed question of the Silesian debts and Austro-Prussian commercial relations were again discussed. Frederick repudiated most of the outstanding Silesian debts except those guaranteed by the Silesian Estates and payable to Prussian subjects. Maria Theresa showed no inclination to make any tariff concessions which might benefit the trade of Silesia. The Treaty of Hubertusburg merely repeated the provisions of the Treaty of Dresden concerning the encouragement of mutual trade and these vague undertakings were valueless.

The Austro-Prussian tariff war entered a new phase in 1764 when Austria prohibited the importation of a number of goods from Silesia. There were, however, occasions on which particular consignments of Silesian goods were admitted to Bohemia on payment of import duties. The Austrians continued their efforts to prevent the transit traffic between Poland and Saxony from passing through Silesia. The Breslau Chamber of Commerce reported in the 1760's that low Austrian transit dues had attracted to Bohemia and Moravia some traffic that had formerly passed through Silesia.

The changes that were made in Poland's frontiers in 1772 enabled the Austrians to harm Silesia's export trade in another way. The annexation of Galicia and Bukowina enabled Austria to levy transit dues on Silesian textiles which were sent to the Ukraine by way of Cracow and Lemberg. Frederick retaliated by imposing prohibitions or high duties on Austrian exports to Prussia and by levying higher dues at Magdeburg on Austrian traffic on the River Elbe.

Silesia did not suffer as much as might have been expected from the long Austro-Prussian tariff war. Opportunities for exporting linens and woollens to the Habsburg territories declined but Silesia expanded her markets both in Prussia and in Poland. Frederick fostered the expansion of Silesia's farms, manufactures and mines. Large numbers of new settlers were brought to the province, a land mortgage bank was established, the textile industries were encouraged, ironworks were set up at Malapane, and a lead-silver mine was opened at Tarnowitz. The output of linen cloth rose from 85,000 pieces in 1755 to 125,000 pieces in 1775. In spite of the tariff war the economic links between Silesia, Bohemia, Moravia and Galicia were not entirely severed. From time to time both the Austrian and the Prussian authorities issued licences which allowed particular transactions to be completed. And smuggling—sometimes on a large scale—enabled goods to cross the Austro-Prussian frontier despite the prohibitions and high duties. Mirabeau declared that at the end of Frederick's reign Silesia had 'une population, une culture et une industrie vraiment immense' while Dr Fechner, who made a detailed study of Austro-Prussian economic relations in the second half of the eighteenth century, considered that 'Silesia had no reason to be dissatisfied with Frederick's commercial system'.

(iii) *Saxony*[1]

The Electorate of Saxony was a small state in central Germany

[1] J. Falke, *Die Geschichte des deutschen Zollwesens* (1869), pp. 269-320; J.

with a population of about 1,750,000.[1] It lay in the valleys of the Elbe, the Saale, the Mulde and the Elster. The Erzgebirge formed the southern frontier of the Electorate and divided Saxony from Bohemia. Prussian territories lay to the east (Silesia), the north (Brandenburg), and the west (Mansfeld and the Saalkreis).

Saxony was one of the leading industrial and commercial regions of Germany in the eighteenth century and its merchants handled a considerable volume of trade. Several factors had fostered the development of craft industries in Saxony. The Electorate was well endowed with a variety of raw materials. It had large flocks of sheep and wool of a high quality was obtained from the merino 'Electoral sheep' which had been brought from Spain to the Elector's estates at Hohnstein and Stolpen. In certain years there was a surplus of wool which was exported but Saxony was sometimes also an importer of fine wools and yarn from Bohemia and Silesia. The flax, hides and clay required by the linen, leather and porcelain industries were available within the Electorate. Vegetable dyes and fuller's earth were available for the manufacture of textiles. The Electorate was rich in minerals, such as silver and iron ore,[2] and also in timber and coal.

Capital for industrial expansion had come from various

Ziekursch, *Sachsen und Preussen um die Mitte des 18en Jahrhunderts* . . . (1904); R. Forberger, *Die Manufaktur in Sachsen vom Ende des 16en bis zum Anfang des 19en Jahrhunderts* (1958); R. Forberger, 'Zur Aufnahme der maschinellen Fertigung durch sächsische Manufakturen' (*Jahrbuch für Wirtschaftsgeschichte* 1960, Part 1); and H. Schlechte, *Die Staatsreform in Kursachsen* (1958). For the peasant clearances in Saxony see K. Blaschke, "Das Bauernlegen in Sachsen" (*Vierteljahrschrift für Sozial -und Wirtschaftsgeschichte.* XCII, 1955, Heft ii) W. Boelcke, *Bauer und Gutsherr in der Oberlausitz* (1957), R. Lehmann *Die Verhältnisse der neiderlausitzischen, Herrschafts- und Gutsbauern in der Zeit vom 30- jährigen Kriege bis zu den preussischen Reformen* (1956); R. Lehmann, *Quellen zur Lage der Privatbauern in der Niederlausitz im Zeitalter der Absolutismus* (1957).

[1] K. Kretschmer, *Historische Geographie von Mitteleuropa* (1904), p. 614. Heinitz estimated Saxony's population at 1,960,000 (for 1755) and 1,940,000 (for 1775). Canzel estimated the population at 1,616,000 (for 1755) while Büsching estimated the population at 1,695,000 (for 1775). There appears to have been little increase in Saxony's population between 1755 and 1775.

[2] Iron ore was mined in the Erzgebirge both on the Saxon and on the Bohemian sides of the mountain range. There were some 40 ironworks in Saxony in the eighteenth century.

9

sources. Some had been supplied by great nobles who had developed mining and other industrial enterprises on their own estates. The Löwendal family, for example, had established the Lauchhammer ironworks at Mückenberg in 1725[1] and they were expanded by the able and energetic Detlev von Einsiedel.[2] These were among the very few ironworks on the Continent in which experiments in the puddling process were made in the eighteenth century.[3] Some capital had come from the exploitation of Saxony's rich silver, lead and tin mines.[4] Some had come from local merchants who had invested in industry the profits derived from commercial ventures. Merchants from south Germany, particularly entrepreneurs from Nürnberg and Augsburg, had played a significant role in the development of Saxony's textile industries. High standards of craftsmanship were maintained both by the Saxon workers themselves and by immigrants who had been encouraged by the government to settle in the Electorate. The technical knowledge and skill of the miners of Freiberg, the textile workers of the Voigtland and the Lausitz, the porcelain workers of Meissen, the ironworkers of Lauchhammer, and the armament workers of Suhl were known far beyond the frontiers of Saxony.

As was customary at this time the State tried to stop the export of native raw materials which might promote the expan-

[1] F. Redlich, 'A German Eighteenth Century Ironworks during its first Hundred Years' (*Bulletin of the Business Historical Society*, Vol. XXVII, 1953, pp. 69-96, 141-157, and 231-259. The first history of a firm to be written was an account of the Lauchhammer ironworks: see J. F. Trautscholdt, *Geschichte und Feier des ersten Jahrhunderts des Eisenwerkes Lauchhammer* (1825).

[2] Karl von Weber, 'Detlev von Einsiedel, Königlich Sächsischer Cabinets-Minister' (*Archiv für die Sachsische Geschichte*, Vol. I, 1863) and E. Johnson, 'Zur Lebensgeschichte des Kabinetts Ministers Detlev, Graf von Einsiedel' (*Neues Archiv für Sächsische Geschichte*, Vol. XII, 1891).

[3] L. Beck, *Die Geschichte des Eisens*, Vol. III (1897), p. 699 and pp. 899-904. Beck states that there were about 40 ironworks in Saxony in 1780. See also C. Schiffner and W. Gärtner, 'Alte Hütten und Hämmer in Sachsen' (in *Freiberger Forschungshefte*, No. XIV, 1960) and S. Sieber, 'Erzgebirgische Bergfabriken' (in *Forschungen und Fortschritte*, Vol. XXXIV, October 1960, Heft 10, p. 292).

[4] For the silver, lead and tin mines of Saxony see J. F. Daubuisson, 'Mémoire sur la partie économique et administrative des mines de la Saxe' (*Journal des Mines*, Vol. XI, 1801-2, pp. 63-90) and J. Köhler, *Die Keime der Kapitalismus im sächsischen Silberbergbau . . .* (1955).

sion of rival manufacturers abroad and it endeavoured to assure to native craftsmen a monopoly of the home market by prohibiting the importation of manufactured goods. The state set up industrial establishments of its own, such as the famous works at Meissen for the production of 'Dresden china'.[1] Financial assistance was given to private industry. Saxony's most important exports were textiles. Linens, woollens, cottons and silks were sold both on the Continent and overseas. Other exports were goldware and silverware, porcelain, arms and musical instruments.

Saxony was not only an industrial region but also an important centre of commerce. The location of the Electorate at the junction of great commercial routeways encouraged the development of transit trade. Traffic moving along the valley of the River Elbe between Hamburg and Austria and traffic moving across the Continent between Poland and the Rhineland passed through the Electorate. It might have been expected that Dresden, situated on the Elbe, would have become a great commercial city. In fact it was Leipzig, which lay in the lowlands between the Saale and the Mulde, that developed into the commercial capital of the country and its international fairs were visited by merchants from all over the world. The town was a small one in the eighteenth century and Mirabeau stated that a horseman could ride round its walls in five or six minutes. It was sufficiently distant from Dresden to be free from domination by the court, the nobles and the administration. The Leipzig merchants largely managed their own affairs and the town enjoyed a considerable measure of local self-government. Leipzig was also a university city and a centre of the German book trade. Its great fairs were visited by large numbers of merchants—variously estimated at between 3,000 and 7,000—and between a fifth and a quarter of them

---

[1] Victor Böhmert, 'Urkundliche Geschichte und Statistik der Meissener Porzellanmanufaktur von 1700 bis 1800 . . .' (*Zeitschrift des k. Sächsischen Statistischen Bureaus*, Vol. XXXVI, 1880 (Heft i and ii)); K. Berling, *Das Meissener Porzellan und seine Geschichte* (1900); E. Zimmermann, *Die Erfindung und Frühzeit des Meissener Porzellans* (1908); the *Festschrift zur 200-jährigen Jubelfeier der ältesten Porzellanmanufaktur Meissen* (1910); and *250 Jahre staatliche Porzellan Manufaktur Meissen* (1960).

were Polish Jews.[1] But the roads and rivers which brought trade to the city in peacetime also brought hostile armies in time of war for 'the plain in the hollow of Leipzig is the most memorable field of battles on German soil'.

In the first half of the eighteenth century Saxony played a more important part in European affairs than might have been expected from so small a state. Between 1697 and 1764, with only brief interruptions, its rulers were kings of Poland. Augustus II and Augustus III were more powerful than they would have been as rulers of a German Electorate. Only a limited measure of success attending their efforts to take advantage of the situation by exploiting Poland's economic resources for the benefit of Saxony. Brühl's attempt to secure for Saxony a dominant position in eastern Europe through her connection with Poland involved the Electorate in four European wars and contributed to bring about its ruin. Between 1732 and 1756 Saxony's national debt grew from 3·4 million thalers to 28·5 million thalers and the burden of interest payments became increasingly heavy. The Seven Years War completed the financial ruin of the country and when Augustus III and Brühl both died in 1763 the Electorate was virtually bankrupt.

Frederick the Great took full advantage of the fact that there was a small country on his frontier which was rich in economic resources but poor in political leadership. He was particularly anxious to divert to Prussia the trade between Saxony and Hamburg and between Saxony and Poland. Soon after his accession he imposed transit tolls upon goods from Saxony passing through Magdeburg by road or by water on their way to Hamburg. In 1747 he revived Magdeburg's staple rights and forced ships coming from Saxony to transfer their cargoes to Prussian vessels.[2] When the merchants of Leipzig sent some of their goods

---

[1] For Leipzig at the end of the eighteenth century see F. G. Leonhardi, *Geschichte und Beschreibung der Kreis- und Handelsstadt Leipzig nebst der umliegenden Gegend* (1799).

[2] Between 1685 and 1747 Dresden ships had sailed past Magdeburg on their way to Hamburg and had not been forced to unload their goods. When Frederick the Great visited Magdeburg in 1747 he re-established the ancient staple rights of the city. Henceforth ships from Dresden had to stop at Magdeburg and transfer their cargoes to a Magdeburg vessel. See Martin Kriele, *Die Regulierung der Elbeschiffahrt 1819-1821* (1894), p. 8.

to Hamburg by a new 'detour route' through Brunswick and Hanover — a road which avoided Prussian territory — Frederick's officials entered Brunswick and forced the Saxon carts to go to the nearest Prussian town.

The conquest of Silesia enabled Frederick to interfere with the trade route linking Poland and Saxony. By levying high tolls at Breslau he tried to divert to Prussian fairs the goods taken by Jewish merchants from Warsaw, Cracow and Lemberg to Leipzig. In 1755 the government of Saxony retaliated by banning nearly all Prussian goods from the Electorate.

After the Seven Years War negotiations between Prussia and Saxony took place at Halle an der Saale in the hope of ending the tariff war between the two countries. But they broke down mainly because Frederick refused to lift his restrictions upon trade between Poland and Saxony passing through Silesia. After the first partition of Poland Frederick forced the Poles to agree to a commercial treaty which contained provisions designed to foster the trade of Frankfurt an der Oder at the expense of that of Leipzig. There is, however, evidence to suggest that many Jewish merchants continued to visit the Leipzig fair.

It was not only Saxony's commerce and transit trade which suffered from Frederick's aggressive policy. The economic penetration of the Electorate by its powerful neighbour was seen in the purchase of a considerable number of Saxon national debt bonds by Prussian investors and in the enticing of skilled artisans from the Electorate to Prussia. Cottbus, a Prussian enclave in the Lower Lausitz, was one of the main recruiting centres for Saxon textile workers.[1] During the War of the Austrian Succession there was an organised migration of some 270 skilled textile workers from the Electorate to Berlin, Potsdam and Silesia and similar migrations occurred during the Seven Years War.

In time of war Frederick used Saxony as a base of military operations. From his various headquarters in the Electorate he

---

[1] See H. Kublick, *Die Siedlungspolitik Friedrichs des Grossen im Kreise Cottbus* (1934) and F. Schmidt, *Die Entwicklung der Cottbuser Tuchindustrie* (1928). But it is probable that more Saxon textile workers migrated to Bohemia than to Prussia in the eighteenth century.

defended Prussia against attack from the west and threatened to move up the valley of the Elbe against the Austrians in Bohemia. From Saxony he secured men, money and supplies with which to prosecute his military operations. At the beginning of the Seven Years War Frederick occupied Saxony, surrounded the army of the Electorate at Pirna, and incorporated many of the troops in his own army. He collected the normal taxes due to the Elector and levied heavy additional war contributions in cash and in kind.

During the War of the Austrian Succession when Frederick's troops threatened to occupy Meissen at the end of 1746 the Saxon authorities evacuated the leading porcelain experts to Dresden and dismantled or hid much of the equipment. When the Prussians reached Meissen they sent 250 boxes of chinaware to Berlin and used the workshops as a temporary military hospital. On Christmas day Podewils informed Frederick that the Saxon authorities had complained that Meissen and its porcelain works would be ruined if the sick and wounded stayed in the town much longer. The King replied that the wounded could not be moved until they were fit to travel.[1] The Prussians, however, had evacuated the premises by 18 January 1746 and the porcelain works resumed production.

Ten years later Frederick again occupied Meissen. He seized the contents of the porcelain warehouse and sold them to Schimmelmann who auctioned some of them in Hamburg. Several skilled workers migrated from Meissen to Berlin where Wegely and Gotzkowsky had set up porcelain factories. During the Seven Years War the output of silks in Leipzig declined since Raabe's workshops closed down and many of the weavers settled in Prussia and in Austria. At this time the Prussians cut down large quantities of Saxon timber for sale abroad.

By the end of the Seven Years War Saxony had been stripped bare not only by the Prussians but by her own allies.[2] There had

---

[1] The Saxons long remembered what they had suffered at the hands of the Prussians at this time. A Swiss journeyman who worked in Chemnitz in 1792 declared that his master detested the Prussians 'because of all the harm that they had done to his Fatherland during the Seven Years War' (Karl Schib (ed.). *Johann Conrad Fischer, 1773-1854: Tagebücher*, Schaffhausen, 1951, p. 13).

[2] *Politische Correspondenz Friedrichs des Grossen*, Vol. IV (1880), p. 388.

been a serious decline in population. Fortunately her territories survived intact since Frederick had been unable to seize the Lausitz. Prince Xaver[1] initiated a programme of reconstruction which eventually enabled the country to recover from the effects both of a disastrous war and of the previous misrule of Brühl. Saxony no longer aspired to the role of a Great Power. A Reconstruction Commission (1762-3) prepared plans for the economic revival of the Electorate, its leading member being Thomas von Fritsch who was a civil servant of exceptional ability. In February 1764 a new Department of State (*die Landes-Oeconomie-Manufactur-und-Commercien-Deputation*) was set up to put into effect the recommendations of the Reconstruction Commission. The administrative system was overhauled; the national finances were put in order; and a vigorous policy of state aid to industry was adopted.

Between 1760 and 1784 over seventy new industrial establishments were set up. The Meissen porcelain works were started again by Helbig who raised enough capital to buy back from Schimmelmann many of the porcelain articles which he had acquired from the Prussian authorities. The Leipzig silk industry revived when new establishments were founded by Stiehler to fill the gap caused by the disappearance of the firm of Raabe. The quality of Saxon wool was improved when a flock of Spanish merino sheep was imported in 1765. The efficiency of the mining industry was improved in the following year when Heinitz set up a mining academy at Freiberg.[2] The roads of the Electorate were greatly improved by Klumpp and Günther.[3] In spite of tariff wars with Prussia[4] and Austria, and the harvest failure of the early 1770's, the measures taken after the Seven

[1] Prince Xaver was Regent of the Electorate of Saxony between 1763 and 1768.

[2] See J. F. Daubuisson, 'Mémoire sur la partie économique et administrative des mines de la Saxe' (*Journal des Mines*, Vol. XI, 1801-2, pp. 63-90); the *Festschrift zu hundertjährigen Jubiläum der königl. Sächs, Bergakademie zu Freiberg am 30 Juli 1866* (Dresden, 1866); and W. Herrmann, *Beiträge zur Geschichte des Freiberger Bergbaues und der Bergakademie Freiberg* (1953).

[3] H. Schlechte, *Die Staatsreform in Kursachsen, 1762-3* (1958), p. 469.

[4] The correspondence between Marie Antonie of Saxony and Frederick shows that Marie Antonie pleaded in vain for some relaxation of Frederick's restrictions on the transit of goods through Prussia to the international fair at Liepzig.

Years War contributed to the economic revival of the country and laid the foundations of Saxony's industrial progress in the nineteenth century.

CHAPTER V

The Prussian Economy in the 1780's[1]

THE rise of Germany in the nineteenth century to the position of the leading manufacturing state on the Continent was due largely to the expansion of the Prussian economy. It was in the great industrial regions of Prussia that most of Germany's mines, plants and factories were to be found. Prussia's central location on the Continent gave her control over the most important German rivers and trade routes. And it was the Prussian authorities who took the initiative in establishing the customs union which played so important a part in bringing about the economic unification of the country. But the origins of the industrial revolution are to be sought in the second half of the eighteenth century rather than in the nineteenth century. It was the age of Frederick the Great that saw the rise of Prussia not only as a leading military power but also as a manufacturing country. When Frederick came to the throne Prussia had an agrarian economy. Her main exports were grain and timber. The manufacture of woollen cloth in the Mark Brandenburg and the production of metal goods in the

[1] For Frederick the Great's economic policy see the documents in J. D. E. Preuss, *Friedrich der Grosse* . . . (10 parts in 4 vols., 1832-4); C. O. Mylius, *Corpus Constitutionum Marchicarum, 1298-1750* (6 vols., and 4 supplementary vols., 1737-55); the *Politische Correspondenz Friedrichs des Grossen* (1879-1912); and the following volumes in the *Acta Borussica: Handels, -Zoll- und Akzisenpolitik* (2 vols. in 3 parts, 1911-28); *Münzwesen* (4 vols., 1904-13) and *Seidenindustrie* (3 vols., 1892). See also Freiherr von Knyphausen's statistics of factories and workshops in Hildegard Hoffman, *Die gewerbliche Produktion Preussens im Jahre 1769* . . . (typescript of Ph.D. thesis in the library of the Humboldt University, Berlin, 1957); F. G. Leonhardi, *Erdbeschreibung der Preussischen Monarchie* (3 vols., in 4 parts, 1791-4); Mirabeau, *De la monarchie prussienne sous Frédéric le Grand* (4 vols., 1788 and German translation edited by Jakob von Mauvillon); E. F. von Hertzberg, *Huit dissertations . . . lues dans les assemblées publiques de l'Academie Royale . . . de Berlin . . . 1780-7* (1787); R. Koser, *Geschichte Friedrichs des Grossen* (2nd edn., 4 vols., 1921-5); and A. Zottmann, *Die Wirtschaftspolitik Friedrichs des Grossen* (1937). For a discussion of Mirabeau's book on Prussia see H. Reissner, *Mirabeau und seine 'Monarchie Prussienne'* (1926).

County of Mark were virtually the only industrial activities of more than local importance. As centres of commerce and manufactures Berlin, Stettin, Frankfurt an der Oder, Magdeburg and Halle an der Saale could not be compared with Hamburg, Cologne, Leipzig or Frankfurt am Main.

When Frederick died the position was very different. In Silesia he had gained one of the greatest centres of manufactures east of the Elbe. In West Prussia he had secured a link between East Prussia and the Mark Brandenburg. In Emden he had secured a window to the North Sea. He had seized a long stretch of the Baltic coast and Prussia now controlled the important trade routes of the Oder and the Vistula. He had promoted the economic expansion of both the hereditary provinces and the recently acquired territories by setting up the Bank of Berlin, the Overseas Trading Corporation and several privileged commercial companies. He had constructed great public works: he had attracted thousands of farmers and artisans to his dominions; he had opened up new mines and had fostered the establishment of many industrial enterprises. In 1785 the value of Prussia's output of manufactured articles was estimated at 30 million thalers.[1]

An important factor in promoting Prussia's economic expansion was the long period of peace between 1763 and 1786. The grievous losses suffered in the Seven Years War were repaired in 23 years of peaceful reconstruction. Those years saw only the minor military actions in Poland and in the campaign against the Austrians in 1778-9.

After the Seven Years War Frederick sought to achieve his aims by diplomacy. For sixteen years the cornerstone of his policy was the alliance with Russia which was signed in 1764. This agreement secured Russia's recognition of Prussia's annexation of Silesia and paved the way for the first partition of Poland. In 1769 the alliance was renewed until 1780.

Frederick's efforts to secure an agreement with Austria were less successful. He twice met Joseph II and secured his assent

[1] This estimate excludes the output of the shipbuilding, lumber and flour-milling industries. See F. G. Leonhardi, *Erdbeschreibung der preussischen Monarchie*, Vol. I (1791), Introduction: section 12. Krug's estimate for industrial output in 1789 was 48 million thalers.

to a joint offer of mediation in the Russo-Turkish war. He also secured the co-operation of Austria in the first partition of Poland. But he failed to persuade Austria to relax her prohibitive tariff and in 1778 Prussia was again at war with the Habsburgs. Frederick was not prepared to see Austria extend her territories at Bavaria's expense. His intervention saved Bavaria from partition but ended any hopes of reconciliation between Prussia and Austria.

In 1781 Frederick once more found himself without an ally since—although he had joined the Armed Neutrality sponsored by Russia against Britain—Catherine failed to renew for a second time the agreement of 1764 and concluded an alliance with Austria for eight years. Frederick now turned to the German princes and in 1785 succeeded in establishing the *Fürstenbund* between Prussia, Saxony and Hanover to safeguard the frontiers and the rights of all members of the Empire. Frederick's diplomacy in the second half of his reign had secured for Prussia a much needed respite from war. And when he died Prussia's position as Austria's rival for the leadership of the German states was stronger than ever.

(i) *Population*

The growth of the population was a factor of major importance in promoting the economic expansion of the country. In Frederick's reign the population of his dominions rose from 2,785,000 to 5,629,000[1] despite a decline of about 500,000 during the Seven Years War.[2] The density of population in-

[1] Mirabeau's estimate. Slightly different estimates for Prussia's population in the 1780's were given by Hertzberg in his address to the Berlin Academy on 27 January 1785 and by the author of the *Acht statistische Tabellen zur bequemen Übersicht der Grösse . . . der vornehmsten europäischen Staaten* (second edition, 1783). Koser gives an estimate of 5,868,000.

[2] Frederick the Great's estimate in his *Oeuvres historiques* (2 vols., 1847) Part VI, p. 74. In the first draft of chapter 2 (*Des Finances*) of his *Mémoires depuis la paix de Hubertusburg* Frederick stated that Prussia's population had declined by 'about 600,000'. Koser considers that even the revised figure of 500,000 to be too high. Statistics compiled by the General Directory show a decline of only 332,582 for the principal provinces (the Mark Brandenburg, the New Mark, Pomerania, East Prussia and Silesia). See Reinhold Koser, 'Zur Bevölkerungsstatistik des preussischen Staates von 1756-86' (*Forschungen zur Brandenburgischen und Preussischen Geschichte*, Vol. XVI (1903), pp. 583-9).

creased from 18·7 per square kilometre in 1740 to nearly 30 in 1793. But the distribution of the population as between town and country remained steady throughout Frederick's reign. A little over a quarter of the people were townsmen and a little under three quarters were countrymen. The expansion of Prussia's population—particularly after 1763—was due to the excess of births over deaths, the acquisition of new provinces, and the arrival of thousands of new settlers in Frederick's dominions.

Hertzberg[1] claimed in the 1780's that Prussia's population was increasing more rapidly than in any other country on the Continent. He stated that births exceeded deaths by 59,000 in 1785. When Frederick the Great died the territories which he had annexed had a population of over 2,000,000, the largest being Silesia with nearly 1,500,000 inhabitants. Between 300,000 and 350,000 persons emigrated to Prussia in Frederick's reign and by 1786 every fifth inhabitant was a colonist.[2] Some came of their own accord. Some 40,000 immigrants from Saxony and Bohemia came to Prussia in the early 1770's because the harvest had failed. There were also religious refugees from Bohemia who sought an asylum under a king who granted freedom of worship to all his subjects. About 16,500 Czech Protestants migrated to Silesia where they planned to establish a settlement at Münsterberg. Eventually they split into several groups and found new homes in various parts of Silesia while a few settled in the Mark Brandenburg at Berlin and Köpenick.[3]

Most of the immigrants, however, came to Prussia at the King's invitation and were settled in Brandenburg, the New

[1] Ewald Friedrich Graf von Hertzberg (1725-95) entered the service of Frederick the Great in 1747 and became a Minister of State in 1763. He was in charge of the royal archives; he collected materials for the king's historical writings; and he was an expert in foreign affairs.

[2] M. Beheim-Schwarzenbach, *Hohenzollersche Colonisation* (1874) estimates the total number of migrants at 300,000. A higher estimate is given by Conrad Matschoss, *Friedrich der Grosse als Beförderer des Gewerbefleisses* (1912) and a lower estimate by J. D. E. Preuss, *Friedrich der Grosse. Eine Lebensgeschichte*, Vol. III (1833), p. 87. Hertzberg, in an address to the Berlin Academy on 27 January 1785, stated that 539 new villages had been established in Frederick's reign and that 42,000 immigrant families had settled in Prussia.

[3] M. Beheim-Schwarzenbach, *Geschichte der Hussitenansiedlung unter Friedrich II als Mittelpunkt der böhmischen Glaubens-Colonie in Preussen* (1874).

Mark, Pomerania, West Prussia, Upper Silesia and Magdeburg. Immigration officials were stationed at Frankfurt am Main and at Hamburg while other agents—some acting for the government and others for merchants or landowners—visited various parts of the Continent to find new settlers for the King. Attractive inducements were offered to farmers and artisans to persuade them to settle in Prussia. These included the payment of the fare to Prussia; exemption from military service; land, a cottage, equipment and stock for smallholders; a house, a workshop, tools and trading privileges for craftsmen. Some smallholders were granted long leases on the royal domain; some were leased land near new villages established as a result of drainage schemes or the improvement of former wasteland. Others secured smallholdings close to towns where there was a growing demand for vegetables, fruit and dairy produce.

The artisans who came to Prussia included miners, metalworkers, linenweavers, silkworkers and makers of porcelain. The arms factories at Spandau and Potsdam; the porcelain workshops of Berlin; the foundries and forges of Neustadt-Eberswalde and Malapane; and the silkworks of Berlin and Potsdam all employed some immigrants. The leading merchants of Berlin—men like Splitgerber and Gotzkowsky—co-operated with the King to attract skilled workers to Prussia.

Important settlements were established on fenland reclaimed from the valleys of the Oder, the Havel, the Warthe and the Netze and also around Lake Madü (between Pyritz and Altendamm) and on Usedom Island. In frontier regions the King's agents were particularly assiduous in their efforts to attract foreign immigrants. Saxon families from the Lower Lausitz—who combined farming with flax spinning and weaving—were settled in the Cottbus district which was an enclave in Saxony.[1] Peasants from the Voigtland who regularly sought harvest-work in the Duchy of Magdeburg were persuaded to settle permanently in the district. When West Prussia was annexed Frederick increased the German population of his Polish province by settling large numbers of people—mainly from Danzig and Württemberg—both on the land and in the towns.

[1] H. Kublick, *Die Siedlungspolitik Friedrichs des Grossen im Kreise Cottbus* (1934) and F. Schmidt, *Die Entwicklung der Cottbuser Tuchindustrie* (1928).

Some immigrants brought little with them except their skill. Others did not come empty-handed. It was estimated that the new settlers brought with them 2,000,000 thalers in cash; 20,000 sheep; 6,300 horses; 7,800 cattle and 3,200 pigs. Frederick's policy of internal colonisation met with opposition both at home and abroad. Local officials seldom relished the prospect of having to deal with large groups of settlers who might be unable to speak German and whose religion and way of life might be very different from those of their neighbours. Both townsmen and peasants tended to look upon immigrants as unwelcome intruders and potential competitors. The rulers of Austria, Saxony and Poland did their best to prevent their subjects from emigrating to Prussia. Frederick the Great, however, brushed all opposition aside and pushed forward vigorously with his plans to increase the population by bringing new settlers into the country. Some immigrants settled down successfully in their new homes and their skill as craftsmen and farmers helped to promote the economic expansion of Prussia. Others proved to be a liability rather than an asset. A contemporary stated that certain settlers in East Frisia were lazy and worthless immigrants. Twenty years after coming to the province they were still notoriously idle and were continually in trouble with the police.

(ii) *Agriculture*

In so far as the growth of Prussia's population at this time was due to immigration and to the excess of births over deaths it was necessary to expand agricultural production to provide additional food for the increased population. To secure new farmland the drainage of fens and the cultivation of waste land was undertaken on a large scale. Among the most important fen districts which were reclaimed were the *Oderbruch*, the *Warthebruch*, and the *Netzebruch*. In 1740 the valley of the lower Oder between Oderberg and Küstrin was a vast swamp supporting only the fishermen whose cottages were situated on high land above the marshes. A grandiose improvement scheme —drawn up by the Swiss mathematician Leonhard Euler and the engineer von Haerlem—was undertaken in the 1740's and

1750's. Troops were used to expedite the work. The construction of a new bed for the river was completed in 1753 and some 150,000 acres of fenland were drained. There were protests from the fishermen who declared that their livelihood would be injured but the King rode roughshod over all opposition and the boats of the villagers were requisitioned to assist in the transport of men and materials. By 1763 over 1,000 smallholders and their families—over 6,000 persons—had been settled on the fertile soil reclaimed from the marshes. Forty villages had been built or extended—nearly all between 1755 and 1761—of which 20 were constructed by the King and 20 by owners of large estates.[1] Many of the new settlers were Protestant refugees from Bavaria and the Palatinate. Farther down the River Oder between Schwedt and Stettin many more families were settled on reclaimed lands. Frederick declared that the new settlements in the Oder valley was 'une nouvelle petite province que l'industrie conquit sur l'ignorance et la paresse'.

The drainage of the marshes in the valleys of the Warthe and the Netze—between Küstrin and Driesen—was under-taken as part of Frederick's policy of reconstruction after the Seven Years War. The plan was drawn up by Lieutenant Colonel Petri and its execution was entrusted to Brenkenhof,[2] one of Frederick's ablest officials. Although he had received

[1] Of the 20 settlements established by the King on the royal domains, at a cost of at least 600,000 thalers, 15 were new villages while 5 were additions to villages which already existed. For the *Oderbruch* land reclamation scheme see F. W. Noeldechen, *Oekonomische und staatswirtschaftliche Briefe über den Niederoderbruch* (1800); S. Maire, 'Beiträge zur Besiedlungsgeschichte des Oderbruchs' (*Archiv der 'Brandenburgia' Gesellschaft für Heimatkunde der Provinz Brandenburg*, Vol. XIII, 1911); H. K. Kramm, 'Der preussische Absolutismus und seine Bedeutung für die ökonomisch- und siedlungsgeographischen Verhältnisse im Gebiet des heutigen Bezirks Frankfurt an der Oder' (*Wissenschaftlichte Zeitschrift der Pädagogischen Hochschule Potsdam*, Vol. V, 1959-60, pp. 33-42) Albert Detto, 'Die Besiedlung des Oderbruches durch Friedrich den Grossen' (*Forschungen zur Brandenburgischen und Preussischen Geschichte*, Vol. XVI (Part I), 1903, pp. 163-205) and P. F. Mengel, *Das Oderbruch* (Eberswalde, 1930).

[2] A. G. Meissner, *Leben Franz Balthasar Schönberg von Brenkenhof* (Leipzig, 1782), Spude, *Franz Balthasar Schönberg von Brenkenhof* (1880; reprinted from *Brandenburgisches Provinzialblatt*); Rehmann, 'Kleine Beiträge zur Charakteristik Brenkenhofs' (*Schriften des Vereins für Geschichte der Neumark*, XXII, 1908) and P. Schwartz, 'Brenkenhofs Berichte über seine Tätigkeit in der Neumark' (*ibid.*, X, 1907).

little or no schooling Brenkenhof was a thoroughly competent surveyor, engineer and administrator. The district was a labyrinth of marshes and ditches in which huntsmen stalked their game. Part of the region lay close to Poland and when Brenkenhof first inspected it the frontier had not been clearly defined. At the time of the first partition of Poland Frederick seized the Netze District and rectifications of the frontier to Prussia's advantage were secured later. The work of reclaiming the Netze-Warthe fens between 1766 and 1776 cost the King 750,000 thalers. About 3,500 families were settled in the district and in a few years the population of the reclaimed fenlands rose to 15,000. The names of some of the new villages —Stuttgart, Neu Dresden and Klein Mannheim—show that the immigrants came from Württemberg, Saxony and the Palatinate.[1] Smaller land-improvement schemes included the draining of the Drömling marshes (in the Alt Mark), the re-claiming of some of the low-lying parts of the valley of the Havel, and the cultivation of numerous heaths and sandy districts such as the wastelands on the road between Schöneberg and Charlottenburg and the sand dunes between Küstrin and Bromberg.

Frederick not only financed land reclamation schemes but he also made substantial annual grants and loans to estate owners and farmers to enable them to pay their debts and to improve their properties. He adopted a plan suggested by the Berlin merchant Büring[2] and set up three agricultural credit banks.[3] The first served Silesia (1769-70), the second the Mark

---

[1] For the reclamation of the valleys of the Warthe and Netze and the establishment of new villages see E. Neuhaus, *Die friderizianische Kolonisation im Warthe- und Netzebruch* (*Schriften des Vereins für Geschichte der Neumark*, Heft 18, 1906); Dannemann, *Die Melioration des Warthebruchs* (1866); L. F. Hahn, 'Historische Nachrichten von der Bewallung und Urbar-machung des Netzebruches, 1780' (in *Die Neumark. Mitteilungen des Vereins für Geschichte der Neumark*, Vol. IV, 1925).

[2] Büring's plan was eventually printed in the *Schlesische Provinzialblätter*, March 1799.

[3] For the Prussian land banks see Rabe, *Darstellung des Wesens der Pfand-briefe in den königlich preussischen Staates* (2 vols., 1818); Kohlschütter, 'Über landesschaftliche Kredit-systeme' (*Archiv der politischen Ökonomie*, New Series, Vol. I, 1843); Bülow-Cummerow, *Über Preussens landwirtschaftliche Creditvereine . . .* (1843); and H. Mauer, *Das Landschaftliche Kreditwesen Preussens . . .* (1907).

Brandenburg and the New Mark (1777), and the third Pomerania (1781).[1] They provided owners of large estates with additional capital by the issue of mortgage bonds. These securities bore interest and were readily transferable. In Silesia the first issue was for 20 million thalers and Frederick claimed that this sum—to which he added a grant of 200,000 thalers—saved some 400 landed gentry from bankruptcy. An English observer subsequently remarked that 'in a country where no government funds were in existence, or none in which the public had much confidence, these (*sic*) kind of securities became the natural deposits of such accumulations of money as were not intended to be exposed to any risks'.[2]

In some districts—such as Upper Silesia—most of the land was owned by great feudal families but in others medium-sized farms and smallholdings were also to be found.[3] While in Mecklenburg and in Swedish Pomerania the landed proprietors were clearing the peasants off the land[4] in Frederick's dominions no such clearances were allowed.[5] In 1777 serf tenure was made hereditary so that when a serf died his smallholding did not revert to the Crown but remained the inheritance of the next of kin.[6] The King not only made serf tenure more secure. He

[1] Shortly after Frederick the Great's death land mortgage banks were set up in West Prussia (1787) and in East Prussia (1788).

[2] W. Jacob, *Report on the Trade in Foreign Corn* (1826), p. 42.

[3] Members of the Prussian nobility were not always owners of great estates. Brenkenhof reported that in Czarndamero, a village in Pomerania, the population consisted of twelve noble families who were all smallholders. Only the cowherd and the night watchman were not of noble birth though both had married the daughters of nobles. See A. G. Meissner, *Leben Franz Balthasar Schönberg von Brenkenhof* (1782), p. 57.

[4] For the peasant clearances in Mecklenburg see J. Nichtweiss, *Das Bauernlegen in Mecklenburg* (1954); F. Mager, *Geschichte des Bauerntums and der Bodenkultur in Mecklenburg* (1955): P. Steinmann, *Bauer and Ritter in Mecklenburg* (1960); and G. Heitz, "Feudales Bauernlegen in Mecklenburg in 18en Jahrhundert" (*Zeitschrift für Geschichtswissenschaft*, VII, 1960, Heft vi).

[5] That the great landlords of Prussia undertook peasant clearances in the years before the accession of Frederick the Great may be seen from the fact that in the Ukermark and in the lordship of Beeskow-Storkow about 2,000 smallholders lost their lands between 1624 and 1746.

[6] For serfdom in Prussia in the eighteenth century see J. Nichtweiss, "Zur Frage der zweiten Leibeigenschaft und des sogenannten preussischen Weges der Entwicklung des Kapitalismus in der Landwistschaft" (*Zeitschift für Geschichte*, 1953, Heft III, p. 704 et se) and J. Kuczynski, "Zum Aufsatz

131

helped peasants who were in difficulties to keep their holdings and he tried to increase their number by welcoming immigrants. In his political testament of 1776 the King claimed that he was spending 3·7 million thalers a year on public works, land improvements and compensation for disasters. According to Hertzberg the King's grants to the provinces in the last twenty years of his reign amounted to over 24 million thalers. This included grants towards major land-reclamation and forestry schemes, payments to local authorities, and gifts and loans to landed proprietors and peasants. There are differences of opinion concerning the total sum distributed by the King but the list of the many projects to which he gave financial aid is an impressive one. The lion's share of the royal bounty went to the owners of large estates. Smallholders and peasants generally secured assistance only when they were in danger of being driven off the land by enemy action in wartime or by fire, floods, storms or crop-failures in peace time.

Frederick made strenuous efforts to improve the standard of agriculture in Prussia. He complained that the conservatism of the farmers delayed the introduction of new farming techniques. He made enquiries concerning up to date methods of agricultural production in England[1] and in Holland and he invited Dutch farmers to settle in his dominions to expand the output of dairy products. He favoured the consolidation of scattered strips and the enclosure of common fields though this might harm the interests of the smallholders whom he professed to support. Hertzberg stated in 1785 that the abolition of common fields and pastures had been carried out in hundreds of villages.

The King tried to improve the breeding of horses, cattle and sheep. The royal stud at Trakehnen, founded by Frederick William I in 1732, was largely responsible for maintaining the high reputation enjoyed by the horses of East Prussia at this

von Johannes Nichtweiss über die zweite Leibeigenschaft" (*ibid.*, 1954, Heft iii, pp. 467-471 and reply by Nichweiss pp. 471-476).

[1] Two examples may be given: (i) Count Kamecke paid a visit to an estate at Nottingly near Ferrybridge (Yorkshire) to study English farming methods. See letters from Sir Andrew Mitchell to Lord Rochford (Berlin, 29 April 1769) in H. Ellis, *Original Letters illustrative of English History*, Vol. IV, p. 518 and Wilhelm Roscher, *Geschichte der National-Oekonomik in Deutschland* (1874), p. 398. (ii) A farmer named Sydow, after visiting England with his son, grew turnips and lucerne on his farm at Kolbatz (Pomerania).

time. Pedigree rams and bulls were distributed to landed proprietors to raise the quality of Prussia's flocks and herds.
Merino sheep were imported from Andalusia. But Frederick did
not succeed—as the rulers of Saxony succeeded—in developing
a native breed of sheep which produced wool of really high
quality.[1] Prussian farmers were encouraged to keep their cattle
under cover during the winter. Seeds were distributed to secure
the growing of a greater variety of crops. The output of potatoes,
flax, turnips, clover, woad and tobacco was increased. In
Pomerania and in the New Mark Brenkenhof played an important part in raising the standard of farming. In Silesia
Count Reichenbach purchased a derelict estate in 1771 for
20,900 thalers and had improved it to such an extent in nine
years that he was able to sell it for 80,000 thalers. He cultivated
the land intensively, exploited its mineral resources, and secured
the maximum services from his serfs. Subsequently he twice
bought estates, greatly improved them and then sold them at
enhanced prices. Jeremias Forster, a peasant's son, did so well
as a farmer that he became the owner of seven farms and was
ennobled in 1786.[2]

The problem of making the best use of the sandy soil of
Brandenburg was tackled in various ways. On one of the royal
estates an English expert grew turnips and allowed them to rot
in the ground. He then planted the fields with various grasses
and clover and turned them into pastures on which cattle and
sheep could graze. The fields subsequently supported one third
more cattle than before. On soil too sandy for either arable or
dairy farming, trees were planted. About 13,000 acres of pine
were planted between 1776 and 1782. The King took vigorous
measures to preserve the forests in his kingdom and to regulate
the timber industry. During the Seven Years War the forests
had been neglected and mismanaged and the country's reserves
of timber had been depleted by illegal felling. After 1763 new
edicts were issued to limit felling and to provide for reafforesta-
tion. Tobacco was among the new—or relatively new—crops

[1] In Frederick's reign there were about 1.7 million sheep in the Mark
Brandenburg and the New Mark and about 1.8 million sheep in Silesia.

[2] J. Ziekursch, *Hundert Jahre schlesischer Agrargeschichte* ... (second edition
1927), p. 12 *et seq.*, and Wolfgang Treue, 'Der landwirtschaftliche Unternehmer in Ostdeutschland' (*Tradition*, Vol. III. February 1958, p. 37).

which were grown in Prussia at this time. Frederick the Great encouraged the growth of the tobacco plant in Silesia and the Ukermark in the hope of saving some of the money spent in purchasing American tobacco in England or Hamburg. The quality of the homegrown tobacco, however, was much inferior to that of Virginian tobacco. In 1780 the chemist, Achard[1] was asked to conduct experiments with a view to discovering whether American tobacco plants could be acclimatised in Prussia. His efforts appear to have achieved some success since he was granted a pension of 500 thalers a year 'in recognition of his services in improving the cultivation of tobacco' in Prussia.

The success of Frederick's agricultural policy was seen in 1770-1 when the harvest failed and there was a serious grain shortage in many parts of Germany. Saxony[2] and Bohemia suffered so severely that 40,000 persons migrated to Prussia where more food was available. This was partly because Prussia normally had a surplus of cereals which was exported and partly because the King kept considerable supplies of grain and flour stored in royal warehouses. Normally the reserve was used to keep grain prices stable and to prevent them from rising above one thaler a bushel. If war broke out or the harvest failed, grain and flour were released to meet the emergency. The annexation of West Prussia in 1772 rendered the position of Frederick's dominions more secure from the point of view of grain supplies. Frederick observed in his memoirs that the chief advantage which he gained from the first partition of Poland was that he was now 'master of the Vistula' and consequently 'master of Poland's commerce'.[3] He added that since Poland exported large quantities of grain Prussia no longer feared 'either shortage or famine'. Grain supplies from other parts of central Europe also had to cross Prussian territory if they were transported to Danzig, Stettin, or Hamburg. In some Continen-

---

[1] Achard's greatest achievement was his success in refining beet-sugar.
[2] In the Saxon Erzgebirge over 50,000 persons died of starvation at this time.
[3] After the first partition the Poles still held three small harbours on the Baltic—Polangen, Libau and Windau—in the provinces of Samogitia and Courland but they were of little value since the main routes of Polish trade followed the valleys of the Vistula and the Niemen and these routes were now effectively controlled by Prussia.

tal countries a poor harvest was a disaster but Prussia now had exceptional opportunities of securing grain or flour even in lean years.[1]

In 1786 farming standards varied considerably in different parts of the country. Some districts in the maritime provinces —forest, swamps and sandy heaths—were unsuitable for farming while others had light soil which did not yield heavy crops. Unfavourable climatic conditions, particularly the long, hard winters, added to the farmer's difficulties. The more fertile districts were to be found in the valleys and deltas. The land between the Vistula and the Nogat and the valleys of the Pregel, the Oder, the Warthe and the Netze were regions of improved farming. East Prussia was noted for its cereals, horses and cattle. There were substantial exports of grain from this province to various Baltic ports and also to Hamburg and Holland. Some of the grain was grown in East Prussia and some came from Poland.

Although much of its soil was poor the standard of farming in the Mark Brandenburg was improving because of the incentive provided by urbanisation. Not only Berlin but Potsdam, Neustadt-Eberswalde, Zehdenick and many other towns were expanding centres of domestic manufactures. Hence mixed farming—grain, vegetables, dairy products—developed to meet the demands of the townsmen. Frederick encouraged this development. Thus he forbade the import of eggs so as to force the Brandenburg farmers to increase their output sufficiently to satisfy the needs of the towns.

In the inland provinces the most fertile districts were in Lower Silesia, Magdeburg and the *Hellweg* (in the County of Mark). The main agricultural products of Lower Silesia were flax and wool. Silesian linens were of high quality and were one of Prussia's most important exports at this time. Most of the clip of Silesia's 1·8 million sheep was sold at Breslau, about half of the wool being bought by local clothiers and half by Berlin merchants. Considerable quantities of grain and potatoes were grown in Silesia.[2] In the Duchy of Magdeburg

[1] See W. Naudé, 'Die brandenburg-preussische Getreidehandelpolitik 1713-1803' (*Schmoller's Jahrbuch*, Vol. XXIX, 1905).
[2] For agriculture in Silesia see J. Ziekursch, *Hundert Jahre schlesischer Agrargeschichte vom Hubertusburger Frieden bis zum Abschluss der Bauernbefreiung* (first edn., 1915, second edn., 1927).

there were rich arable lands and pastures in the valleys of the Elbe and the Saale which were noted for their grain, potatoes, flax and cattle. During the Seven Years War Frederick declared that only the foresight of Schlabrendorf—who had fostered the extension of potato growing in Silesia—saved his armies from starvation. The neighbouring County of Halberstadt was also a prosperous farming region. In the County of Mark cereals were grown in the *Hellweg* district but the adjacent Sauerland was an arid region.[1]

(iii) *Industry*

Frederick the Great considered that the expansion of manufactures was just as important as the improvement of agriculture. When he came to the throne Germany's main manufacturing and commercial regions—Saxony, Silesia, Westphalia, the Palatinate and the Saar—lay outside Prussia. The territories of the Hohenzollerns were underdeveloped from an industrial point of view. Prussia's exports consisted mainly of foodstuffs such as grain and raw materials such as timber, flax, hemp and wax. Woollen and linen cloths were almost the only Prussian manufactured articles to be sold abroad. On the other hand Prussia depended upon foreign countries for supplies of many industrial products and semi-manufactured articles such as pig-iron from Sweden and textiles and hardware from England. Tobacco, wines, raw silk, spices and fruits were also imported. When Fäsch took charge of the Department of Manufactures he submitted a report to the King in which he argued that a number of goods which were imported could be made in Prussia. He wrote: 'We have harbours, rivers and transport facilities. What we need is a little more energy and a few big merchants of our own who are rich enough to run the new industries'.[2]

Frederick promoted the expansion of manufactures in many ways. He annexed the industrial province of Silesia, he seized

[1] For Frederick the Great's agricultural policy see R. Stadelmann, *Preussens Könige in ihre Tätigkeit für Landeskultur*, Part II *Friedrich der Grosse* (Publicationen aus den K. Preussischen Staatsarchiven, Vol. XI, 1882).

[2] Fäsch's report to the King was entitled *Idée générale du commerce de ce pays-ci* (1 October 1749).

new ports such as Elbing and Emden, and he gained control over the Vistula trade-route. He adopted a fiscal policy designed to reduce imports, to encourage exports, and to make Prussia as self-sufficient as possible. He waged tariff wars upon Austria and Saxony in the hope of injuring the commerce of rival states.[1] He improved Prussia's communications by building canals and harbours. He established State mines, foundries and workshops, porcelain works, sugar refineries and other factories. He tried to attract skilled foreign artisans to his dominions. He established new organs of administration to control industrial developments, the most important being the Department of Manufactures (1740), the Royal Bank of Berlin (1765), the General Administration of Customs and Excise (1766), the Department of Mines and Ironworks (1768), the Forestry Department (1771). the Overseas Trading Corporation (1772) and the offices which administered the salt, tobacco and coffee monopolies. Some able ministers and civil servants, such as Marschall, Fäsch, Hagen, Heinitz, de Launay, and Struensee served the King in these organisations.[2]

There were several reasons why Frederick the Great endeavoured to foster the development of industry and commerce. He considered that the expansion of manufactures would increase Prussia's strength and would help to raise her to the position of a Great Power. He wished to be certain that his army should always have the arms and supplies necessary to wage immediate war. He was determined that Prussia should herself produce the cannon, muskets, small arms, munitions and woollen cloth which were essential to an efficient fighting force. He wished Prussia to have a favourable balance of commodity trade. Not only staple products (textiles, metals, salt) but luxury industries (silks and porcelain) were fostered so as to expand Prussia's exports. He wanted a favourable balance

[1] For Prussia's commercial relations with Austria and Saxony in Frederick the Great's reign see H. Fechner, *Die handelspolitischen Beziehungen Preussens zu Oesterreich . . . 1741-1806* (1886) and M. Schröpfer, *Friedrich der Grosse und Kursachsen nach dem Siebenjährigen Kriege 1763-6* (1913).

[2] For administrative changes in Prussia in Frederick the Great's reign see H. Haussherr, *Verwaltungseinheit und Ressorttrennung vom Ende des 17en bis zum Beginn des 19en Jahrhunderts* (1953) and W. L. Dorn, 'The Prussian Bureaucracy in the Eighteenth Century' (*Political Science Quarterly*, Vol. XLVI, 1931 and XLVII, 1932).

of payments in international trade and tried to save the money that was paid to Sweden for pig-iron, to Berg for cutlery and to Hamburg for refined sugar. He hoped that increased exports would be paid for not only in commodities but also in silver. And a large supply of silver in his war chest was essential if Prussia were always to be ready to wage war.

The branches of industry to which Frederick devoted most attention were textiles, metalworking, armaments, mining, porcelain and sugar-refining. Textiles were the largest group of manufactures in Prussia at the end of his reign.[1] According to Hertzberg they produced goods worth over 21 million thalers a year[2] and gave employment to over 150,000 workers. They accounted for two-thirds of the total output (by value)[3] and over 90 per cent of the industrial labour force of the country.

The manufacture of linens was the most important branch of Prussia's textile industries. The spinning and weaving of flax gave employment to some 80,000 workers and the annual output of linens in the 1780's was valued at 9 million thalers.[4] After 1740 linen cloth was by far the most important manufactured product which Prussia exported. By securing a substantial share of Germany's great export trade in linens Prussia changed the pattern of her international commerce. Instead of exporting only raw materials and grain she now exported also one of the most important manufactured products of the eighteenth century. By sending her linens to British, French, Spanish and Portuguese colonies she was in a position to purchase sugar, coffee, tea, tobacco, cotton, ivory and other products from the tropics and so she was able to raise her stan-

---

[1] For the textile industries in the Mark Brandenburg in the reign of Frederick the Great see Konrad Scherf, 'Die brandenburgische Textilindustrie im 18en und 19en Jahrhundert und ihre standortbildenden Fakturen' (*Wissenschaftliche Zeitschrift der Pädagogischen Hochschule Potsdam*, Vol. V, 1959-60, pp. 43-65).

[2] Mirabeau considered that Hertzberg's estimate was too high. Mirabeau thought that the value of the annual output of textiles in Prussia in the 1780's was only 15.6 million thalers.

[3] In Silesia in 1800 textiles accounted for three quarters of the total industrial output of the province: see *Schlesische Provinzialblätter*, Vol. XXIV (1801), p. 554, *et seq.*

[4] Hertzberg's estimate with which Leonhardi agreed. Mirabeau's estimate was seven million thalers for the year 1785.

dard of living. Prussia's exports of linens were valued at 6 million thalers in 1785.[1]

It was the annexation of Silesia which enabled Prussia to export linens on a large scale.[2] Frederick the Great compared the wealth that accrued to his dominions from the export of Silesian linens to the wealth which flowed to Spain from the silver mines of Peru. Hertzberg estimated that the value of Silesia's output of linens was 7 million thalers a year while all the other Prussian provinces produced linens worth only 2 million thalers.

Linens were manufactured in many parts of Silesia but in the eighteenth century the most important centres of production were villages in the Riesengebirge, the mountain range separating Silesia from Bohemia. The industry was intimately connected with the feudal order of society since many of the workers were serfs who no longer tilled the lands of their feudal lords but divided their time between farming and industry. Many families of serfs grew their own flax and then spun it and wove it into linen cloth. They paid their feudal dues either in

[1] Hertzberg's estimate. Preuss valued Prussia's linen exports at 4.3 million thalers in 1780 and at 6 million thalers a year in the prosperous period 1795-98.

[2] For the linen industry of Silesia in the eighteenth century see Alfred Zimmermann, *Blüthe und Verfall des Leinengewerbes in Schlesien* (1885), Lujo Brentano, 'Über den grundherrlichen Charakter des hausindustriellen Leinengewerbes in Schlesien' (*Zeitschrift für Sozial- und Wirtschaftsgeschichte*, Vol. I, 1893, p. 333); Curt Frahne, *Die Textilindustrie im Wirtschaftsleben Schlesien . . .* (1905); Herman Fechner, *Wirtschaftsgeschichte der preussischen Provinz Schlesien in der Zeit ihrer provinziellen Selbstständigkeit 1741-1806* (1907); Gustav Croon, 'Zunftzwang und Industrie im Kreise Reichenbach' (*Zeitschrift des Vereins für Geschichte und Alterthum Schlesiens*, Vol. XLIII, 1909, p. 104); Hermann Aubin, 'Die Anfänge der grossen schlesischen Leinenweberei und- handlung' (*Vierteljahrschrift für Sozial- und Wirtschaftsgeschichte*, Vol. XXXV, 1942); Elizabeth Zimmermann, 'Der schlesische Garn und Leinenhandel im 16en und 17en Jahrhundert' (*Economisch-Historisch Jaarboek. Bijdragen tot de economische geschiednis van Nederland*, Vol. XXXVI, 1956, pp. 208-17 and pp. 247-52); Herbert Kisch, 'The Textile Industries in Silesia and the Rhineland: a comparative study in Industrialisation' *Journal of Economic History*, December 1959); W. Dlugoborski and K. Popiolek, 'A Study of the Growth of Industry and the History of the Working Classes in Silesia' (*Annales Silesiae*, Vol. I, No. 1, Breslau 1960, pp. 82-112); John Horner, *The Linen Trade of Europe during the Spinning Wheel Period* (1920). See also Joseph Partsch, *Schlesien, eine Landeskunde für das deutsche Volk auf wissenschaftliche Grundlage* (Breslau, 1896).

kind (flax, yarn or linen) or in cash (earned by producing linen).[1]

Early in the sixteenth century there was already a flourishing trade in the export of Silesian linen cloth. The principal centre of the linen trade at that time was the town of Jauer. The expansion of the export of linens was due largely to the enterprise of foreign merchants who purchased linens from the great landlords and from the domestic workers of Silesia and supplied them to Dutch, English and Spanish exporters. Eventually the cloth was sold in colonial territories, particularly in the Spanish possessions in South America. The foreign merchants and middlemen were able to extend considerable credit to the purchasers of linens—credit which the Silesian producers were not in a position to grant.

The foreign entrepreneurs had to face opposition both from their German rivals and from the spinners and weavers. The Silesian merchants, anxious to maintain their trade privileges, complained that the alien factors were avoiding the urban markets and were dealing directly with the landlords and the village textile workers who produced linen yarn and cloth in the country districts. The weavers complained that the foreign merchants paid very low prices for yarn and cloth and habitually indulged in fraudulent practices. The feudal lords, however, supported the foreign capitalists against both the town gilds and the rural weavers. Some Silesian merchants were able to compete successfully with the interlopers but the domestic weavers found no remedy against the exploitation of their labour by the middlemen.

Important changes took place in the Silesian linen industry between 1600 and 1740. There was a shift in the location of the industry. After the destruction of Jauer in the Thirty Years War new centres of production developed in the foothills of the Riesengebirge at Hirschberg, Landeshut, Schmiedeberg, Greiffenberg, Schweidnitz and Bolkenhain. Hirschberg became both the main centre for the manufacture of lawns and the principal trading town in the province. This move was associated with a decline in the number of the urban workers and an increase in the number of the rural workers. The growth of the linen

[1] The feudal tax on weavers was known as the *Weberzins*.

industry in the mountain villages was due partly to the fact that more timber was available for fuel in this region than in the lowlands around Jauer. There was also a considerable expansion in the labour force owing to the arrival of Protestant refugees from Bohemia (after 1627) and from France (after 1685). The great expansion in the manufacture of linens and the growth of a prosperous export trade turned Silesia into one of the richest provinces in Germany but the wealth derived from the industry was unequally divided. There was a marked contrast between the high incomes of the landlords and the entrepreneurs and the low wages earned by the spinners and weavers. The fact that so many workers were available helped to keep piece-rates down while the failure to replace the distaff by the spinning wheel restricted the amount of yarn which spinners could produce.[1]

The annexation of Silesia by Frederick the Great had far-reaching effects upon the development of the linen industry. Formerly the linen manufacturing districts of Silesia and Bohemia had virtually formed a single textile region. Sometimes flax was spun in Silesia, woven in Bohemia and bleached in Silesia. Now the two sides of the Riesengebirge were separated by an international frontier and the economic unity of the district was disrupted. Moreover the Silesian linen manufacturers lost one of their former markets in the long tariff war between Austria and Prussia. The campaigns of the Seven Years War caused serious devastation in Silesia and checked the progress of the linen industry.

Frederick the Great tried to mitigate the adverse economic effects of the annexation of Silesia and of the dislocation caused by the War of the Austrian Succession. He hoped to secure a substantial expansion in the output of linens so as to increase the volume of Silesia's exports. Additional capital was advanced to the landed proprietors in the form of royal grants and of loans from the mortgage bank set up in 1769. Skilled foreign textile workers were settled in the province; numerous spinning

[1] Oddy, writing in 1805, observed that 'the yarn of which the Silesian linen is made is spun by means of the spindle (distaff) which makes it look like cotton and requires less time to bleach than any other'. He also stated that Silesian cloth was 'generally three or four months in bleaching'. See A. J. Warden, *The Linen Trade* (1864), p. 269.

schools were established; flax growing was encouraged; bleachworks were put in order; and regulations were issued concerning the maintenance of the quality and the price of linen yarn and cloth.[1] Formerly fine linen yarn from Silesia had been sent to Holland to be bleached. Now the export of yarn was prohibited. The only exception to this rule was that yarn might be sent to Bohemia to be woven provided that it was eventually sent back to Silesia to be bleached. The number of linen looms in Silesia rose from 19,800 in 1748 to 28,700 in 1790. In the same period Silesia's exports of linens increased in value from 3·5 million thalers to 5·9 million thalers.[2] Little success, however, attended Frederick's efforts to expand the production of damask and creas in Silesia.[3]

Frederick's encouragement of the linen industry in Silesia received the support of the local feudal magnates and the entrepreneurs. But the condition of the workers remained unsatisfactory and there was much unrest in the 1780's. The expansion of the labour-force, the survival of primitive methods of production, and the liability to make substantial annual payments to their feudal lords made it impossible for the linen workers to secure any improvement in their standard of living. Soon after the death of Frederick the Great the prosperity of Silesia's great export trade was threatened by competition from Lancashire cotton piece goods and Scottish and Irish linens.[4] These economic factors—coupled with the ferment brought about by the French Revolution—led to serious riots in the mountain villages of the Riesengebirge in the spring of 1793.

Linen was also manufactured in other parts of Prussia. Westphalia was one of Germany's most important centres for the production of linen cloth and Prussia's territories in this region were noted for their linen yarns and cloths. In the County of Ravensberg fine linens of the highest quality were

---

[1] For the regulations of 1765 concerning the production of linens in Silesia see C. Gill, *The Rise of the Irish Linen Industry* (1925) pp. 117-119.

[2] Alfred Zimmermann's statistics (which include brown linen, white linen, and lawns): see J. Horner, *The Linen Trade of Europe* . . . (1920), p 407.

[3] For Frederick's attempt to develop the manufacture of damask in Silesia see C. Gill, op. cit., pp. 104-6. 'Creas' are coarse unbleached linen cloths.

[4] Exports of linens from Ireland rose from 14.9 million yards in 1781 to 45.5 million yards in 1792; see C. Gill, op. cit., Appendix 2.

made at Bielefeld and Steinhager. The bleachworks of Bielefeld had been destroyed by French troops in 1757 but had subsequently been re-established. Exports of yarn and cloth from this district were valued at 425,000 thalers in 1775. The County of Tecklenburg produced a strong durable cloth made entirely from hemp. Linen yarns and cloths were also manufactured in the districts of East Frisia, Minden, Halberstadt and Magdeburg.

In the King's hereditary dominions the Mark Brandenburg,[1] the New Mark, Pomerania and East Prussia all produced yarn and linens. Yarn from Ermland in East Prussia was exported from Braunsberg to Hull and Dundee. The linen yarn exported from Elbing and Danzig included some spun in Prussia and some spun in Poland. By the end of the eighteenth century linens accounted for about a quarter of Prussia's total exports.[2]

The second largest textile industry in Prussia in the 1780's was the manufacture of woollen cloth. It was an old-established industry and had for many years been controlled and fostered by the State. The clothiers had been given a monopoly of the home clip by prohibiting the export of raw wool. The Great Elector and his successor had tried to improve the quality of Prussia's sheep and wool and had regulated both the production and the sale of wool, yarn and cloth. Frederick William I had subsidised Johann Andreas von Kraus, who had established a Wool Warehouse in Berlin in 1713. This establishment bought large quantities of wool and employed many weavers in the small towns and villages of the Mark Brandenburg—such as Brandenburg, Neuruppin and Treuenbrietzen—to make army cloth. Frederick William I granted privileges to the Russia Company of Berlin which gained contracts to supply the Czar's military authorities with cloth in the years 1725-38.[3]

Frederick the Great pursued a similar policy to that of his father to encourage the expansion of the woollen industry.

---

[1] Cottbus and Peitz were important as linen centres in the Mark Brandenburg.

[2] In 1799 Prussia's exports of linens are valued at £2,000,000. In the same year Irish exports of linens were valued at £2,500,000.

[3] For the wool industry in Frederick William I's reign see C. Hinrichs (ed.), *Die Wollindustrie in Preussen unter Friedrich Wilhelm I* (*Acta Borussica: Denkmäler der Preussischen Staatsverwaltung*, 1933).

When he ascended the throne he found that wool was being sold abroad so he imposed a new prohibition on the export of fells, wool and yarn. The prohibition was repeated in 1766 and again in 1774 when the death penalty could be imposed for its infringement. He wanted the whole of the home-clip to be spun and woven in his own dominions. Some merino sheep were introduced into Prussia at this time but no new breed was developed from them. The annexation of Silesia increased the number of sheep in Prussia and added a new woollen industry to those already established in Brandenburg[1] and elsewhere. Reichenbach and Silberberg were important centres in which the finishing processes were carried out. The trade in Silesian woollen cloths flourished in the 1740's. There was some decline in output and exports during the Seven Years War but the loss of the Austrian market was nearly balanced by increased sales in Poland.[2]

The existence of a large standing army stimulated the production of woollen cloth in Prussia. Both the Berlin Wool Warehouse and many independent clothiers received regular orders from the military authorities. The spinners and weavers of Beeskow, Storkow, Strausberg, Neustadt-Eberswalde and Fürstenwalde, were almost exclusively engaged in making army cloth. Prussian woollen cloths were exported to various parts of Germany and were regularly sold at the great fairs. Hertzberg stated in 1785 that the value of Prussia's exports of woollens amounted to 4 million thalers. The growth of the

[1] In the Mark Brandenburg at this time the most important centres for the manufacture of cloth were Brandenburg, Rathenow, Neuruppin, Wusterhausen an der Dosse, Gransee, Beeskow, Storkow, Strusberg, Neustadt-Eberwalde, Fürstenwalde, Nowawes, Köpenick, Luckenwalde, and Cottbus. In Cottbus 538 persons (one tenth of the population) were engaged in the manufacture of woollens in 1785. For the Cottbus woollen industry see F. Schmidt, *Die Entwicklung der Cottbuser Tuchindustrie* (1928). For the Nowawes woollen industry see W. Spatz, *Chronik von Nowawes-Neuendorf* (1907); A. Wichgraf, *Geschichte der Webercolonie Nowawes bei Potsdam* (1862); and G. Vogler, *Zur Lage und zum Klassenkampf der Weber und Spinner in Nowawes in der zweiten Hälfte des 18en Jahrhunderts* (Institut für Deutsche Geschichte der Humboldt Universität, Berlin, 1956).

[2] For the Silesian woollen industry in the eighteenth century see F. von Schrötter, 'Die schlesische Wollenindustrie im 18en Jahrhundert' (*Forschungen zur Brandenburgischen und Preussischen Geschichte*, Vols. X, XI and XIV). For the neighbouring industry on the Bohemian side of the Riesengebirge see J. Grunzel, *Die Reichenberger Tuchindustrie* . . . (Prague, 1898).

weaving branch of the industry was so considerable that there was a shortage of spinners. Efforts were made to attract spinners from abroad and to persuade the wives of soldiers to take up spinning.

When it was suggested that English spinning machines should be introduced to increase output Frederick adopted a cautious attitude. He allowed the importation of only a limited number of machines to spin fine wool or cotton. He considered that if machinery were introduced too quickly there would be a danger of unemployment among the Prussian woolworkers.[1]

Frederick the Great established the manufacture of a thin combed unfulled cloth (known as *Zeug*) at Luckenwalde in the Mark Brandenburg in the early 1780's. The soft water of the River Nuthe, the proximity of sheepfarms, and easy access to the fairs of Leipzig and Frankfurt an der Oder favoured the expansion of clothmaking at Luckenwalde. A small group of skilled Thuringian weavers, rendered homeless by a great fire in Gera, were settled in Luckenwalde. The King built a warehouse costing 72,000 thalers—popularly known as the 'big factory'—which included a combing-room, a yarn storehouse, a dyeing room, a finishing workshop and a house for the manager (*Verleger*). The establishment was run by Thomas de Vins who came from Frankfurt am Main and by 1785 about 200 outworkers were employed.[2] Thomas de Vins had to deal with much labour unrest in the 1780's. Many of the outworkers complained bitterly of low piece-work rates of pay and long periods of unemployment without wages.[3]

Hertzberg estimated that there were 58,000 woolworkers in Prussia in 1788. The value of the cloth produced at that time

[1] C. Ergang, 'Friedrich der Grosse in seine Stellung zum Maschinenproblem' (*Beiträge zur Geschichte der Technik und Industrie,* edited by Conrad Matschoss, Vol. III, 1910, pp. 78-82).

[2] See J. Feig, 'Die Begründung der Luckenwalder Wollindustrie durch Preussens Könige im 18en Jahrhundert' (*Forschungen zur Brandenburgischen und Preussischen Geschichte,* Vol. X. 1898, p. 79 *et seq.*) and L. Bamberger, Beiträge zur Geschichte der Luckenwalder Textilindustrie' (*Forschungen zur Brandenburgischen und Preussischen Geschichte,* Vol. XXIX, 1916, p. 407 *et seq.*) Although the 'big factory' was sold in 1806 the manufacture of woollens had by that time been firmly established in Luckenwalde.

[3] See documents in H. Krüger, *Zur Geschichte der Manufakturen und der Manufakturarbeiter in Preussen* (1958), p. 573 *et seq.*

was estimated at 8 million thalers,[1] this being only a little less than the output of the linen industry. The value of the exports of woollen cloth was estimated at 4 million thalers.[2]

The cotton industry was established in Berlin in Frederick's reign. The first calico printing works were set up—with the aid of a royal subsidy—in 1741. Three years later cotton yarn was spun and cotton cloth was woven in the Prussian capital. In 1756 Johann Georg Sieburg set up calico works in Berlin which eventually employed 700 workers. He was largely responsible for the expansion of the Berlin cotton industry and introduced many important technical improvements. He brought various foreign experts to Berlin who introduced the manufacture of chintz, the spinning of cotton yarn by English machines, the printing of calicoes with copper plates, and the growing of madder (on a royal estate at Wilmersdorf) for the production of red dye. Another branch of the industry—the production of cotton velvet—was introduced by the Overseas Trading Corporation in 1775 and these works were soon taken over by Thomas Hotho and Karl Welper. It has been estimated that by the end of Frederick's reign the value of the output of cotton goods in Prussia was 1·2 million thalers. About 7,000 workers were employed in the industry.[3]

The manufacture of silks in Prussia[4] was located in two widely separated parts of the kingdom. In the Berlin-Potsdam area the industry was subsidised by the State but in Crefeld it was left to private enterprise. The production of silks was on a much smaller scale than that of linens and woollens. At the end of Frederick's reign the value of the silks produced was 3 million thalers,[5] the number of workers employed was 6,000

[1] Leonhardi accepted Hertzberg's estimate. Mirabeau gave a rather lower estimate (6.5 million thalers).

[2] J. D. E. Preuss, *Friedrich der Grosse. Eine Lebensgeschichte*, Vol. III (1833), p. 42.

[3] J. D. E. Preuss, op. cit., pp. 56-58. Leonhardi gives the same figures. See also the brief account of Sieburg's career given by Kosmann and Heinsius and quoted by H. Krüger, *Zur Geschichte der Manufakturen und der Manufakturarbeiten im Preussen* (1958), p. 530.

[4] For the silk industry in Frederick the Great's reign see Gustav Schmoller and Otto Hintze, *Die Preussische Seidenindustrie im 18en Jahrhundert* (*Acta Borussica*, 3 vols., 1892).

[5] Hertzberg's estimate with which Leonhardi agreed: Mirabeau's estimate was 1.3 million thalers.

and the number of looms was 3,000. Before 1740 little success had attended the efforts of the Prussian kings to establish the silk industry in their dominions. When Frederick came to the throne the only works of any importance were those of David Hirsch (Potsdam) and the brothers von der Leyen (Crefeld).

Frederick tried to introduce the production of raw silk in Prussia but the climate was unsuitable and the largest output in any one year was only a little over 11,000 lbs. (1784).[1] He established a Central Industrial Fund (1745) to finance new silkworks and a royal Silk Warehouse (1749) in which supplies of raw silk and yarn—purchased for the most part in Italy— could be stored. The King subsidised entrepreneurs who set up silkworks. He brought skilled foreign silkworkers to Prussia and he protected the industry by prohibiting the import of foreign silks.

The Berlin merchant Gotzkowsky established a new velvet manufactory in 1746 and he subsequently took over other silk-works in the Prussian capital. But he had many other business interests and went bankrupt during the commercial crisis of 1763. His silkworks then passed into the hands of two Jewish entrepreneurs. Owing to the difficulties which faced the silk industry after the Seven Years War Frederick decided to encourage the establishment of silkworks in towns other than Berlin and Potsdam such as Magdeburg[2] and Bernau. Nevertheless Berlin and Potsdam continued to be the largest centres for the production of silks in Frederick's dominions, the most important firms being those of Hirsch, Michelet, Baudouin, Gardemain, and Bernhard.[3] The value of the output of silks in Berlin in 1782 was estimated at over 700,000 thalers.[4] At the end of the eighteenth century Berlin and Potsdam had 4,000 silklooms operated by 5,500 workers.

[1] About two-thirds of this raw silk was produced in the Mark Brandenburg and the New Mark.

[2] For the Magdeburg silk industry see F. Vester, 'Seidenbau und Seidenfabrikation in Magdeburg im achtzehntzen Jahrhundert' (*Magdeburgs Wirtschaftsleben in der Vergangenheit* (Madgeburg Chamber of Commerce), Vol. I, 1925, p. 495 *et seq.*).

[3] The Potsdam merchant Isaac Bernhard is remembered not only as a pioneer of the silk industry but also as the patron and employer of the philosopher Moses Mendelssohn (grandfather of the Composer).

[4] Nicolai's estimate.

147

In Crefeld the silk industry had expanded in Frederick's reign without any help from the State. It was virtually free from government control. The presence of linen workers in the district created a reserve of relatively cheap labour for the silk industry. The von der Leyen enterprises[1] almost had a monopoly of the production of silks in Crefeld. In 1786 these undertakings employed 3,300 workers[2] and made silks to the value of 700,000 thalers, Mirabeau ascribed the continuous prosperity enjoyed by the Crefeld silk workshops to the fact that they had been at liberty to 'run along natural lines'.

In fostering the textile industries Frederick the Great particularly favoured his capital.[3] By the end of the eighteenth century. Berlin had developed into a textile centre of some importance. Some 21,000 of its citizens were employed in the textile industries.[4] The Court patronised the silk industry and the army provided a market for coarse woollen cloth.

The mining and metal industries, which eventually became so important a factor in Prussia's expansion as a manufacturing country, were of relatively minor importance in the reign of Frederick the Great.[5] In 1785 Hertzberg estimated the value of their output at 2 million thalers which was about the same level of production as that attained by the sugar refineries, the leatherworks and the porcelain works. In the eighteenth century most of Germany's pig-iron and other metal products came from the Eifel, the Hunsrück, the Siegerland, the Harz,

[1] W. Kurschat, *Das Haus Friedrich und Heinrich von der Leyen in Krefeld . . . 1794-1814* (1939) and T. Riedl, *Die Ursache für den Aufstieg der Krefelder Seidenindustrie im 17en und 18en Jahrhundert* (dissertation: Cologne, 1952). The decline of the silk industry in Cologne was a factor which favoured the expansion of the manufacture of silks in Crefeld.

[2] This figure presumably includes the outworkers in villages near Crefeld.

[3] For the industrial development of Berlin in the reign of Frederick the Great see H. Rachel, *Das Berliner Wirtschaftsleben im Zeitalter des Frühkapitalismus* (1931) and F. Dopp, *Uber die Entwicklung der Berliner Industrie im achtzehnten Jahrhundert* (1904).

[4] Growth of the Berlin textile industries in Frederick the Great's reign.

	Number of Looms			
	Silk	Wool	Cotton	Linen	Total
1750. . . .	292	2,880	81	284	3,537
1761. . . .	1,185	3,082	627	184	5,078
1780. . . .	2,220	2,286	1,018	228	5,752

[5] See Friedrich Anton Heinitz, *Mémoire sur les produits du régne minéral de la monarchie prussienne* (1786).

the Erzgebirge, Thuringia, Styria and Carinthia. Prussia's output of these products was insufficient for her needs so she imported pig-iron from Sweden[1] and from the Harz. According to Mirabeau the value of Prussia's imports of pig-iron and metal products in the 1780's was between 550,000 thalers and 600,000 thalers a year. At this time small quantities of coal were mined in the Ruhr valley but the vast deposits which lay to the north of the River Ruhr and in Upper Silesia were not exploited.

As the head of a great military state Frederick was anxious to increase the output of pig iron and of those branches of the metal industries which were concerned with the production of arms and munitions. In 1768 he established a Royal Mining Office and two years later at a conference with his ministers he emphasized the importance of developing the coal resources of Silesia. But it was not until Heinitz[2] was placed in charge of the national mining administration in 1778 that real progress was made. Heinitz was one of the leading mining experts of his day and he had served as a mining official in Saxony and Brunswick. He reorganised the mining administration of Prussia and appointed exceptionally able men to promote the expansion of the mining and metal industries in the various regions of Prussia. Towards the end of his reign the King set aside 260,000 thalers to foster the development of these industries. He appreciated the need for introducing the most modern techniques into Prussia and encouraged his officials to study English methods of ironsmelting and working in metals. Reden, Stein and Eversmann were among those who visited England in the 1770's and 1780's for this purpose.[3]

In the early years of his reign Frederick concentrated his

[1] Hertzberg stated in 1786 that the annual value of East Prussia's imports of Swedish pig-iron amounted to 34,000 thalers. These imports were not high grade iron from Dannemora but low grade iron from Gefle. The import of Swedish iron into other Prussian provinces had been forbidden in November 1779.

[2] For Heinitz see A. Schwemann, 'Friedrich Anton von Heinitz' (*Beiträge zur Geschichte der Technik und Industrie*, edited by Conrad Matschoss, XII, 1922).

[3] Towards the end of Frederick's reign the first steam pump to be installed in a Prussian mine was erected by Bücking at Hettstedt in the district of Burggörner (County of Mansfeld). It was set to work on 23 August 1785 in the presence of Heinitz. See L. Beck, *Die Geschichte des Eisens*, Vol. III (1897), pp. 540-3.

efforts on the improvement of the metalworks and armament factories of the Mark Brandenburg. The most important works to be set up or expanded were the furnaces, forges, rolling and slitting mills, copperworks, brassworks and cutlery workshops of Neustadt an der Dosse, Neustadt-Eberswalde, Zehdenick, Peitz and Hegermühle and the small arms factories at Potsdam and Spandau. They were royal manufactories which were either operated by the State or were leased to private entrepreneurs such as Splitgerber and Daum. The production of copper in the County of Mansfeld and the Saalkreis was expanded. Then the King turned his attention to Silesia. On the advice of Rhedanz new ironworks were established near Oppeln (Lower Silesia) at Malapane[1] and Kreuzburg (1754) and later at Krascheow, Jedlitz (1775) and Dembiohammer (1784). Deposits of lead and silver were found at Tarnowitz in Upper Silesia in 1784. Reden, the recently appointed head of the regional mining office for Silesia, was responsible for opening up the Frederick Mine (*Friedrichsgrube*) and the smelting and refinery works (*Friedrichshütte*) at Tarnowitz in 1786. Both were operated by the State.[2]

Meanwhile in the County of Mark a revised mining code, introduced in 1766, gave the authorities wide powers to control the management and regulate the day to day working of the privately owned mines in the Ruhr. The regulation of the River Ruhr in the 1770's improved the facilities for exporting coal and metal goods. These exports were valued at one million thalers in 1785.[3] In 1784 Stein was sent to the western provinces of Prussia to supervise the mines and workshops. Two years later Heinitz gave the King an encouraging report on the prospects of the Ruhr as a coalmining region and of the Sauerland as a centre for the production of pig-iron and metal goods.[4]

[1] For the Malapane ironworks see L. Wachler, *Geschichte des ersten Jahrhundert der Königlichen Eisenhütten-Worke in Malapane* . . . (Glogau, 1856).

[2] For Reden's work in Silesia see W. O. Henderson, *The State and the Industrial Revolution in Prussia 1740-1870* (1958), pp. 1-20; and A. Schwemann, 'Friedrich Wilhelm, Graf von Reden' (*Beitrage zur Geschichte der Technik und Industrie*, edited by Conrad Matschoss, XIV, 1924).

[3] Hertzberg's estimate.

[4] For Stein's work in the County of Mark see W. O. Henderson, *The State and the Industrial Revolution in Prussia 1740-1870* (1958) pp. 21-41.

Other industries were of less importance. The new porcelain industry, with an estimated output of two million thalers in 1785, was one to which Frederick attached great importance. As an export industry it helped to secure for Prussia a favourable balance of payments in international trade. On two occasions when the King's armies occupied Dresden, Frederick tried to learn the secrets of the manufacture of Meissen china. He persuaded Gotzkowsky to set up a porcelain factory in Berlin and some skilled workers from Saxony were employed there. When Gotzkowsky went bankrupt the porcelain works were purchased by the King and became a State enterprise.[1] Sugar, hitherto imported from Hamburg, was refined in Berlin by Splitgerber who was granted a monopoly of its sale in most of Prussia. Mention may also be made of the royal saltworks in the County of Mark at Königsborn (Unna) and in the County of Magdeburg at Halle an der Saale and Schönebeck;[2] the manufacture of pharmaceutical products at the Francke Institute at Halle an der Saale;[3] the royal lime kilns in the Mark Brandenburg;[4] the paperworks at the Francke Institute (Halle) and at Spechthausen,[5] Hegermühle and Wolfswinkel (near Neustadt-Eberswalde); the glassworks in the New Mark at Neustadt an der Dosse;[6] shipbuilding in the Baltic ports;[7] and the felling of timber which was of importance as an export

[1] About 500 workers were employed in the royal Berlin porcelain factory at the end of Frederick's reign. Voltaire wrote to d'Alembert on 13 November 1772: 'Le roi de Prusse vient de m'envoyer un service de porcelaine de Berlin, qui est fort au-dessus de la porcelaine de Saxe et de Sèvres' (J. D. E. Preuss, *Friedrich der Grosse . . .*, Vol. III, 1833, p. 47).

[2] By the end of the eighteenth century the Schönebeck saltworks (founded in 1705) were the largest in Germany.

[3] This institution (the *Francksche Stiftung*) was run by the Lutheran Church. It was partly a welfare organisation (an orphanage and a school) and partly an industrial enterprise (pharmaceutical products and printing). Its press published over 20,000 copies of the Bible annually.

[4] There were lime kilns at Berlin, Spandau, Potsdam, Rathenow, and Beeskow.

[5] *Hundert Jahre der Papierfabrik Spechthausen* (1887). The royal paper mill at Spechthausen was leased first to Jean Dubois (1780), then to P. E. Eisenhardt (c. 1783), and then to J. G. Ebart and M. F. Forster (c. 1787). The royal paperworks at Hegermühle were destroyed by the Russians in 1760.

[6] W. Hoff, *Die Glasshütten der Neumark* (1940).

[7] Ninety ships were built at Königsberg, Pillau and Memel between 1778 and 1782. The Stettin shipyards also enjoyed a boom in that period.

industry. The growth of the tobacco industry was also of some significance because the production and sale of tobacco was made a royal monopoly, the profits of which were a substantial source of revenue for the State.[1]

(iv) *Commerce*

Frederick the Great wished to foster not only agriculture and industry but also internal and foreign commerce. When he came to the throne there was little trade between his scattered provinces though the fairs of Frankfurt an der Oder were not without importance. East Prussia and the County of Mark were isolated provinces with relatively few economic contacts with the Mark Brandenburg. In the contiguous territories bad roads, staple rights, high tolls, and excises were serious barriers to commercial intercourse. And since Prussia had no harbours outside the Baltic, no overseas possessions, no navy and only a small mercantile marine, she could hardly hope to share in the great ocean trades of the world.

Frederick remedied some of these drawbacks by extending the territories of his kingdom. The acquisition of East Frisia gave him a North Sea port (Emden) while the annexation of West Prussia bridged the gap between Brandenburg and East Prussia. He endeavoured to foster overseas commerce by encouraging merchants to establish trading companies, such as the Asiatic Company, and by setting up the Overseas Trading Corporation. Although he had no navy he tried to put pressure on foreign states to respect the rights of Prussian traders and he refused to repay the Silesian loan to English bondholders until the English government had compensated Prussian merchants for losses incurred when their ships and cargoes were seized during the War of the Austrian Succession. It is said that in his later years Frederick founded a secret society called the 'Friends of the Fatherland' which sent Colonel von Schöning to Spain, Portugal and Holland to make confidential reports on the

---

[1] The net profit of the General Tobacco Administration was 1,729,000 thalers in the fiscal year 1785-6. See Dr Charpentier, 'Das alt-preussische Tabaksmonopol. (*Preussische Jahrbücher*, LXI, 1888, pp. 145-163) and E. P. Reimann, *Der Tabaksmonopol Friedrichs des Grossen* (1913).

activities of Prussian traders and government agents and to enter into private commercial negotiations with foreign courts to foster the trade in Prussian linens.[1]

The improvement of communications was an essential feature of Frederick's plans to promote both internal commerce and foreign trade. He saw the necessity of linking the agrarian parts of his kingdom with the provinces which were beginning to be industrialised and he appreciated the need for improving communications between Berlin and the ports of Stettin and Hamburg. Transport facilities were improved by building canals rather than roads.[2] The Plauen Canal between the Elbe and the Havel was opened in 1757 and the reconstruction of the Finow Canal between the Oder and the Havel[3] was completed in 1746. These two waterways linked the Elbe and the Oder and facilitated the movement of goods between the main German North Sea and Baltic ports and such inland commercial centres as Berlin, Magdeburg, Breslau and Frankfurt an der Oder. Both canals carried salt to Berlin—the Plauen Canal from Schönebeck (near Magdeburg) and the Finow Canal from Stettin. Several important foundries, ironworks, and cutlery workshops were established on or near the Finow Canal. Two new waterways were built in the Ukermark—the Templin Canal (1745) and the Fehrbellin Canal (1766). Nearly all the staple privileges of Stettin and Frankfurt an der Oder were abolished and the General Directory was instructed to equalise the tolls payable on the Elbe and the Oder. In the hope of expanding the export of Polish grain through Stettin substantial reductions were made in the Prussian tolls charged on the Oder, the Warthe and the Netze. In 1764-6 improvements were made in the waterways of East Prussia to facilitate the floating of logs to the Baltic. In the region of the Masurian

[1] J. D. E. Preuss, *Friedrich der Grosse*, Vol. III (1833), p. 42 (note i).
[2] Not many new roads were built in Prussia in the reign of Frederick the Great. Frederick was however responsible for constructing some military highways in the mountainous parts of Silesia, such as the roads from Schweidnitz to Glatz and from Schweidnitz to Landeshut.
[3] The first Finow Canal had been opened to traffic in 1620. It ran to Finowfurt and joined the Old Havel at Lake Möllen. Finowfurt was linked to the River Oder by the River Finow. This first canal had been destroyed during the Thirty Years War and a hundred years elapsed before it was reconstructed. The new canal had 18 locks.

lakes there was a vast system of waterways—between Johannis-burg and the River Angerapp—which was successfully used for this purpose.

After the first partition of Poland Frederick put in hand a programme of public works in West Prussia and the Netze District which was designed to improve the navigation of the River Vistula and its tributaries. In this way the King hoped to attract to his dominions as much as possible of the trade of Poland. The Bromberg Canal was built to join the River Brahe to the River Netze. This waterway was 24 miles long and it forged a link between the Oder and the Vistula. Brenkenhof was placed in charge of the enterprise on which a large number of workers were employed. The construction of the new water-way was completed in 16 months. No less than 1,500 men lost their lives while the canal was being built. They worked for long hours up to their armpits in icy cold water and then slept in the open. In the circumstances it is hardly surprising that so many of the workers were struck down by dysentery and other illnesses. The cost of the canal, opened in 1775, was 640,000 thalers. The River Netze was regulated between Nakel and Driesen. The River Nogat was made navigable in the hope of attracting to Elbing some of the trade of Danzig, a port which was still in Polish hands.[1] At the same time at the other end of the kingdom the navigation of the River Ruhr below Langen-scheid was improved (1780) so that the coal and metal goods of the County of Mark could reach the River Rhine more easily.[2]

Frederick the Great appreciated the need for improving the shipping facilities of Stettin which had been acquired from Sweden in 1720. Although it was a comparatively small town when compared with Königsberg or Danzig[3] it was the nearest

---

[1] For the ruthless economic sanctions by which Frederick the Great tried to ruin Danzig see R. Damus, *Die Stadt Danzig gegenüber der Politik Friedrichs des Grossen und Friedrich Wilhelm III* (1887) and Margot Herzfeld, 'Der polnische Handelsvertrag von 1775' (*Forschungen zur Brandenburgischen und Preussischen Geschichte*, XXXII (1920), XXXV (1923) XXXVI (1924)).

[2] This regulation of the River Ruhr was carried out by the Prussian authorities in association with the rulers of Essen, Werden, and Broich (Berg) whose territories lay between the Prussian territories of Mark and Cleves.

[3] Mirabeau gave the following estimates of population at the end of Frederick's reign: Stettin 15,399 (excluding the garrison); Königsberg 54,000 (excluding the garrison); Danzig 60,000.

seaport to Berlin and it handled a substantial volume of trade which moved up and down the River Oder. In 1740 the approaches from the open sea to Stettin were far from satisfactory. Only the most easterly of the three passages linking the Baltic and the Stettiner Haff was normally used by Prussian ships. The western (or Peene) channel was still in Swedish hands and the central passage between the islands of Usedum and Wollin (the Swine Channel) was not very suitable for seagoing vessels. In 1747 the engineer Walrabe completed the task of rendering the Swine Channel suitable for navigation. These works were destroyed by Swedish troops in 1759 and had to be rebuilt after the Seven Years War. New settlers were brought to the fishing village of West Swine and so Swinemünde was established as an outport for Stettin. It was granted municipal rights in 1765. Although Stettin's trade expanded[1] and its timber merchants[2] and shipbuilders[3] enjoyed a boom in the early 1780's, it failed to develop into a port of international significance. It could not compete with Hamburg which offered superior harbour facilities, cheaper insurance rates,[4] and longer credit terms than Stettin. Moreover the existence of a network of commercial treaties between Hamburg and the main commercial nations of the world gave Hamburg vessels and their cargoes a measure of protection in many foreign ports which the ships of Stettin could hardly hope to enjoy.[5]

The acquisition of East Frisia gave Frederick the opportunity he desired to extend Prussia's overseas commerce. He dreamed

[1] One of the most important of Stettin's trades was the export of grain to France and Spain. The Prussian Levant Company, backed by the Berlin banker F. W. Schütze, attempted to develop Stettin's trade with the Near East but the company lasted only from 1765 to 1769. The number of vessels using the harbour of Stettin rose from 79 in 1751 to 147 in 1786.

[2] E.g. the merchant Velthusen who also established sugar refineries at Stettin and Wismar.

[3] The Overseas Trading Corporation (*Seehandlung*) built a number of vessels at its shipyard in Stettin.

[4] Even after the founding of the Marine Insurance Company in Berlin the merchants of Stettin preferred to insure their ships and cargoes in Amsterdam and Hamburg.

[5] For Stettin at the end of the eighteenth century see J. F. Zöllner, *Reise durch Pommern nach der Insel Rügen* (1797).

of turning Emden into a new Amsterdam[1] and granted the city the status of a free port in 1751. In the same year the Asiatic Company was established to trade with China. Sixteen successful trading voyages to Canton were made and not a ship was lost. The company's activities came to an end during the Seven Years War when Dauvet occupied East Frisia. Attempts to revive the company after the war failed[2] though groups of Emden merchants resumed voyages to the Far East in the 1770's. The Bengal Company of Emden was granted a charter in 1753 but its first two voyages were dogged by misfortune and the venture was wound up. The failure of Emden to develop its trade with India and China was due partly to the inexperience of Prussian entrepreneurs and partly to the opposition of England and other maritime states to those who intruded upon their preserves.[3] The merchants of Emden later established a herring company (1769) which secured a monopoly of the sale of herring in certain provinces of Prussia. The company acquired special ships (called *Buyen*) to make three voyages a year to the fishing grounds in the North Sea. Some 500 sailors were employed in the herring fishery. Hertzberg stated in 1785 that the Herring Company had paid 6 per cent interest on its shares.

After the Seven Years War Frederick vigorously promoted the revival of home and overseas trade and twenty years later Prussia had secured a favourable balance of commodity trade.[4]

[1] On 2 November 1776 William Carmichael informed the American Committee of Secret Correspondence that Frederick the Great was 'a prince who for several years has been dreaming of making his port of Emden an Amsterdam'. (F. Wharton, *The Revolutionary Diplomatic Correspondence of the United States* (6 vols., 1889), Vol. II, p. 185). For the port of Emden see W. Kohte, *Westfalen und der Emsmündung (Gesellschaft für Westfälische Wirtschaftsgeschichte*, No. 7, 1960).

[2] Nothing came of the plan of the Amsterdam banker, de Neufville, to establish a new Asiatic Company at Emden.

[3] For overseas trading companies in the reign of Frederick the Great see H. Berger, *Überseeische Handelsbestrebungen und koloniale Pläne unter Friedrich dem Grossen* (1899); V. Ring, *Asiatische Handelsbeziehungen Friedrichs des Grossen* (1890); R. Koser, 'Der Grosse Kurfürst und Friedrich der Grosse in ihrer Stellung zu Marine und Seehandel' (in the *Marine Rundschau*, 1904, reprinted in *Zur preussischen und deutschen Geschichte* (1921), p. 27 *et seq.*); and Annemarie Müller, 'Emdens Seeschiffahrt und Warenhandel 1744-1899' (*Hansische Geschichtsblätter*, Vol. IV, 1930).

[4] Frederick's estimate (1782) was 4.5 million thalers while Heinitz's estimate was 3.5 million thalers.

The King improved Prussia's banking facilities by setting up the Royal Deposit and Loan Bank of Berlin in 1765.[1] Seven branch offices were established in the provinces. The 400,000 thalers initial capital provided by the King was too small to enable the bank to play a very important part in the economic life of the country but the funds at its disposal were increased when the King required trustees to open accounts with the bank. At first the affairs of the bank were mismanaged but it made satisfactory progress after von Hagen took charge. It did not fulfil the function of a central bank and its activities as a bank of issue were modest in extent since notes to the value of only 800,000 thalers were printed and not all of them were put into circulation. But, as Mirabeau remarked, the bank did good business as a 'maison de commerce' and its profits rose from 22,000 thalers in 1767-8 to 216,000 thalers 1785-6.

Immediately after the first partition of Poland the King set up the Overseas Trading Corporation (*Seehandlung*) at Marienwerder in West Prussia so as to expand Prussia's transit trade with Poland.[2] The corporation had an initial capital of 1·2

[1] For the Royal Bank of Berlin see Marcus Niebuhr, *Geschichte der königlichen Bank in Berlin* . . . (1854); articles in the *Zeitschrift des Vereins für deutsche Statistik*, Vol. I (1847), pp. 71-2; *Statistik des preussischen Staates*, Vol. II (1867), p. 28 *et seq.;* and the *Handwörterbuch der Staatswissenschaften*, Vol. II (edition of 1891), pp. 68-71 and Vol. II (edition of 1899), pp. 189-192 (by W. Lexis); H. von Poschinger, *Bankwesen und Bankpolitik in Preussen* (2 vols., 1878-9); O. Noel, *Les banques d'émission en Europe*, Vol. I (1888), p. 246; and C. A. Conant, *A History of Modern Banks of Issue* (sixth edition, 1927).

[2] For the Overseas Trading Corporation (*Seehandlung*) see Christian von Rother, *Die Verhältnisse des Königlichen Seehandlungs-Institut und dessen Geschäftsführung und industrielle Unternehmungen* (1845); article by R. Koch on the *Seehandlung* in the *Wörterbuch des Deutschen Verwaltungsrechts*, Vol. II (1890), pp. 443-4; article by W. Lexis on the *Seehandlungsgesellschaft* in the *Handwörterbuch der Staatswussenschaft*, Vol. V (1893), pp. 260-2; lecture by Dr Schubert, *Zur Geschichte der Kgl. Preussischen Seehandlung* (Berlin, 1904); articles by Dr Nussbaum on 'Die Preussische Seehandlung' in the *Annalen des Deutschen Reiches*, 1905, Heft i (p. 31) and Heft ii (p. 130); article by Dr Obst on 'Die Kgl. Seehandlung in Vergangenheit und Gegenwart' in the *Zeitschrift für Handelswissenschaft und Handelspraxis*, September 1909, p. 202 *et seq.;* Paul Schrader, *Die Geschichte der Königlichen Seehandlung (Preussische Staatsbank)* . . . (1911); Hermann Schleutker, *Die volkswirtschaftliche Bedeutung der Königlichen Seehandlung von 1772-1820* (University of Tübingen dissertation published at Paderborn, 1920); an account of the Overseas Trading Corporation issued on the occasion of its 150th anniversary. *Die Preussische Staatsbank (Seehandlung) 1772-1922* (1922); Rolf Keller, *Christian von Rother als Präsident der Seehandlung* (Rostock University dissertation, 1930); and

million thalers, the King holding all but 300 of the 2,400 shares. The *Landschaft* of the Mark Brandenburg lent the corporation 500,000 thalers and guaranteed a 10 per cent dividend on its shares. The *Seehandlung* was granted a monopoly of the import of foreign salt and the re-export of Polish timber and wax coming down the River Vistula. A recently established salt corporation was absorbed by the *Seehandlung* in 1775. It was hoped that the *Seehandlung* would foster the export of Silesian linens from Stettin to the Spanish colonies and a director of the corporation was stationed at Cadiz for that purpose.

At first it seemed as if the corporation was going to be a success. In November 1775 Frederick congratulated von Goerne on making a profit of 3,300,000 thalers in the financial year 1774-5. But then events took an unfavourable turn and in 1776 James Harris (Lord Malmesbury) ascribed the King's ill humour to the failure of the corporation 'without a probability of redemption'. Delâtre, the former head of the salt company, had been placed in charge of the *Seehandlung*'s vessels and was responsible for the import of salt and the export of linens. He mismanaged this side of the *Seehandlung*'s affairs and returned to France in disgrace. The corporation survived this crisis and in November 1778 Frederick informed von Görne that he was quite satisfied with the most recent balance submitted to him. Shortly afterwards, however, von Görne began to misappropriate the funds of the *Seehandlung*. About 800,000 thalers were missing when von Görne was found out. He was dismissed in January 1782 and received a life sentence. The King advanced the corporation over a million thalers to save it from bankruptcy. Struensee took charge of the corporation in 1782 and gradually placed it on a sound financial footing. Its early promise as a trading concern was not fulfilled but the corporation carried out satisfactorily various business and financial transactions of a kind hitherto handled by private merchants on the King's behalf. It purchased iron and gunpowder for the royal arsenals, cereals for the King's grain warehouses, bullion for the mint, and tobacco and coffee for the royal tobacco and coffee administrations.

W. O. Henderson, *The State and the Industrial Revolution in Prussia 1740-1870* (1958). pp. 119-147.

When the American War of Independence broke out Frederick hoped that Prussian ports would benefit from Britain's inability to retain control over the trade of her American colonies. The activities of privateers made it difficult for British and French merchantmen to operate on the Atlantic trade route. Prussia was a neutral country and her merchant ships tried to gain a foothold in trades hitherto closed to them. Frederick joined the Armed Neutrality against Britain in May 1781 and placed the Prussian mercantile marine under the protection of the Russian navy. Hertzberg stated that during the war 'le pavillon prussienne a gagné une faveur extraordinaire'. Frederick told the head of the Overseas Trading Corporation that, after the war between Britain and her colonies was over, an attempt should be made to establish a direct trade with American ports. He suggested that linens and woollens should be sent to America in exchange for tobacco, sugar, indigo and rice. When the Americans secured their independence Frederick recognised their government and in 1785 a commercial treaty (on the basis of reciprocity) was signed between Prussia and the United States.[1] But it was the merchants of Hamburg and Bremen rather than those of Emden or Stettin who opened up a direct trade between Germany and the United States in the closing years of the eighteenth century.

(v) *Conclusion*

Frederick's economic policy was criticised in his own day and has been criticised since. Manufacturers complained of unfair competition from State enterprises (such as the Wool Warehouse and the Overseas Trading Corporation) and from a small group of favoured merchants (such as Splitgerber and Gotzkowsky) who secured monopolies, privileges and subsidies. Smallholders and peasants, heavily burdened with feudal obligations, complained that it was the owners of great estates

---

[1] See F. Kapp, *Friedrich der Grosse und die Vereinigten Staaten von Amerika* (1871); G. M. Fisk, *Die handelspolitischen . . . Beziehungen zwischen Deutschland und den Vereinigten Staaten* (1897); P. L. Haworth, 'Frederick the Great and the American Revolution' (*American Historical Review* IX, 1903-4); and H.. M. Adams, *Die Beziehungen zwischen Preussen und den Vereinigten Staaten 1775-1870* (1960).

who secured most of the grants paid by the King to foster agricultural expansion. Consumers complained of the rising cost of living—particularly the high prices charged for salt, sugar, coffee, tobacco and beer—which was brought about by state monopolies, private monopolies and high excise rates. Frederick's projects for land reclamation, canal building, the construction of harbours and internal colonisation were resented because of the hardships inflicted upon people whose way of life was ruthlessly upset by these schemes. The depreciation of the coinage during the Seven Years War led to inflation and the consequent rise in prices and in rents caused much distress. Frederick's policy of accumulating a treasure was criticised since the money saved was withdrawn from circulation. The rigorous methods of collecting the excise employed by the *Regie* was bitterly resented.

James Harris (Lord Malmesbury) declared that the King of Prussia could never understand that 'a large treasure lying dormant in his coffers impoverishes his kingdom; that riches increase by circulation; that trade cannot subsist without reciprocal profit; that monopolies and exclusive grants put a stop to emulation, and of course to industry; and, in short, that the real wealth of a sovereign consists in the ease and affluence of his subjects'.[1] Lord Dalrymple, the British Minister in Berlin, declared in 1786 that Frederick's system of Protection was 'too complicated and confused to admit of a clear and satisfactory explanation'.[2] Responsible Prussian officials were well aware of the drawbacks of some aspects of Frederick's version of 'mercantilism'. This may be seen from the report by Ursinus on the inefficiency of the Berlin silk industry—an artificial creation of the king's—and from the report by Heinitz on the policy of de Launay's *Regie*.

In spite of all that can be said in condemnation of Frederick's policy the fact remains that his successes at home were as striking as his military and diplomatic achievements. He greatly strengthened the Prussian economy by adding valuable new territories to his dominions; by bringing new farmers and

---

[1] Lord Malmesbury (ed.). *Diaries and Correspondence of James Harris, first Earl of Malmesbury*, Vol. I (1845), p. 123.

[2] Quoted by J. Ehrman, *The British Government and Commercial Negotiations with Europe 1783-1793* (1962), p. 114 (n).

skilled artisans to Prussia; by raising the standard of agriculture; by expanding existing industries and by founding new ones; by encouraging overseas commerce; and by setting up such institutions as the Royal Bank of Berlin and the *Seehandlung*. The great expansion in output and the existence of a favourable balance of commodity trade were achievements of no mean order. But Frederick could not make omelettes without breaking eggs and the Prussians discovered—as the Russians were to find out in the 1930's—that a price had to be paid for rapid economic progress.

Certain aspects of Frederick's policy may be noted in conclusion. There can be no doubt as to what the King was trying to do. His economic policy was clearly outlined in his memoirs, in his private correspondence, and in his letters to ministers and officials. He not merely laid down the principles of his policy but he took an active part in the detailed work of carrying out his plans. The great public works; the settling of colonists; the improvements in farming; the promotion of new industries; the establishment of the Bank of Berlin, the *Seehandlung*, and the land mortgage banks; the introduction of the *Regie*; and many other economic activities received Frederick's personal attention. No contemporary monarch worked so hard to keep in constant touch with his subordinates not only by correspondence but by regularly visiting the provinces.

Frederick was an autocrat whose authority was not restricted by any cabinet, parliament or provincial assemblies so that Prussia's economic policy reflected his personal views. There were however some limits to his powers. He gave Brenkenhof the clearest instructions to abolish serfdom in Pomerania but his orders were not carried out owing to the opposition of the nobles. He told de Launay that customs and excise duties should be levied so that the rich paid more than the poor. In fact indirect taxes bore more heavily upon the peasants and artisans than upon the nobles. And the execution of some of Frederick's schemes was delayed because of the difficulty of finding competent officials to carry them out. The Mining Office, the Bank of Berlin, and the *Seehandlung* had to wait for some time before the King secured the services of men capable of running them satisfactorily.

There was virtually nothing original in Frederick's economic policy. He accepted principles which had been laid down by Colbert and were widely practised in Europe in his day. As Macaulay observed 'he had on his side illustrious examples and popular prejudice. Grievously as he erred, he erred in company with his age.' The pursuit of self-sufficiency; the attempt to produce at home as much food and as many manufactured articles as possible; the encouragement of mining, armaments and luxury industries; the financial assistance given to land-owners and entrepreneurs; the drive to secure a favourable balance of commodity trade; the attempts to promote direct commercial contacts with the Americas, India, China and the Levant; the efforts to attract skilled artisans and farmers; and the founding of privileged monopoly companies were all aspects of a policy that had been practised before Frederick's day. Some of Frederick's achievements, that attracted considerable attention, were traditional aspects of the economic policy of the Hohenzollerns. When he established colonies of Protestant refugees, maintained a network of grain warehouses, and amassed a fund of silver for his war chest Frederick was follow-ing the example of his predecessors.

Roscher has observed that Frederick's ideas on economic affairs not only lacked originality but changed very little during his long reign. 'The creative genius that made Frederick out-standing as a military leader, a diplomat, and a legal reformer was lacking in his handling of economic problems.'[1] In many respects he was an enlightened ruler. He abolished torture and refused to allow his subjects to engage in the slave trade. He gave a home to religious refugees whether they were Protestants or Jesuits. His treatment of the Catholics in Silesia compared very favourably with the way in which the English government treated the Catholics in Ireland. On the royal domains he effectively supervised his tenants and made hereditary the former precarious tenure of his serfs. His judicial and admini-stative reforms were in advance of his age. But he rejected the new principles of economics that were being advocated by the Physiocrats, by Adam Smith, and by J. G. Büsch. The lessons on economics that he had learned as Crown Prince from his

[1] Wilhelm Roscher, *Geschichte der National-Oekonomik* (1874), p. 412.

tutor Hille guided him throughout his life and much of his work was a continuation of that of his father. Mirabeau was one of Frederick's admirers but he regarded the King's economic policy as entirely misconceived.

What was new in Frederick's policy was the vigour and the speed with which he carried out his plans. His predecessors had attracted foreign artisans and peasants to Prussia. But Frederick pursued the policy of internal colonisation on a scale never before attempted. About 1,200 new villages and hamlets were founded and over 300,000 immigrants were settled in his dominions. And it was largely due to Frederick's vigorous policy of reconstruction that Prussia recovered from the Seven Years War far more quickly than Brandenburg had recovered from the Thirty Years War. Another special feature of the Prussian economy in Frederick's day was the unusual role of the armed forces.[1] The army was a large one in relation to the size of the country and a substantial—though a declining—part of the national revenue was devoted to its maintenance. Orders from the military authorities stimulated the expansion of the output of iron products, armaments, woollen cloth and grain. The erection of fortifications and barracks gave employment to the building industry. In peacetime the soldiers were engaged in exercises and manoeuvres for only a few months in the summer. During the rest of the year they—and sometimes also their wives—worked on the land or at a domestic craft. The army was integrated into the national economy as far as possible and some of the King's military expenditure found its way back into the civilian economy.

It may be added that Frederick's efforts to promote the development of manufactures did not affect all his provinces to the same extent. Brandenburg,[2] Silesia, Magdeburg and the County

---

[1] August Skalweit, 'Die Eingliederung des friderizianischen Heeres in den Volks- und Wirtschaftskörper' (*Jahrbücher für Nationalökonomie und Statistik*, Vol. CLX, 1944, pp. 194-220) and A. Zottmann, *Die Wirtschaftspolitik Friedrichs des Grossen mit besonderer Berücksichtigung der Kriegswirtschaft* (1937).

[2] By the end of the eighteenth century about one third of Prussia's manufacturing establishments were situated in Berlin and its vicinity. For the industrial development of two towns in the Mark Brandenburg in Frederick the Great's reign see H. J. Kram , 'Potsdam, eine historisch-geographische Skizze' (*Wissenschaftliche Zeitschrift der Pädagogischen Hochschule Potsdam*, Vol. II, 1955-6, pp. 27-57) and Brigitta Zuckermann, 'Die

of Mark could be described as 'industrialised' by eighteenth century standards. East and West Prussia, however, remained almost entirely agrarian in character. Frederick's attempts to expand industrial production occurred in an age of small workshops and hand-machines. The *manufacture réunie*[1] was exceptional. It was only in the last year of Frederick's reign that Prussia had its first steam-engine in the County of Mansfeld. The King did try to gain some information about the advances on technical knowledge that were being made in England at this time but it was left to Frederick's successors to promote the development of large factories and power-driven machinery. There was no uniformity in the structure of Prussia's industries or the way in which they grew in the second half of the eighteenth century. The textile and mining industries of Silesia were examples of 'feudal capitalism'—industries which were developed by the initiative of great landowners and the labour of serfs. The Berlin silk and porcelain industries were 'artificial' branches of manufacture which might never have existed had the King not decided to establish them. The Ruhr and Sauerland coal and metal industries were in the hands of small entrepreneurs whose activities were fostered and controlled by royal officials. The manufacture of silks in Crefeld was a 'laissez faire' industry which expanded because of the hard work and skill of the von der Leyen family and owed little or nothing to the State. Frederick the Great tried to plan the industrial growth of his dominions but economic, geographical and social factors sometimes produced changes over which he could exercise little control.

The unpopularity of certain aspects of Frederick's economic

ökonomisch-geographische Entwicklung der Stadt Eberswalde' (*ibid.*, Vol. III, 1956-7, pp. 77-102).

[1] A *manufacture réunie* was a large "manufactory" in which craftsmen—who may formerly have had their own small domestic workshops—were collected together in a single building or in a group of buildings. The tools and machines used in this early type of factory were usually manually operated though waterpower was sometimes used. The introduction of machines driven by steampower turned the *manufacture réunie* into the modern factory. In England the works established in the seventeenth century by Ambrose Crowley at Swalwell and Winlaton to produce iron smallwares were a typical *manufacture réunie*. There is no generally accepted term in English for a *manufacture réunie*. It would be convenient to make use of the word "manufactory" for this purpose.

policy caused his successor to make some important changes. Shortly after Frederick's death Hertzberg declared that Frederick William II would 'remove all those tyrannical restrictions on the commerce of foreign nations imposed during the late reign' and a commission was established to revise the system of taxation. De Launay was dismissed and the *Regie* was abolished. An end was made to the tobacco and coffee monopolies. But there was little change in the basic principles of Frederick's policy. His ideas and many of the institutions that he had established survived to play their part in fostering the industrial development of Prussia in the nineteenth century.

LIST OF MAPS

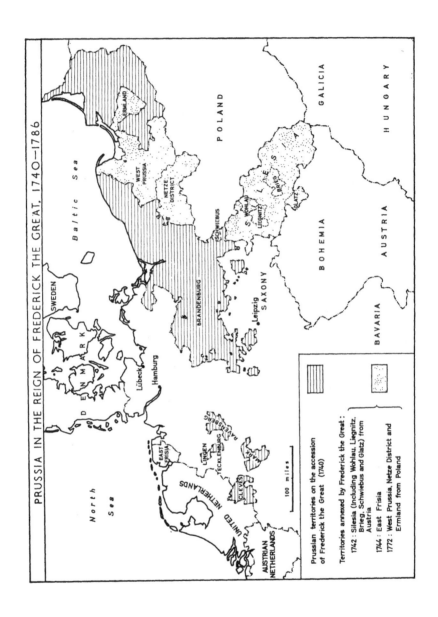

PRUSSIA IN THE REIGN OF FREDERICK THE GREAT, 1740—1786

Prussian territories on the accession
of Frederick the Great (1740)

Territories annexed by Frederick the Great :

1742 : Silesia (including Wohlau, Liegnitz,
Brieg, Schwiebus and Glatz) from
Austria

1744 : East Frisia

1772 : West Prussia, Netze District and
Ermland from Poland

100 miles

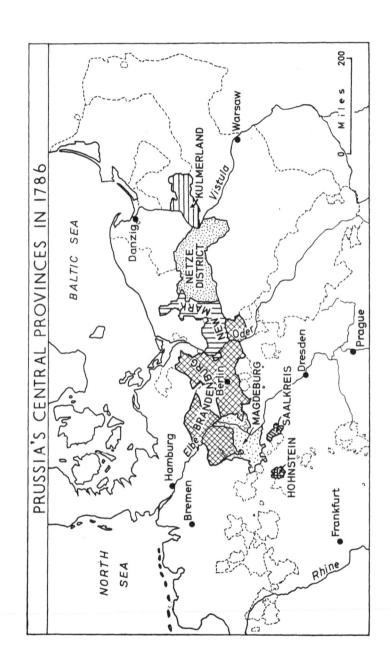

PRUSSIA'S CENTRAL PROVINCES IN 1786

NORTH SEA

BALTIC SEA

KULMERLAND

Vistula

Warsaw

Danzig

NETZE DISTRICT

NEW MARK

Oder

Hamburg

Bremen

Elbe

BRANDENBURG

Berlin

MAGDEBURG

SAALKREIS

HOHNSTEIN

Dresden

Prague

Frankfurt

Rhine

0   Miles   200

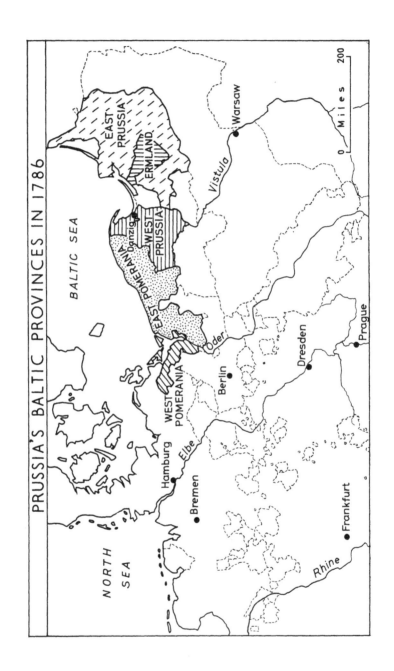

PRUSSIA'S BALTIC PROVINCES IN 1786

NORTH SEA

BALTIC SEA

EAST PRUSSIA

ERMLAND

WEST PRUSSIA

Danzig

EAST POMERANIA

Oder

WEST POMERANIA

Vistula

Warsaw

Berlin

Dresden

Prague

Hamburg

Elbe

Bremen

Frankfurt

Rhine

0   200

M i l e s

170

SILESIA

0 Miles 50

Approximate
extent of coalfield

Schwiebus

Oder

Neisse

Posen

Grünberg

Sagan

SAXONY

Glogau

KINGDOM   OF

POLAND

Steinau

Liegnitz

Wohlau

SILESIA

Lissa

Hohen
friedeberg

Striegau

Breslau

Iser

Bunzelwitz

Schweidnitz

Landeshut

Burkersdorf

Mollwitz

Reichenbach

Brieg

Strehlen

prosna

Warta

Glatz

Neisse

Oppeln

KINGDOM

Elbe

OF

Klein
Schnellendorf

Oder

AUSTRIAN

Kosel

Tarnowitz

Beuthen

NEW

BOHEMIA

SILESIA

Königshütte

Jägerndorf

Ratibor

GALICIA

Troppau

SILESIA

Pless

Vistula

MORAVIA

Teschen

KINGDOM
OF
HUNGARY

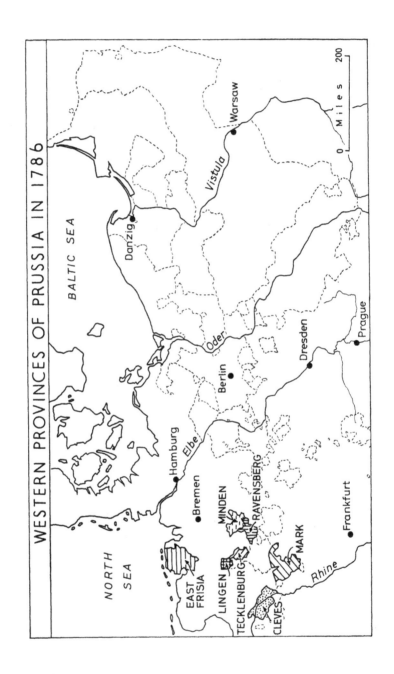

WESTERN PROVINCES OF PRUSSIA IN 1786

BALTIC SEA

NORTH
SEA

Hamburg
Bremen
EAST
FRISIA
LINGEN
TECKLENBURG
CLEVES
MINDEN
RAVENSBERG
MARK
Frankfurt
Rhine

Berlin
Elbe
Oder
Dresden
Prague
Danzig
Vistula
Warsaw

0   Miles   200

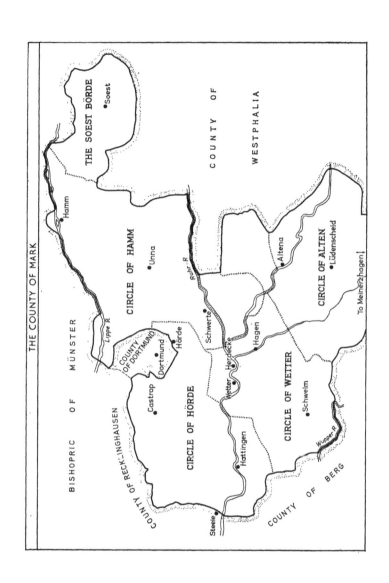

THE COUNTY OF MARK

THE SOEST BÖRDE

• Soest

BISHOPRIC OF MÜNSTER

COUNTY OF RECKLINGHAUSEN

• Hamm

Lippe R.

CIRCLE OF HAMM

• Unna

COUNTY OF WESTPHALIA

Ruhr R.

• Altena

CIRCLE OF ALTEN

• Lüdenscheid

To Meinerzhagen

• Castrop

COUNTY OF DORTMUND

• Dortmund

• Hörde

CIRCLE OF HÖRDE

• Schwerte

Wetter Herdecke

• Hagen

• Hattingen

CIRCLE OF WETTER

• Schwelm

Wupper R.

COUNTY OF BERG

• Steele

173

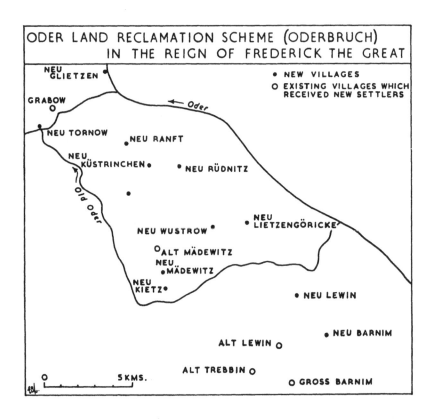

ODER LAND RECLAMATION SCHEME (ODERBRUCH)
IN THE REIGN OF FREDERICK THE GREAT

• NEW VILLAGES
O EXISTING VILLAGES WHICH
  RECEIVED NEW SETTLERS

NEU GLIETZEN

GRABOW

Oder

NEU TORNOW

NEU RANFT

NEU KÜSTRINCHEN

NEU RÜDNITZ

Old Oder

NEU WUSTROW

NEU LIETZENGÖRICKE

ALT MÄDEWITZ
NEU MÄDEWITZ

NEU KIETZ

NEU LEWIN

NEU BARNIM

ALT LEWIN

ALT TREBBIN

GROSS BARNIM

5 KMS.

ODER, WARTHE & NETZE RECLAMATION SCHEMES
IN THE REIGN OF FREDERICK THE GREAT.

NETZE DISTRICT
(To PRUSSIA 1772)

NEW MARK

BRANDENBURG

R. Vistula

BROMBERG
B.
N
NETZEBRUCH
R. Netze
R. Drage
DRIESEN
LANDSBERG NETZE BRUCH
R. Warthe
R. Warthe
WARTBRUCH
New Oder
ODERBRUCH
Old Oder
KÜSTRIN
R. Oder
FRANKFURT AN DER ODER
EBERSWALDE
Finow R. (canal)
WRIEZEN
BERLIN

N = NAKEL

B = R. Brahe

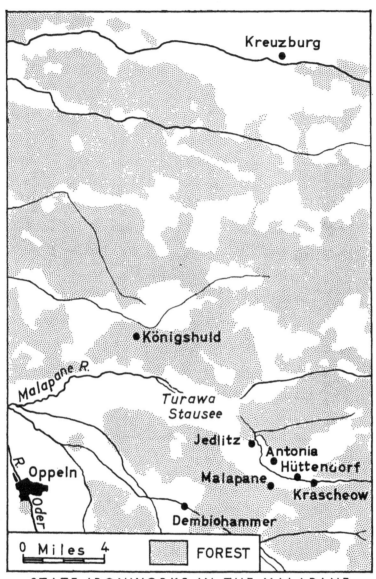

STATE IRONWORKS IN THE MALAPANE
REGION IN THE REIGN OF FREDERICK
THE GREAT

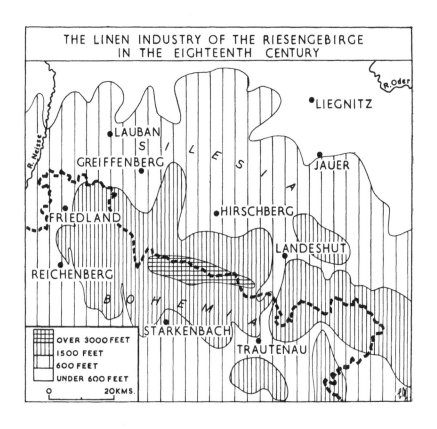

THE LINEN INDUSTRY OF THE RIESENGEBIRGE
IN THE EIGHTEENTH CENTURY

R. Oder

•LIEGNITZ

R. Neisse

•LAUBAN

S   I   L   E   S   I   A

GREIFFENBERG

JAUER

•HIRSCHBERG

FRIEDLAND

LANDESHUT

REICHENBERG

B   O   H   E   M   I   A

STARKENBACH

TRAUTENAU

OVER 3000 FEET
1500 FEET
600 FEET
UNDER 600 FEET

0   20 KMS.

177

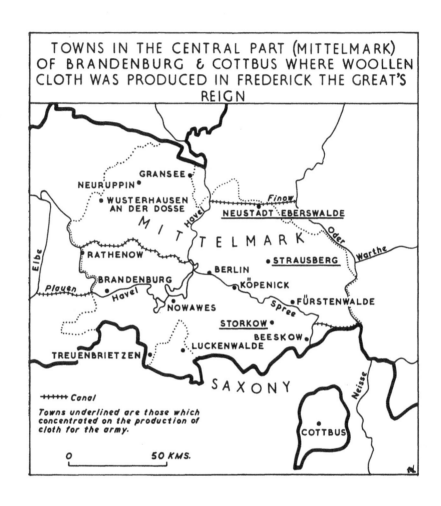

TOWNS IN THE CENTRAL PART (MITTELMARK)
OF BRANDENBURG & COTTBUS WHERE WOOLLEN
CLOTH WAS PRODUCED IN FREDERICK THE GREAT'S
REIGN

GRANSEE
NEURUPPIN
WUSTERHAUSEN
AN DER DOSSE
Finow
NEUSTADT EBERSWALDE
MITTELMARK
Havel
Oder
Warthe
RATHENOW
STRAUSBERG
Elbe
BERLIN
BRANDENBURG
KÖPENICK
Plauen
Havel
Spree
FÜRSTENWALDE
NOWAWES
STORKOW
BEESKOW
LUCKENWALDE
TREUENBRIETZEN
SAXONY
Neisse
+++++ Canal

*Towns underlined are those which
concentrated on the production of
cloth for the army.*

O   50 KMS.

COTTBUS

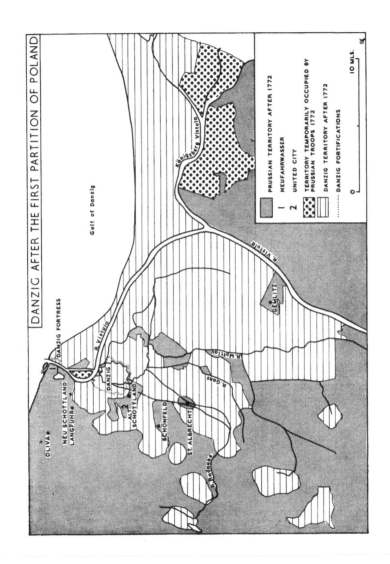

DANZIG AFTER THE FIRST PARTITION OF POLAND

Gulf of Danzig

OLIVA•
NEU SCHOTTLAND
LANGFUHR•
•DANZIG FORTRESS
DANZIG
ALT SCHOTTLAND
SCHÖNFELD
ST. ALBRECHT
GEMLITZ

R. Vistula
Königsberg Vistula
R. Vistula
R. Mottlau
R. Gans
R. Radaune

PRUSSIAN TERRITORY AFTER 1772
NEUFAHRWASSER 1
UNITED CITY 2
TERRITORY TEMPORARILY OCCUPIED BY PRUSSIAN TROOPS 1772
DANZIG TERRITORY AFTER 1772
DANZIG FORTIFICATIONS

0   10 MLS.

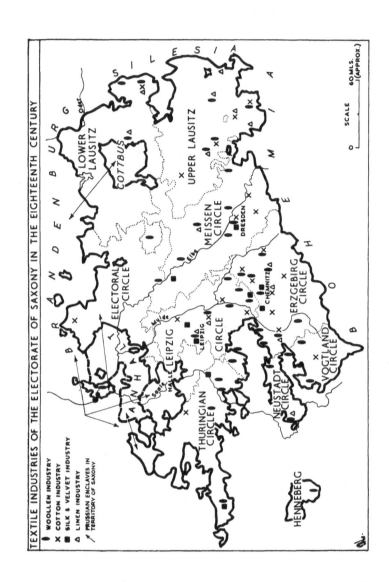

TEXTILE INDUSTRIES OF THE ELECTORATE OF SAXONY IN THE EIGHTEENTH CENTURY

WOOLLEN INDUSTRY
X COTTON INDUSTRY
■ SILK & VELVET INDUSTRY
△ LINEN INDUSTRY
PRUSSIAN ENCLAVES IN TERRITORY OF SAXONY

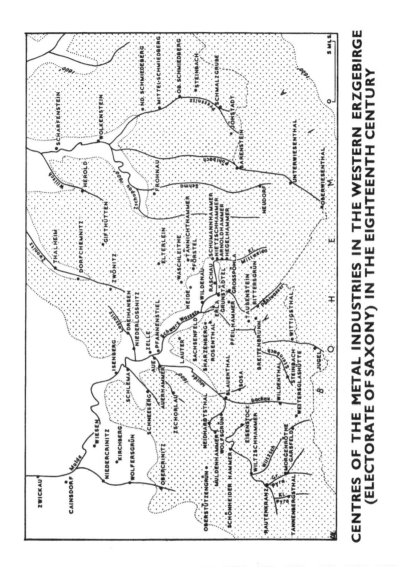

CENTRES OF THE METAL INDUSTRIES IN THE WESTERN ERZGEBIRGE (ELECTORATE OF SAXONY) IN THE EIGHTEENTH CENTURY

POLAND BEFORE THE FIRST PARTITION IN 1772

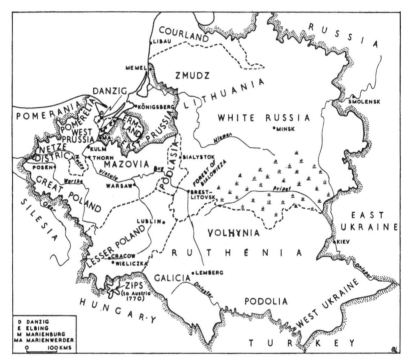

SELECT BIBLIOGRAPHY

A

Askenazy, S. *Danzig and Poland* (1921).

B

Bamberger, L. 'Beiträge zur Geschichte der Luckenwalder Textilindustrie' (*Forschungen zur Brandenburgischen und Preussischen Geschichte*, Vol. XXIX, 1916).

Bär, M. 'Beiträge zur Geschichte der Erwerbung Danzigs' (*Mitteilungen des Westpreussischen Geschichtsvereins*, Vol. X).

Beck, L. *Die Geschichte des Eisens* (5 vols., 1884-1904), Vol. III (1897).

Beheim-Schwarzbach, M. *Hohenzollersche Colonisation* (1874).

Behre, O. *Geschichte der Statistik im Brandenburg-Preussen Staate bis zur Gründung des Königlich Statistischen Bureaus* (1905).

Bensch, A. D. *Die Entwicklung der Berliner Porzellanindustrie unter Friedrich dem Grossen* (1928).

Berger, H. *Überseeische Handelsbestrebungen und koloniale Pläne unter Friedrich dem Grossen* (1899).

Berney, A. 'Die Anfänge der friderizianischen Seehandelspolitik' (*Vierteljahrschrift für Sozial-und Wirtschaftsgeschichte*, Vol. XXII, 1929, pp. 16-31).

Beutin, Ludwig. 'Die Wirkungen des Siebenjährigen Krieges auf die Volkwirtschaft in Preussen' (*Vierteljahrschrift für Sozial-und Wirtschaftsgeschichte*, Vol. XXII, 1929, pp. 16-31).

Bülow-Cummerow. *Über Preussens landwirtschaftliche Creditvereine* . . . (1843).

Büch, J. G. *Versuch einer Geschichte der Hamburgischen Handlung* (1797). Reprinted in *Sämmtliche Schriften*, Vol. XII (1816).

Buss, G. *Geschichte der Berliner Börse von 1689-1913* (1913).

C

Cauer, E. 'Zur Geschichte der Breslauer Messe . . .' (*Zeitschrift des Vereins für Geschichte und Altertum Schlesiens*, Vol. V, 1863, pp. 63-69 and 222-250).

Cavaignac, G. 'L'état social en Prusse jusqu'à l'avénement de Frédéric-Guillaume III . . .' (*Revue Historique*, Vol. XLII, 1890).

Charpentier. 'Das alt-preussische Tabaksmonopol' (*Preussische Jahrbücher*, LXI, 1888, pp. 145-163).

Cohn, T. 'Der Zwangsverkauf von Porzellan an der jüdischen Gemeinde zu Potsdam unter Friedrich dem Grossen' (*Mitteilungen des Vereins für die Geschichte Potsdams*, 1878, p. 317 *et seq.*)

Conrad, J. 'Der Konsum an notwendigen Nahrungsmitteln in Berlin vor 100 Jahren und in der Gegenwert' (*Jahrbücher für Nationalökonomie und Statistik*, New Series, Vol. III, 1881, pp. 509-524).

Coxe, W. *Travels in Poland, Russia, Sweden and Denmark* (3 vols., 1784-90).

Croon, G. 'Zunftzwang und Industrie im Kreise Reichenbach' (*Zeitschrift des Vereins für Geschichte und Alterum Schlesiens*, Vol. XCIII, 1909, p. 98 *et seq.*).

D

Dabinius, G. *Die ländliche Bevölkerung Pomerellens im Jahre 1772* . . . (Marburg, 1953).

Damus, R. 'Die Stadt Danzig gegenüber der Politik Friedrichs des Grossen und Friedrich Wilhelm II' (*Zeitschrift des Westpreussischen Geschichtsvereins*, Vol. XX, 1887, pp. 1-213).

Dorn, W. L. 'The Prussian Bureaucracy in the Eighteenth Century' (*Political Science Quarterly*, Vol. 46 (1931), pp. 403-23 and Vol. 47 (1932), pp. 75-94 and pp. 259-273).

Dorwart, R. A. *The Administrative Reforms of Frederick William I of Prussia* (*1953*).

E

Eichborn, K. F. von. *Das Soll und Haben von Eichborn und Co., in zwei Jahrhunderten* (second edn., 1928).

Eversmann, F. A. H. *Die Eisen und Stahlerzeugung auf Wasserwerken zwischen Lahn und Lippe* (1804).

F

Faden, E. 'Das friderizianische Berlin . . .' (in Crendt, Faden and Gandert, *Geschichte der Stadt Berlin* (1937), pp. 230-80).

Fechner, H. *Wirtschaftsgeschichte der Preussischen Provinz Schlesien in der Zeit ihrer provinziellen Selbständigheit, 1741-1806* (1908.)
'Der Zustand des schlesischen Handels vor der Besitzgreifung des Landes durch Friedrich den Grossen' (*Jahrbücher für Nationalökonomie und Statistik*, New Series, Vol. X, 1885, pp. 209-236).
Die handelspolitischen Beziehungen Preussens zu Östereich während der provinziellen Selbststandigkeit Schlesiens 1741-1806 (1886).
'Die Königlischen Eisenwerke Malapane und Kreuzburger-hütte . . . 1753-1780' (*Zeitschrift für Berg- Hütten- und Salinenwesen im Preussischen Staate*, XLIII, 1795, p. 75 *et seq.*).
'Geschichte des schlesischen Berg- und Hüttenwesens 1741-1806' (*Zeitschrift fur Berg- Hütten- und Salinenwesen im Preussischen Staate*, Vol. XCVIII (1900)), Vol. XLIX (1901) and Vol. L. (1902)).
Feig, J. 'Die Begründung der Luckenwalder Wollindustrie durch Preussens Könige im 18en Jahrhundert' (*Forschungen zur Brandenburgischen und Preussischen Geschichte*, Vol. X, 1898, p. 79 *et seq.*).
Felsch, G. *Die Wirtschaftspolitik des preussischen Staates bei der Gründung der Oberschlesischen Kohlen- und Eisenindustrie, 1741-1871* (1919).
Ford, G. S. *On and Off the Campus* (1938). See p. 183 *et seq.* for Matthew Boulton, *Statement of Facts*, 1787.
Frederick II. *Oeuvres historiques de Frédéric II, Roi de Prusse* (two parts, 1847).
Die Briefe Friedrichs des Grossen an seinen vormaligen Kammerdiener Fredersdorf (edited by J. Richter, 1926).
Politische Korrespondenz Friedrichs des Grossen (1879-1912).
Die politischen Testamente Friedrichs des Grossen (edited by G. B. Volz: supplementary volume to *Politische Korrespondenz*, 1920).
Freymark, H. *Zur Preussischen Handels- und Zollpolitik vom 1648-1818* (dissertation: Halle an der Saale, 1897).
Furger, F. *Zum Verlagssystem als Organisationsform des Frühkapitalismus im Textilgewerbe* (1927).

G

Garnier, Jean-Paul. *La Tragédie de Danzig* (1935).

Gebhard, G. *Die Berliner Börse von den Anfängen bis zum Jahre 1896* (1928).

Geiger, L. *Geschichte der Juden in Berlin* (2 vols., 1871).

Geissler, O. *Die Wirtschaftspolitik Friedrichs des Grossen und der Begriff der Planwirtschaft* (dissertation: Tübingen, 1951).

Glager, B. *Der Potsdamer Steuerat* (dissertation, Berlin 1956).

Goldschmidt, F. and P. *Leben des Staatsrates Kunth* (1881).

Gossler, W. von. '60 Jahre Magdeburger Manufaktur' (*Geschichtsblätter für Stadt und Land Magdeburg*, Jahrgang 72-73 (1937-8), p. 13, *et seq.*).

Gothsche, H. *Die Königlichen Gewehrfabriken* (1904).

Gotzkowsky, J. E. *Geschichte eines patriotischen Kaufmanns* (1768: new edition (ed. by O. Hintze), 1873).

Grünhagen, C. *Schlesien unter Friedrich dem Grossen* (2 vols., 1889-92). 'Die Breslauer Kaufmannschaft im Kampf gegen das Mercantilsystem' (*Zeitschrift des Vereins für Geschichte und Altertum Schlesiens*, XXIX, 1895, p. 113 *et seq.*).

Guibert, J. A. H. *Journal d'un voyage en Allemagne fait en 1793* (2 vols., 1803).

H

Harkort, F. *Ältere Geschichte des Steinkohlenberbaues und der Eisen- und Stahlerzeugung in der Graftschaft Mark* (1855).

Hartung, F. 'Die Epochen der absoluten Monarchie in der neueren Geschichte' (*Historische Zeitschrift*, Vol. CXLV, 1931-32, pp. 46-52).
Der preussische Staat und seine westfälischen Provinzen (*Westfälische Forschungen*, Vol. VII, 1954).
Enlightened Despotism (Historical Association, 1957).

Hassenstein, W. *Zur Geschichte der Königl. Gewehrfabrik in Spandau unter besonderer Berücksichtigung des 18en Jahrhunderts* (*Beiträge zur Geschichte der Technik und Industrie*, Vol. IV, 1912).

Haussherr, Hans. *Verwaltungseinheit und Ressorttrennung vom Ende des 17en bis zum Beginn des 19en Jahrhunderts* (1953).

Heinicke, E. *Die wirtschaftliche Entwicklung der Stadt Halle unter brandenburg-preussischer Wirtschaftspolitik von 1680-1806* (dissertation, Halle an der Saale, 1929).

Heinitz, F. A. *Mémoire sur les produits du régne minéral de la monarchie prussienne* (1786).

Hertzberg, E. F. von. *Huit dissertations . . . lues dans les Assemblées publiques de l'Academie Royale des Sciences et Belles-Lettres de Berlin . . . 1780-7* (Berlin, 1787).

Herzfeld, Margot. 'Der polnische Handelsvertrag von 1775' (*Forschungen zur Brandenburgischen und Preussischen Geschichte*, Vol. XXXII, 1920, p. 57 *et seq.* Vol. XXXV, 1923, p. 45 *et seq.*; Vol. XXXVI, 1924, p. 210 *et seq.*).

Hinrichs, C. 'Das Königliche Lagerhaus in Berlin' (*Forschungen zur Brandenburgischen und Preussischen Geschichte*, Vol. XLIV, 1932, pp. 46-69).

Hintze, Otto. 'Zur Agrarpolitik Friedrichs des Grossen' (*Forschungen zur Brandenburgischen und Preussischen Geschichte*, Vol. X, 1898).

'Friedrich der Grosse nach dem Siebenjährigen Kriege und das Politische Testament von 1768' (*Forschungen zur Brandenburgischen und Preussischen Geschichte*, Vol. XXXII, 1920, pp. 1-50).

'Ein Berliner Kaufmann aus der Zeit Friedrichs des Grossen' *Schriften des Vereins fur die Geschichte Berlins*, Heft XXX, 1893, pp. 1-18.

'Die Industrialisierungspolitik Friedrichs des Grossen' (in *Historische und Politische Aufsätze*, Vol. II, p. 131 *et seq.*).

'Eine Denkschrift über Berliner Manufakturverhältnisse aus dem Jahr 1801' (*Schriften des Vereins für die Geschichte fur die Geschichte Berlin*, Vol. XXXI, 1894, p. 101 *et seq.*).

'Zwei Denkschriften aus dem Jahre 1800 über die preussische Seidenindustrie' (*Forschungen zur Brandenburgischen und Preussischen Geschichte*, VII, 1895, p. 103 *et seq.*).

Hinze, K. *Die Arbeiterfrage zur Berlin zu Beginn der modernen Kapitalismus in Brandenburg-Preussen* (1927).

Hoff, W. *Die Glashütten in der Neumark* (dissertation, Berlin 1940).

Hoffmann, Hildegard. *Die gewerbliche Production Preussens im Jahre 1769* . . . (dissertation, 1956; typescript in the Humbolt University Library, Berlin). (Based on statistics collected by Freiherr von Knyphausen).

Hofmann, F. H. *Das Porzellan der europäischen Manufakturen in achtzehnten Jahrhundert* (1932).

J

Jars, Gabriel. *Voyages métallurgiques* (3 vols., 1774-81).

K

Kalisch J. and Gienowski J. *Um die Polnische Krone* (1962).

Kapp, F. *Friedrich der Grosse und die Vereinigten Staaten von Amerika* (1871).

Kisch, Herbert. 'The Textile Industries in Silesia and the Rhineland . . .' (*Journal of Economic History*, December 1959).

Kliche, W. *Die Schiffahrt auf der Ruhr und Lippe im achtzehnten Jahrhundert* (1904).

Klingenborg, Melle. 'Das Berliner Mietsedikt vom 19 April 1765' (*Forschungen zur Brandenburgischen und Preussischen Geschichte*, Vol. XXVI, 1915, pp. 179-189.

Koch, Hugo. *Denkschrift zur Feier des hundertjährigen Bestehens des Königlichen Blei- und Silbererzbergwerkes Friederichsgrube . . .* (1884).

Kohlschütter. 'Über landesschaftliche Kreditsysteme' (*Archiv der politischen Okonomie*, New Series, Vol. I, 1843).

Kolb, G. *Geschichte der königlichen Porzellanmanufaktur zu Berlin* (1863).

König, A. B. *Versuch einer historieschen Schilderung der Hauptveränderungen der Religion, Sitten, Gewohnbeiten, Künste, und Wissenschaften der Residenzstadt Berlin seit den ältesten Zeiten bis 1786* (5 vols., 1793-8).

Koser, R. 'Der preussische Staatsschatz von 1740-56' (*Forschungen zur Brandenburgischen und Preussischen Geschichte*, Vol. IV, pp. 529-181).

'Die preussischen Finanzen im Siebenjährigen Kriege'. (*Forschungen zur Brandenburgischen und Preussischen Geschichte*, Vol. XVI, 1903. pp. 445-476.)

'Die Epochen der absoluten Monarchie in der neueren Geschichte' (*Historische Zeitschrift*, Vol. LXI, 1889 pp. 246-287).

Geschichte Friedrichs des Grossen (4 vols., edn. of 1921-5; abridged edn. in one volume, 1925).

Kramm, H. K. 'Der Preussische Absolutismus und seine Bedeutung für die ökonomisch- und siedlungs-geographischen Verhältnisse im Gebiet des heutigen Bezirkes Frankfurt an der Oder'. (*Wissenschaftliche Zeitschrift der Pädagogischen Hochschule Potsdam*, V, 1959-60, pp. 33-42).

Krug, L. *Topographisch-statistisches-geographisches Wörterbuch der sämmtlichen preussischen Staaten* (13 parts, 1796-1803).

Kublick, H. *Die Siedlungspolitik Friedrichs des Grossen im Kreise Cottbus* (1924).

Kunzel, G. *Die politischen Testamente der Hohenzollern* (2 vols., second edn., 1919-20).

Kurschat, W. *Das Haus Friedrich und Heinrich von der Leyen in Krefeld* (1933).

L

Lamprecht, G. R. von. *Von der Kameralverfassung und Verwaltung der Handwerke, Fabriken und Manufakturen in den preussischen Staaten . . .* (1933).

Lehmann, R. *Die Verhältnisse der niederlansitzischen Herrschafts- und Gutsbauern in der Zeit vom 30-jährigen Kriege bis zu dem preussischen Reformen* (Vol VI of *Mitteldentshse Forschungen* (1956)).

Lehndorff, E. A. H. von. *Dreissig Jahre am Hofe Friedrichs des Grossen . . .* (ed. by K. E. Schmidt-Lötzen, 1907: supplementary volume appeared in 1910).

Lenz and Unholtz. *Die Geschichte des Bankhauses Gebrüder Schickler* (1912).

Leonhardi, F. G. *Erdbeschreibung der Preussischen Monarchie* (3 vol. in four parts, 1791-4).

M

Malmesbury, Lord (ed.). *Diaries and Correspondence of James Harris, First Earl of Malmesbury*, Vol. I (1945).

Matschoss, Conrad. *Friedrich der Grosse als Beförderer des Gewerbefleisses* (1912).

Mauer, Hermann. *Die private Kapitalanlage in Preussen während des 18en Jahrhunderts* (1921).
Das landschaftliche Kreditwesens Preussens . . . (1907).

Mehring, Franz. *Historische Aufsätze zur Preussische-Deutschen Geschichte* (1952).
Deutsche Geschichte vom Ausgang des Mittelalters (1952).

Meissner, A. G. *Leben Franz Balthasar Schönberg von Brenkenhof* (1782).

Meyer, M. *Geschichte der preussischen Handwerkerpolitik* (2 vols., 1888).

Mirabeau, H. G. R. Comte de. *De la monarchie prussienne sous Frédéric le Grand* (4 vols., 1783). German edition: Jakob von Mauvillon, *Schilderung der preussischen Monarchie nach Mirabeau bearbeitet* (4 vols., 1793-5).

Moeglin, H. 'Das Retablissement des adlingen Grundbesitzes in der Neumark durch Friedrich den Grossen' (*Forschungen zur Brandenburgischen und Preussischen Geschichte*, Vol. XLVI, 1934, pp. 28-69 and 233-74).

Mylius, C. O. *Corpus Constitutionem Marchiocorum* . . . 1298-1750 (10 vols., 1737-55).

N

Naudé, W. *Getreidepolitik* (*Acta Borussica*, 4 vols., 1896-1911). 'Die Brandenburg-preussische Getreidehandelspolitik' (*Schmollers Jahrbuch*, Vol. XXIX, 1905).

Nicholai, C. F. *Beschreibung der Königlichen Residenzstädte Berlin und Potsdam* . . . (3 vols., 1786).

Niebuhr, Marcus. *Geschichte der Königlichen Bank in Berlin* . . . (1834).

O

Otto, Franz. See Spamer, Otto.

Overmann, A. 'Die Entwicklung der Leinen- Woll- und Baumwollindustrie in der ehemaligen Grafschaft Mark unter Brandenburg-Preussischer Herrschaft . . .' (*Münsterische Beiträge zur Geschichtsforschung*, Vol. XIX, 1909).

P

Parker and Pounds. *Coal and Steel in Western Europe*, (1957).

Pfeiffer, J. F. *Die Manufakturen und Fabriken Deutschlands* . . . (2 vols., 1780).

Philippson, M. *Geschichte des preussischen Staatswesens vom Tode Friedrichs des Grossen bis zu den Freiheitskriegen* (2 vols., 1880-2).

Preuss, J. D. E. *Friedrich der Grosse. Ein Lebensbild* (4 vols., 5 supplementary volumes of documents, 1832-4).

R

Rachel, Hugo. *Das Berliner Wirtschaftsleben im Zeitalter des Frühkapitalismus* (1931).
Handels-Zoll- und Akzisenpolitik (Acta Borussica, 3 vols. in 4 parts, 1911-28).
'Der Merkantilismus in Brandenburg-Preussen' (*Forschungen zur Brandenburgischen und Preussischen Geschichte* Vol. XL, 1927, p. 221 *et seq.*).
'Die Juden im Berliner Wirtschaftsleben' (*Zeitschrift für die Geschichte der Juden in Deutschland*, Vol. 2, 1930 (p. 175 *et seq.*).
Rachel, Papritz and Wallich. *Berliner Grosskaufleute und Kapitalisten* (3 vols., 1934-8). (The second volume covers the period 1648-1806).
Rehfeld, P. 'Die preussische Rüstungsindustrie unter Friedrich dem Grossen' (*Forschungen zur Brandenburgischen und Preussischen Greschichte*, Vol. LV 1944, pp. 1-31).
Rehmann. 'Kleine Beiträge zur Charakteristik Brenkenhofs' (*Schriften des Vereins für Geschichte der Neumark*, Vol. XII, 1908).
Reimann, E. P. *Das Tabaksmonopol Friedrichs des Grossen* (1913).
Reissner, H. *Mirabeau und seine 'Monarchie Prussienne'* (1926).
Reidel, A. F. *Der brandenburg-preussische Staatshaushalt in den beiden letzten Jahrhunderten* (1866).
Reidl, T. *Die Ursache für den Niedergang des Kölner Seidengewerbes und für den Aufstieg der Krefelder Seidenindustrie im 17en und 18en Jahrhundert* (dissertation: Cologne, 1952).
Reuter, O. *Die Manufaktur im fränkischem Raum* (1961).
Ring, Victor. *Asiatische Handelskompagnien Friedrich des Grossen* (1890).
Rödebeck, K. H. S. *Beiträge zur Bereichgung und Erläuterung der Lebensbeschreibungen Friedrich Wilhelms I und Friedrichs des Grossen* (2 vols., 1836-8).
Rosenmöller, B. *Schulenburg-Kennert unter Friedrich dem Grossen* (1914).

S

Scherf, K. 'Die brandenburgische Textilindustrie im 18en und 19en Jahrhundert und ihre standortbildenden Fakturen'

14

(*Wissenschaftliche Zeitschrift der Pädagogischen Hochschule Potsdam*, Vol. V, 1959-60, pp. 43-65).

Schlütker, H. *Die volkswirtschaftliche Bedeutung der königlichen Seehandlung von 1772-1820* (1920).

Schmidt, F. *Die Entwicklung der Cottbuser Tuchindustrie* (1928).

Schmoller, Gustav. 'Die Epochen der preussischen Finanz-politik' (*Schmollers Jahrbuch*, Vol. I, 1877, p. 33 *et seq.*).
'Die Einführung der französischen Regie durch Friedrich den Grossen' (*Sitzungsbericht des Kgl. Preuss. Akademie der Wissen-schaften zu Berlin*, 1888 (Part I), p. 63 *et seq.*). See also article in the *Deutsche Rundschau*, April 1888).
'Die geschichtliche Entwicklung der Unternehmung' (*Schmollers Jahrbuch*, Vol. XIV, 1890, p. 735 *et seq.* and p. 1053 *et seq.* and Vol. XV, 1891, p. 1 *et seq.*, p. 633 *et seq.* and p. 963).
'Die preussische Seidenindustrie im 18en Jahrhundert' (supplement to the *Allgemeine Zeitung*, Munich, 1892).
Umrisse und Untersuchungen zur Verfassungs-, Verwaltungs- und Wirtschaftsgeschichte, besonders des preussischen Staates im 17en and 18en Jahrhundert (1898).
The Mercantile System (1931). Appendix I on the Prussian silk industry.

Schmoller and Hintze. *Die preussische Seidenindustrie im 18en Jahrhundert* (*Acta Borussica*, 3 vols., 1892).

Schönborn, T. '*Die Wirtschaftspolitik Osterreichs in Schlesien im 17en und im Anfang des 18en Jahrhundert*' (*Jahrbücher für Nationalökonomie und Statistik* (New Series). Vol. X, 1884).

Scholze, G. 'Die volkwirtschaftliche Bedeutung des Refuge für die Stadt Magdeburg' (*Magdeburgs Wirtschaftsleben in der Vergangenheit*, Magdeburg Chamber of Commerce, I, 1925, p. 373, *et seq.*).

Schön, Theodor von. *Studienreisen eines jungen Staatswirths in Deutschland . . .* (1879).

Spangenthal, S. *Geschichte der Berliner Börse* (1903).

Schrader, Paul. *Die Geschichte der königlichen Seehandlung . . .* (1911).

Schrötter, F. von. *Münzwesen* (*Acta Borussica*, 3 vols., 1902-11).
'Die schlesische Wollenindustrie im 18en Jahrhundert' (*Forschungen zur Brandenburgischen und Preussischen Geschichte*,

Vol. X, 1898, p. 129 *et seq.*; Vol. XI, 1899, p. 375 *et seq.*; and Vol. XIV, 1900, p. 531 *et seq.*).

'Das preussische Münzwesen in 18en Jahrhundert' (*Forschungen zur Brandenburgischen und Preussischen Geschichte*, Vol. XXII, 1909).

Schultze, W. 'Ein Angriff des Minister von Heinitz gegen die französische Regie' (*Forschungen zur Brandenburgischen und Preussischen Geschichte*, Vol. V, 1892, pp. 191-202.) *Geschichte der preussischen Regieverwaltung, 1766-86*, Vol. I. (1888).

Schulze-Briessen, M. *Der preussische Staatsbergbau im Wandel der Zeiten* (2 vols., 1933).

Schulze-Gaevernitz, G. von. 'Die industrielle Revolution' (*Archiv für Sozialwissenschaft und Sozialpolitik*, LXV, 1931).

Schwartze, P. 'Die neumärkische Städte nach dem Siebenjährigen Kriege' (*Schriften des Vereins für Geschichte der Neumark*, Vol. VIII, 1899).

'Brenkenhofs Berichte über Seine Tätigkeit in der Neumark' (*Schriften des Vereins für Geschichte der Neumark*, 1907).

Schwemann, A. 'Friedrich Anton von Heinitz' (*Beiträge zur Geschichte der Technik und Industrie*, edited by Conrad Matschoss, XII, 1922).

'Friedrich Wilhelm, Graf von Reden' (*Beiträge zur Geschichte der Technik und Industrie*, edited by Conrad Matschoss, XIV, 1924).

Seidel, P. 'Friedrich der Grosse und seine Porzellan-Manufaktur' (*Hohenzollern Jahrbuch*, Vol. VI, 1902, pp. 175-206).

Serin, Max. *Geschichte der preussisch-deutschen Eisenzölle* (1882), Appendix, I, pp. 264-271.

Serlo, A. *Beitrag zur Geschichte des schlesischen Bergbaues in den letzten hundert Jahren* (1869).

Serlo, W. 'Des Freihern vom Steins Verdienste um die Bergwirtschaft' (*Zeitschrift für das Berg- Hütten- und Salinenwesen im Preussischen Staate*, Vol. LXXIX, 1931).

Skalweit, August. 'Agrarpolitik Friedrichs des Grossen' (*Forschungen zur Brandenburgischen und Preussischen Geschichte*, Vol. XXI, 1908).

Höhe und Verfall der friderizianischen Getreidehandelspolitik und Getrehandesverfassung (1931).

'Die Eingliederung des friderizianischen Heeres in den Volks- and Wirtschaftskörper' (*Jahrbücher für Nationalökonomie und Statistik*, CLX, 1944, pp. 194-220).

Skalweit, S. *Die Berliner Wirtschaftskrise und ihre Hintergründe* (1937).

Small, A. W. *The Cameralists: The Pioneers of German Social Policy* (1909).

Sobieski, W. *Der Kampf um die Ostsee* (1933).

Spamer, Otto. *Der Kaufmann zu allen Zeiten* . . . Vol. III (1869), pp. 213-236. Appeared under pen name Franz Otto.

Spatz, W. *Chronik von Nowawes-Neuendorf* (1907).

Stadelmann, R. *Preussens Könige in ihrer Tätigkeit für die Landeskultur* (in 4 parts, 1878-87), Part II *Friedrich der Grosse* (*Publicationen aus den K. Preuss. Staatsarchiven*, XI, 1882).

Steinecke, Otto. 'Des Minister von Heinitz mémoire sur ma gestion du 4e et 5e département' (*Forschungen zur Brandenburgischen und Preussischen Geschichte*, Vol. XXII, 1909, pp. 183-191).

Steinmann, P. *Bauer und Ritter in Mecklenburg* (1960).

Stephan, H. *Geschichte der preussischen Post* (1859).

T

Tollin, H. *Geschichte der französischen Colonie von Magdeburg* (3 vols., 1887).

Treue, Wilhelm. 'David Splitgerber . . . 1685-1764' (*Vierteljahrschrift für Sozial- und Wirtschaftsgeschichte*, Vol. XLI (iii), 1954, p. 253-67).

Tröger, H. *Die kurmärkischen Spinnerdörfer* (dissertation, Leipzig, 1936).

V

Vester, F. 'Seidenbau und Seidenfabrikation in Magdeburg im 18en Jahrhundert' (*Magdeburgs Wirtschaftsleben in der Vergangenheit*, Vol. I, 1925, p. 495 *et seq.*).

Vogler, G. *Zur Lage und zum Klassenkampf der Weber und Spinner in Nowawes in der zweiten Hälfte des achtzehnten Jahrhunderts* (Institut für deutsche Geschichte der Humboldt Universität, Berlin, 1956).

Voltz, H. *Die Bergbau- und Hüttenverwaltung des Oberschlesischen Industrie-Bezirks* (1892).

Voss, G. 'Der grosse König und die Berliner Porzellanmanufaktur' (*Mitteilungen des Vereins für die Geschichte Berlin*, 1912).

W

Wachler, L. *Geschichte des ersten Jahrhunderts der königlichen Eisen- und Hüttenwerke in Malapane* . . . (G1 gan, 1856).

Wichgraf, A. *Geschichte der Webercolonie Nowawes bei Potsdam* (1862).

Wiedfeldt, O. *Statistische Studien zur Entwicklungsgeschichte der Berliner Industrie von 1720 bis 1890* (1898).

Wintzer, E. 'Die Wegelysche Porzellanfabrik in Berlin' (*Schriften des Vereins für die Geschichte Berlin*, Vol. XXXV, 1898, pp. 1-65).

Wirth, Max. *Geschichte der Handelskrisen* (1890), pp. 86-95.

Z

Ziekursch, J. *Beiträge zur Charakteristik der preussischen Verwaltungsbeamten in Schlesien bis zum Untergang des friderizianischen Staates* (Darstellungen und Quellen zur schlesischen Geschichte, Vol. 4, 1904).

'Zur Charakteristik der schlesischen Steuerräte 1742-1809' (*Zeitschrift des Vereins für die Geschichte Schlesiens*, Vol. XLIII, 1909, p. 131 *et seq.*).

Sachsen und Preussen um die Mitte des achtzehnten Jahrhunderts . . . (1904).

Hundert Jahre schlesischer Agrargeschichte vom Hubertusburger Friede bis zum Abschluss der Bauernbefreiung (1915 and 1927).

Zimmerbach, F. *Die Begründung der oberschlesischen Eisenindustrie unter Preussens Königen* (1911).

Zimmerman, A. *Blühte und Verfall des Leinengewebes in Schlesien* (1892).

Zöllner, J. F. *Reise durch Pommern nach der insel Rügen* (1797). *Briefe über Schlesien* . . . (2 vols., 1792-3).

Zorn, W. *Handels- und Industriegeschichte Bayerisch-Schwabens* 1648-1870 (1961).

Studies in the Economic Policy of Frederick the Great

Zottman, A. *Die Wirtschaftspolitik Friedrichs des Grossen* (1937). *Festschrift des Oberbergamtes Halle: 150 Jahre Bergverwaltung im mitteldeutschen Bergbau* (1925).

'Königlich Berlin' 1763-1913 (*Gedenkblatt zum 150-jährigen Jubiläum der Konigl. Porzellan-Manufaktur Berlin,* (1914). *Die Preussische Staatsbank (Seehandlung), 1772-1922* (1922).

Index

Names frequently mentioned in the text such as Frederick the Great, Germany and Prussia have not been included in the index.